Classic
JUNIOR LEAGUE®
COOKBOOK COLLECTION

CHARLESTON RECEIPTS

COLLECTED

BY

THE JUNIOR LEAGUE

OF

CHARLESTON

CHARLESTON, SOUTH CAROLINA

1950

**JUNIOR LEAGUE OF
CHARLESTON, SC**
Women building better communities

 Favorite

D1153580

One of the criteria to be considered for the Classic Junior League Cookbook
Collection is the original publication date; the cookbook must be at
least 25 years old. As a result of the length of time in print, some titles have
gone through revisions and updates; others have been intentionally
left in their original context in order to preserve the integrity and authenticity
of the publication. This printing has been taken from the most recent
edition. We hope you enjoy this American icon.

For more than 70 years, Junior League cookbooks have been sought out and collected by both novice and seasoned home cooks. Turned to again and again for their tried-and-true recipes, these cookbooks are a testament to the Junior League volunteers who dedicate themselves to improving the quality of life within their communities. These treasured cookbooks have played a significant role both in raising funds to help fulfill the organizations' missions and by documenting and preserving regional culinary traditions.

Favorite Recipes® Press, a longtime friend and partner of the Association of Junior Leagues International, is proud to present the *Classic Junior League Cookbook Collection*. The inaugural collection is comprised of six Junior League cookbooks that define all that is *Classic;* each serves as a standard of excellence and is considered an authentic and authoritative work on the foods and traditions of its region.

Enjoy,

Sheila Thomas

Executive Editor
Favorite Recipes Press

HISTORY OF CHARLESTON RECEIPTS

Charleston Receipts, first published November 1, 1950, is the oldest Junior League cookbook still in print. The cookbook was originally compiled as a fund-raising project by a committee of twenty-one Sustainers. The editors were Mary Vereen Huguenin and Anne Montague Stoney. The proceeds from the cookbook supported the Charleston Speech and Hearing Center, which was the first center of its kind in South Carolina. In May, 1991, The Junior League of Charleston, Inc. was awarded the Distinguished Service Award from the American Speech-Language-Hearing Association for its significant contribution to the fields of speech-language pathology and audiology.

The 350 page cookbook contains 750 receipts, Gullah verses, and sketches by Charleston artists. No changes have been made in the original cookbook except for a supplement added in the Third Printing (1951) and a revision of the index in the Seventeenth Printing (1971). The Sixteenth Printing (1970) was dedicated to the Tricentennial. The contents of the cookbook were reviewed for the Twentieth Printing (1975). An explanation and translation of the original Gullah phrases was included in the Twenty-Sixth Printing (1989).

The initial investment in the project was approximately $150.00. It took the committee one month to collect the receipts from a number of Charleston residents, two months to test the receipts, and four months to organize and compile the cookbook. The First Edition of 2,000 copies was sold out in only four days. The retail cost per copy was $2.50. Over 750,000 copies have been printed and we are currently in the Thirty-fourth Printing.

After two years, the management of *Charleston Receipts* was turned over to the Actives as a permanent fund-raising project. The proceeds from the sale of the cookbook are ultimately returned to the community through projects undertaken in response to community needs.

In 1990, *Charleston Receipts* was selected for inclusion in the Walter S. McIlhenny Hall of Fame for Community Cookbooks. This special award honored the contribution of *Charleston Receipts* in preserving our American local and regional culinary customs while benefitting the community in a substantial way.

TWO FLOWER WOMEN

Receipt vs. Recipe

———

Throughout this book, as you will see,
We never mention *recipe*,—
The reason being that we felt,
(Though well aware how it is spelt!),
That it is modern and not meet
To use in place of old *receipt*
To designate time-honored dishes
According to ancestral wishes.

L. F. K.

COOK BOOK COMMITTEE

The Sustaining Members of the Junior League of Charleston

EDITORS

Mary Vereen Huguenin   Anne Montague Stoney

GULLAH
THE SPECIAL INGREDIENT

For over 35 years, Gullah phrases have added a distinctive flavor of Charleston to *Charleston Receipts* and have contributed to its reputation as a classic in the world of cookbooks.

Special dishes like Champagne Punch (page 15), James Island Shrimp Pie (page 71) and Dah's Browning (page 128) were generally prepared and served by Lowcountry cooks and butlers. The Gullah lines allow readers to meet these special people, share their humor and "hear" their language.

I use the term "language" advisedly. Gullah is not Black English, neither is it a dialect of any other language. It is a legitimate creole language with its own grammar, phonological system, idiomatic expressions and an extensive vocabulary. It is one of six languages known as the English-derived Atlantic Creoles and is the only one spoken on the U.S. mainland today. About 200,000 Afro-Americans, descendants of the slaves, who live in the Lowcountry of South Carolina and Georgia, still speak Gullah. Many of these people live in Charleston and on nearby sea islands.

Through their language, the Afro-American people have made a unique and substantial contribution to our American heritage, but little is being done to preserve this language. Most native speakers of Gullah are unable to write it, and as older speakers die, some of the language is lost with them. Gullah is in danger of "language death."

By using Gullah in *Charleston Receipts*, the Junior League of Charleston is helping record and document a fascinating part of America's heritage. And by including my standard English translations, it is allowing readers to understand and appreciate the appeal of the language.

Virginia Mixson Geraty
Gullah Instructor
College of Charleston

The Junior League of Charleston, Inc. is an organization of women committed to promoting voluntarism and to improving the community through effective action and leadership of trained volunteers. Its purpose is exclusively educational and charitable. The Junior League of Charleston, Inc. reaches out to women of all races, religious and national origins who demonstrate an interest in and commitment to voluntarism.

For more than forty years, proceeds from the sale of *Charleston Receipts* have been used to support the following community projects.

ARTS IN EDUCATION
ASHLEY HALL WOMEN IN LEADERSHIP
BASE
BEGINNINGS
BUSINESS EDUCATION PARTNERSHIP
CAROLINA YOUTH DEVELOPMENT CENTER
CHARLESTON MUSEUM "DISCOVER ME" ROOM
CHARLESTON MUSEUM LIBRARY RESTORATION
CHARLESTON NURSERY AND DAY CARE CENTER
CHARLESTON SPEECH AND HEARING CENTER
COMPREHENSIVE EMERGENCY SERVICES
CHILD GUIDANCE BUREAU
CHILDREN AT RISK
ENVIRONMENTAL SCHOOL OF THE YEAR
FAMOUS ARTISTS SERIES
GUARDIAN AD LITEM SPECIAL PROJECT
HANDS ON
HERITAGE MINI CONFERENCE
HOMEWORK HELPERS
HORIZON HOUSE

HOSPICE
HOUSEWISE-STREETWISE
I'M SPECIAL
KIDS ON THE BLOCK
"LIVELY ARTS" BROCHURE AND CALENDAR
LOW VISION BOOK FAIR
LOWCOUNTRY CHILDREN'S CENTER
MIDDLETON GARDENS TEAROOM
MOTHERS AND COMPANY
MUSIC IN THE SCHOOLS
NATIONAL TRUST CONFERENCE
OUR CHARLESTON
PARENT YOUTH ASSOCIATION
PENNSYLVANIA BALLET
ROPER HOSPITAL ROLLING LIBRARY
SAFETY VILLAGE
SAGE DAY
SATURDAY SOUP KITCHEN
SWAMP
TEEN OUTREACH
V.I.E. PROJECT
VOLUNTARY ACTION CENTER
WOMAN TO WOMAN

Foreword

There was a time when folks had cooks,
   Who never did depend on books
   To learn the art of cooking.
The help knew all the tunes by ear,
   And no one dared to interfere;
   They brooked no overlooking.

But times have changed, for worse we fear,
   Housewives handle the kitchen ware,
   And must learn how to cook.
With that in mind, we've dug and delved,
   And unearthed treasures long been shelved,
   And placed them in this book.

It represents a world of toil,
   And burning of the midnight oil;
   Correction and suggestion.
At long last it's completed now,
   And offered with the hope, somehow
   'Twill aid to good digestion.

People have been more than kind,
   In writing us on what they dine,
   And just how you should cook it.
If at times a family tree,
   Has intruded for all to see,
   Why you must overlook it.

Gifted artists have unstinting,
   Lent their works for our printing
   In this volume new.
You may feast your eyes while reading
   Some receipt you may be needing,
   For the punch you wish to brew.

The proceeds from this book will go,
   To projects of the League, you know;
   That is why we sell it.
'Twas lots of work, but a lot of fun,
   And if you think our book's well done,
   Don't hesitate to tell it.

                                        A. J. S.

7

ILLUSTRATIONS

*Courtesy of Gibbes Art Gallery/Carolina Art Association

Gullah Lines — Mary Deas Ravenel
Louise Frierson Kerr

Chapter Verses — Louise Frierson Kerr

References concerning the literary works of our contributors were com-
posed by the Cook Book Committee.

In order to insure the greatest possible accuracy, finished proofs of receipts
were submitted to contributors for correction before being sent to press.

Trade names of products are given only when necessary.

CONTENTS

MILES BREWTON HOUSE 1765

BEVERAGES

"Ef yuh teck a heapa haa'd likker, yuh gwine tink deep en' talk strong."

Ratifia is a drink
That ought to make you pause and think.
The drink is thimble-sized, it's true,
But what that thimble does to you ! ! !
Remember, e'er you grow too bold,
That David knocked Goliath cold!

Beverages

Most of these old Charleston receipts, reflecting the pleasant living of past generations, are here presented for the first time. In adapting the punch formulas to modern use, the following comments may prove helpful.

The unit of measure designated herein is the quart, since most of the "spirits" used by our ancestors were imported in casks and bottled in this country in quarts. (The contents of the casks were partially aged by the rolling in the holds of sailing ships—even our domestic liquors were shipped around the Horn for "improvement"). Now most spirits, imported and domestic, come in "fifths."

Many of these original receipts specified Jamaican rum, however, today Puerto Rican and other good rums are often used. Nowadays triple sec is frequently substituted for curacao, and brandy for cognac.

And never forget that punch stock should be poured over a block of ice and served cold, cold, cold!

St. Cecilia Punch

6 lemons	1 quart green tea
1 quart brandy	1 pint heavy rum
1 pineapple	1 quart peach brandy
1½ pounds sugar	4 quarts champagne

2 quarts carbonated water

Slice lemons thin and cover with brandy. Allow to steep for 24 hours. Several hours before ready to serve, slice the pineapple into the bowl with the lemon slices, then add the sugar, tea, rum and peach brandy. Stir well. When ready to serve, add the champagne and water. 80-90 servings.

Charleston Light Dragoon Punch

1 quart grenadine syrup	1 quart bottle red cherries
1 bottle curacao syrup	1 quart can white cherries
1 quart raspberry syrup	1 quart can sliced pineapple
3 gallons rye whiskey	6 dozen oranges
2 quarts light rum	6 dozen lemons
¼ pound green tea leaves	Carbonated water

First secure an 8 gallon crock. Put in the juice of the oranges and lemons and stir thoroughly. Continue to stir and slowly pour in the grenadine, curacao and raspberry syrups, then the green tea, which is made as described below. Add red cherries, white cherries, pineapple and their juices. Stir thoroughly, and slowly add the rye whiskey and light rum. Bear in mind the necessity of constantly stirring as this is the only way to blend the punch properly.

To make the tea: Boil the orange and lemon skins in 2 quarts of water, then use the orange and lemon flavored water to draw the tea. Cool before using.

This punch stock (6¼ gallons) should be made at least 4 days before using and stirred from time to time. First serving should be 2 parts of punch stock to 1 part carbonated water poured over ice. Then 1 part punch stock to 1 part carbonated water can be served. 300-350 servings.

JOHN LAURENS

Otranto Club Punch

1 pound loaf sugar	1 pint peach brandy
1 quart strong green tea	1 quart heavy or light rum
Juice of 12 lemons, strained	2 quarts brandy or
1-3 quarts carbonated water	rye whiskey

Dissolve the sugar in the tea; add the lemon juice, peach brandy, rum and the brandy or whiskey. Use an abundance of ice, adding a liberal quantity of carbonated water. 50-70 servings.

LOUIS Y. DAWSON, JR.

Cotillion Club Punch

(As served at the Club's last dance some years ago.)

¼ lb. gun powder (green) tea (makes 5 quarts)
1 quart cherries
2 dozen lemons (juice)
Fruit syrup (about ½ pint)

12 quarts carbonated water
6 or 8 qts. rye whiskey
½ pint rum
1 lb. sugar made into thick syrup

Pour 5 quarts boiling water onto the tea, bring this to a boil; remove from fire at once and let stand until strong enough. Strain and, when cool, add juice of lemons, syrup from the cherries and also the rye and rum. Sweeten to taste with any fruit syrup; add sugar syrup and cherries. Bottle this stock and keep on ice until ready to serve. Pour over block of ice, add 1 quart of carbonated water to 1 quart of stock. This stock can be kept indefinitely if bottled and sealed. Yield: 275-300 servings.

A CHARLESTON GENTLEMAN

Champagne Punch

½ pound best green tea (makes 10 qts.)
10 bottles brandy
10 bottles light rum
5 dozen lemons

12 pounds sugar
12 quarts carbonated water
12 quarts champagne
1 quart maraschino cherries
2 cans pineapple chunks

Make syrup of the sugar with 1 quart of water and boil until slightly thick, add the juice from the pineapple chunks and let come to a boil. To make tea, bring 10 parts of water to a boil and pour onto tea; let stand until strong, then strain and when cool add syrup, rum, brandy, juice of lemons, cherries, and pineapple chunks. Make this at least 5 days before using . Chill stock and champagne, and when ready to serve, mix 3 quarts stock to 1 quart champagne and 1 quart carbonated water. (Three quarts of carbonated water may be used for the ladies' punch.) Stock should be kept in tightly corked bottles. 600-650 servings.

(FROM A CHARLESTON LADY'S RECEIPT BOOK OF THE 1890's)

Regent's Punch

(As mixed at Lewisfield Plantation, 1783)

¼ pound rock candy	½ bottle sherry
High grade green tea	1 tumbler brandy
1 bottle champagne	1 lemon, sliced

Dissolve rock candy in approximately 1 pint hot tea. When cold, add other ingredients and serve with ice. 20-25 servings.

R. BENTHAM SIMONS

Legaré Street Punch

"This mixture makes a very palatable drink with plenty of authority"

1 quart sauterne	1 pint cognac
2 quarts champagne	Ice
1 quart carbonated water	

Mix the sauterne and cognac, adding last the champagne and carbonated water. Pour over ice and serve immediately. 36-40 servings.

WILLIAM A. HUTCHINSON

Frost Punch

1 pint strong green tea	1 wineglass of curacao
Peel of 4 lemons, pared thin	1 pint brandy (cognac)
Juice of 8 lemons	½ pint heavy rum
1 pineapple, sliced thin	2 pints soda water
1 pound sugar	2 quarts champagne, chilled

Mix all ingredients but soda water and champagne. Add soda water and champagne just before serving. 50-60 servings.

MISS ELLEN PARKER

16

Champagne Punch for the Wedding

1 bottle champagne   1 ounce cognac
½ ounce curacao

To every bottle of champagne: use cognac and curacao in above proportions, mixed several hours beforehand. When ready to serve, pour necessary amount of this mixture over a block of ice in a cold punch bowl and add thoroughly chilled champagne. Stir and serve at once without ladling back and forth over ice, as this eliminates the bubbles. (1 bottle good dry white wine, chilled, may be substituted for every third bottle of champagne.) Allow 3 servings per guest, 3 ounces to the punch cup.

A CONNOISSEUR

Kinloch Plantation Special

For each serving:
½ heaping teaspoon orange   A little water
    marmalade   Generous portion of whiskey
Nutmeg   Cracked ice

Dissolve marmalade with a dash of nutmeg in water; add whiskey, more nutmeg, ice and shake well. Serve in an old-fashioned glass with another dash of nutmeg on top.

EUGENE duPONT

Potent Potion

½ pint water   1 teaspoon angostura bitters
½ pint vermouth   5 teaspoons sugar
1 pint rye whiskey   Rind of ½ lemon

This can be kept indefinitely, but lemon rind should be taken out after three days. 16 servings.

MISS MARY DEAS RAVENEL

Tradd Alley Punch

2 quarts sherry   4 tablespoons sugar
½ pint good brandy   Juice of 2 lemons
½ pint rum   Maraschino cherries

Add cherries to stock and pour over ice in punch bowl. 25-30 servings.

MISS MARY DEAS RAVENEL

Rum Punch

"This was the punch my father made for all the debutante parties of my generation."

1 gallon brandy	2 quarts black tea
½ gallon heavy or light rum	2 dozen lemons
1 pint peach brandy	Sugar to taste

5-6 quarts carbonated water

Add carbonated water just before serving, more or less according to the strength punch is to have. 1 pint curacao or maraschino as well as strawberries, cherries or a few slices of pineapple may be added. 130-140 servings.

Mrs. Ralph Hanson (Eleanor Rutledge)

Simons' Special

If using **heavy** rum:
 1 part rum
 3 parts gin
If using **light** rum:
 1 part rum
 2 parts gin
Lemon mixture:
 1 part lemon juice
 3 parts water
 Sugar to taste

Using the gin and rum mixture as above, use 1 part of this and add 3 parts lemon mixture sweetened so it is just off the tart side. Do not sweeten too much as a rum drink does not need much sugar.

W. Lucas Simons

Charleston Cup (winter version)

For each serving:

2 ounces light rum   ½ ounce orange juice
1 ounce orange curacao 1 teaspoon sugar

To the rum, add curacao, then orange juice with sugar dissolved. Mix well and pour over ice in a bowl. Serve in chilled cups.

DANIEL RAVENEL

Cool o' the Evening (summer version)

For each serving:

1 sprig mint   ½ teaspoon sugar
Juice of ½ lemon   2 ounces light rum

Crush mint in shaker; add other ingredients, using finely chopped ice, and shake until frost forms. Serve in chilled glasses.

DANIEL RAVENEL

Lazy Man's Old Fashioned

For each serving:

1 teaspoon orange marma- 1 finger (measured hori-
 lade   zontally) light (dark)
3 dashes angostura bitters rum or whiskey
   Crushed ice (not too fine) to fill glass

Stir until it tastes right; add spirits, if necessary, to the result.

SAMUEL GAILLARD STONEY

Gin and Sherry Cocktail

1 part gin   Dash angostura bitters
1 part dry sherry   Ice

Shake well with ice and serve immediately.

MRS. AUGUSTINE T. S. STONEY (Louisa Jenkins)

Mint Julep

For each cold goblet use:

Several mint leaves	Crushed, dry ice
Sugar syrup	2 ounces bourbon
(2 or 3 teaspoons)	1 sprig mint

Crush leaves and let stand in syrup. Put this into a cold, silver julep cup or glass and add ice, which has been crushed and rolled in a towel to dry. Pour in whiskey. Stir, not touching the glass, and add sprig of mint. Serve immediately.

MRS. CHARLES S. DWIGHT (Lucille Lebby)

Colonel Aiken Simons' Mint Julep

Having ready as many thin highball glasses as necessary, proceed as follows:

Take a pitcher or jug of suitable size and place therein a teaspoonful of sugar for each julep to be mixed, add just enough water to dissolve the sugar: about an equal volume of water to the sugar will do if you stir enough. Then pour in a whiskey glass of spirits for each julep and stir up with the syrup. Select 4 or 5 fine sprigs of mint and put them into the mixture. Whether this mint is to be crushed or not is controversial and depends on the strength of the mint and the taste of individuals. Crush the mint and let stand awhile.

Then fill each glass with broken ice, taking care not to get the outside of the glass wet as that would interfere with frosting. Divide the contents of the pitcher among the glasses and stir each vigorously. The ice will have subsided and the glasses must be filled up with ice and again stirred briskly. The frost by this time has formed a thick white coating on the glass, so the glass should be handled cautiously to avoid marring the frost which is the pride and joy of a Julep Artifex. Then choose very fine sprigs of mint for the garnishing; stick one in each glass and serve.

ALBERT SIMONS

Plantation Toddy

1 lump sugar   Small piece lemon skin
2 cloves   1 pony rye whiskey
Pour into toddy glass with a little cracked ice. Add a shake of nutmeg.

WILLIAM A. HUTCHINSON

Plantation Greeter

1 jigger of bourbon or rye   Dash of grenadine
Dash of lemon juice   Dash of Benedictine
Stir in ice until cold and serve in a stem glass with a maraschino cherry.

DANIEL RAVENEL

Captain S. G. Stoney's Claret Sanger

2 claret glasses of claret   Juice of one small lime
Sugar to taste
Pour into large goblet and serve with crushed ice.

MRS. ALBERT SIMONS (Harriet Stoney)

Sherry Bolo

3 sherry glasses of sherry   Juice of 1 lime
Sugar to taste
Serve with crushed ice.

S. DAVID STONEY

Sauterne Cup

1 bottle sauterne or   3 lemons or 6 limes
    white wine   1 tablespoon maraschino
1 quart carbonated water   Bunch of mint
Sugar
Make a syrup to taste of lime or lemon juice and sugar. Have wine and water on ice. Mix just before serving. Put mint in top of pitcher. 20 servings.

MRS. JOHN BENNETT (Susan Smythe)

Flip

This refreshing drink was in vogue in England in the 18th century and was brought to Carolina when settled by the Lords Proprietors. The South Carolina Society of Colonial Dames owns a Flip bowl or glass. It is of glass, small at the bottom and gradually widens to the top. It holds about a quart.

4 jiggers whiskey	4 teaspoons sugar
4 egg yolks	1 quart rich milk

Nutmeg to taste

Beat yolks, sugar, and seasoning together. Add milk and whiskey. Shake well with crushed ice, strain and serve in stemmed glasses with a dash of nutmeg on top. 8-10 servings.

MISS ELLEN PARKER

Cherry Bounce

1 quart wild cherries	1 quart whiskey

1 cup sugar

Go to Old Market in June and get a quart of wild cherries. Wash same and put in a large-mouthed jar with a full cup of sugar. Let stand until juice draws, then add a quart of whiskey. Cover lightly and steep about ten days, then pour off liquor and bottle.

R. BENTHAM SIMONS

Mrs. William Huger's Orange Cordial

50 oranges	4 pounds sugar

1 gallon whiskey

Peel oranges very thin. Put peels in the gallon of whiskey and let them soak for 6 weeks. Pour off whiskey and then make a syrup of 4 pounds of sugar with just enough water to keep sugar from burning. While *hot*, add to whiskey and stir.

MRS. WILLIAM S. POPHAM (Louisa Stoney)

Cotton Hall Plantation Eggnog

5 dozen eggs	1 pint coffee cream
4 cups granulated sugar	1½ quarts rye whiskey
1½ quarts whipping cream	1 pint rum

½ teaspoon salt

Beat egg yolks with sugar; add liquor, then whites of eggs beaten very stiff, and salt. Whip cream and add last. 90-100 servings.

MISS MAY MARTIN

Charleston Eggnog

1 pint rye whiskey	10 egg whites
1 quart heavy cream	10 egg yolks

¾ cup granulated sugar

Cream sugar and egg yolks thoroughly. Add whiskey slowly, stirring constantly, the cream (unwhipped), then the stiffly beaten egg whites. 20-25 servings.

MRS. GAMMELL WARING (Annie Gammell)

Simple Eggnog

1 fresh country egg	1 tablespoon good whiskey
Sugar to taste	or brandy
1 cup rich milk	1 teaspoon vanilla
	Pinch of salt

Separate the egg, beating both the yolk and white. Add the sugar and salt to the yolk, then the whiskey or brandy, milk and vanilla. Lastly add the white of the egg. Mix and strain into a tall glass and serve cold. Grate a touch of nutmeg on top.

MRS. AUGUSTINE T. S. STONEY (Louisa Jenkins)

Mrs. A. H. Mazyck's Ratifià (c. 1830)

Take 1 gallon best brandy, 1 quart madeira wine, 1 quart muscat wine, 1 pint orange-flower water, 3 pounds loaf sugar, 1 pint rose water, 1000 peach kernels. Put in a crock and keep in the sun for 4 or 5 weeks.

MRS. ROBERT L. KERR (Louise Mazyck Frierson)

Rice Wine

1 box seeded raisins	1 orange, sliced
1½ pounds of raw rice	1 yeast cake
2½ pounds granulated sugar	1 gallon tepid water

Put in stone crock and cover three weeks to one month, depending on temperature. Stir with wooden spoon daily for a week, every other day the second week, then not at all. Strain. Next day, filter. Set aside six months to a year.

FREDERICK A. TRAUT

Blackberry Wine

7 quarts blackberries	1 egg white
3½ quarts water	7 pounds sugar
2 quarts water	

To mashed blackberries, add 3½ quarts water and let stand for 24 hours, then strain through thin cloth. Beat egg white, add sugar and 2 quarts water. Boil 5 minutes. Skim. When syrup is cool, add to blackberry juice. Stir well and place in jar. Skim each morning for 10 days, followed by a good stir each time; then put in demi-john. (Do not cork.) Cover with cloth and leave until it ceases to ferment. Siphon off and bottle.

MRS. WILLIAM B. GADSDEN (Ruth Walker)

Mrs. L. J. Walker's Scuppernong Wine

8 quarts grapes	2 quarts boiling water
3 pounds sugar	

Mash the grapes. Pour on the boiling water. Let stand 36 hours. Strain and add sugar. Bottle and let stand uncorked until all fermentation is over, keeping bottles full.

MISS MARGARET B. WALKER

Elderberry Flower Wine

1 quart flowers	3 gallons boiling water
9 pounds sugar	3 pounds raisins
2 yeast cakes	2 teaspoons lemon juice

Cut blossoms from stems with scissors leaving as little stem as possible. Put blossoms in jar, cover with boiling water and sugar which have been boiled together. When cool, add yeast and lemon juice. After 9 days, strain through double cheese cloth then put in keg; add raisins. SHAKE, SHAKE, SHAKE for several days, then put in a firm spot where it will not be disturbed until December. Bottle then.

MRS. WILLIAM B. GADSDEN (Ruth Walker)

Southern Spiced Tea

8 cups boiling water	Juice of 6 oranges
5 tablespoons tea leaves	2 cups of sugar
Juice of 1 lemon	8 cups of water

1 teaspoon whole cloves

Add the boiling water to the tea leaves, let stand 5 minutes and strain. Make a syrup by boiling the sugar, cloves, and water together; add this and the fruit juice to the tea. (About 18 cups).

MRS. S. EDWARD IZARD, JR. (Anne Kirk)

Coffee Punch

1 gallon strong coffee	2 quarts vanilla ice cream
1 quart cream	5 teaspoons vanilla

5 tablespoons sugar

Chill coffee. Whip cream; add sugar and vanilla. Place ice cream and whipped cream in punch bowl and pour coffee over it. Mix well before serving. (If block ice cream is used, slice it into thin slices before placing in the punch bowl.) 50-60 servings.

MRS. LOUIS Y. DAWSON, JR. (Virginia Walker)

Fruit Punch

6 oranges
6 lemons
2 quarts tea or grape juice
1 quart can pineapple juice
   or grated pineapple

1 large bottle maraschino
   cherries
2 cups sugar
4 quarts ginger ale
Large lump of ice

Squeeze oranges and lemons; cover skins with boiling water and let stand until cool. Strain. Use this water with sugar to make syrup; add tea and fruit. Add ginger ale just before serving. 70-80 cups.

MRS. LOUIS T. PARKER (Josephine Walker)

Fruit Punch with Sherbet

1 pint fresh orange juice
1 pint canned pineapple
   juice

2 cups fresh lime juice
2 quarts ginger ale
1 quart orange ice

Mix fruit juices, pour over a block of ice and add a quart of orange ice. When ready to serve, add the ginger ale. Garnish with fresh mint and slices of orange. 40-45 servings.

MRS. T. LADSON WEBB, JR. (Ann Moore)

Combination Punch

1 quart can pineapple
   juice

1 quart can orange juice
1 quart apple juice

2 quarts ginger ale

Mix the juices and let stand an hour or two to blend the flavors. Pour in ginger ale and serve over ice. This is a delicious and refreshing summer drink. 50-60 servings.

MRS. MALCOLM L. McCRAE (Ena Mae Black)

Strawberry Shrub

12 pounds fruit

2 quarts water

5 ounces tartaric acid

1½ pounds powdered sugar
to each pint of juice

Acidulate water with tartaric acid; place fruit in jar, cover with the acidulated water and let remain 48 hours. Strain without bruising fruit. Measure juice and add sugar proportionately. Stir to dissolve sugar and leave a few days. Bottle and cork lightly. If slight fermentation takes place, leave cork out a few days. Process all cold. Stand bottles erect.

MRS. NATHANIEL I. BALL, JR. (Anne Barnwell)

Cassina Tea

This is one of the most delicious native drinks and compares favorably with most imported teas if brewed properly.

In the spring of the year, strip the young green leaves from the Cassina or Christmas Berry Bush. Toast them in a hot oven, turning them constantly with a fork until they are brown and crisp enough to crumble in the hand. Put them immediately into cans, covering tightly.

To make the tea, pour boiling water over the leaves in the morning and let them steep all day long. Serve hot or iced in the evening.

MARIA GREEN (from the Belleview-Bermuda Plantation)

Blackberry Acid

1 gallon blackberries   1 ounce tartaric acid
   (unwashed)   Sugar

Put berries in stone jar, cover with water and add acid. Let stand for 24 hours, then strain. To each pint of liquid add a pound of sugar; boil 20 minutes . Bottle hot, and keep in a dry, cool place. Serve ice cold, diluted with water or else over crushed ice.

MRS. AUGUSTINE T. S. STONEY   (Louisa Jenkins)

Francis Marion Reception Punch

1 quart can frozen   2 (No. 5) cans pineapple
   orange juice   juice
3 quarts ice water   4 quarts carbonated water
1 (6 ounce) can frozen   or ginger ale
   lemon juice or juice   2 cups sugar, dissolved in
   of 18 lemons   2 cups water (if
                           desired)

Mix stock thoroughly and chill. When ready to serve, pour half the quantity over large lump of ice in punch bowl and add 2 quarts carbonated water or ginger ale. Use other half of stock and two more quarts of carbonated water or ginger ale as needed. (This keeps the punch "alive"). Add the sugar only if more sweetening is desired. (If to be used as a base for punch "with spirits", omit sugar and substitute alcoholic beverage for pineapple juice—about 4 quarts). 100 servings.

MRS. KATHERINE HERMAN (Katherine Sheridan)

Soirée Punch

2 quarts ginger ale   1 quart orange sherbet

Have ginger ale very cold. Pour one quart over sherbet in punch bowl ½ hour before serving; add second quart when ready to serve. 16-20 servings.

MRS. HENRY C. ROBERTSON, JR. (Elizabeth Lebby)

CANAPES

"Young married 'ooman een dis day she nebbuh sattify wid ole time dish; dey allways want fuh mek some kine ob new mixture."

> The guests arrive at cocktail time.
> On tempting trays, my board displays
> Delectable varieties
> Of canapés. I yearn for praise
> But none comes forth. My busy guests
> They talk and laugh and gaily quaff
> And stretch unseeing hands to 'take
> My handicraft as though 'twere chaff!

Benne (Sesame) Seed "Cocktailers"

This is the original benne seed biscuit of which the New York Times says, "A cocktail biscuit that should revolutionize cocktail parties."

2 cups flour (unsifted)	¾ cup shortening or oleo
1 teaspoon salt	Ice water (¼ cup, approx.)
Dash of cayenne pepper	1 cup roasted benne seed
Additional salt	(see p. 356, No. 51)

Mix dry ingredients; cut in shortening; add enough ice water to make a dough the consistency of pie crust, add seed. Roll thin, cut into small round wafers. Place in biscuit pan and cook slowly in oven (about 300°) for 20 or 30 minutes. Before removing from pan and while hot, sprinkle with salt. These may be kept in a covered tin or cracker jar, and before serving, run into a slow oven to crisp. Makes several dozen.

W. Lucas Simons

Benne Seed Canapé

Squares of melba toast	Benne seed
Butter	Salt

Butter toast generously. Sprinkle benne seed to cover. Sprinkle with salt to taste. Heat in oven until seeds are brown.

Mrs. David Maybank (Marion Taber)

29

Shrimp Paste

1 plate or 1½ pounds
  shrimp
¼ pound butter
Dash of mace

¼ to ½ teaspoon dry
  mustard
Salt and black pepper
10 drops onion juice

1 tablespoon sherry wine

Boil shrimp in salted water, peel and pound in mortar or run through fine meat grinder. Mix thoroughly with butter and add rest of ingredients. Let chill in refrigerator until ready to serve.

Mrs. Lawrence Lucas (Nell Hall)

Shrimp Mold or Paste

2 pounds shrimp
¼ pound butter
¼ teaspoon lemon juice
Dash of mace

3 tablespoons mayonnaise
1 teaspoon Worcestershire
  sauce
Few drops red pepper sauce

Salt and black pepper

Put shrimp through meat grinder twice. Then rub butter and shrimp well together and add enough mayonnaise to soften slightly. Season well with ground mace, lemon juice, salt, pepper and sauces to taste. Chill mixture and serve with crackers or thin, crisp toast. Mayonnaise may be omitted and celery seed used instead of mace. This makes a delicious dish served with hominy for breakfast.

Mrs. C. Stuart Dawson (May Hutson)

Shrimp and Curry Mold

4 pounds shrimp
3 slices lemon
2 bay leaves
1 onion (chopped)
1 teaspoon salt

2 teaspoons curry powder
1½ cups mayonnaise
Juice of 2 lemons
2 onions (grated)
Salt and pepper

Grind shrimp which have been cooked with 3 slices of lemon, bay leaves, 1 chopped onion and teaspoon of salt. Add curry powder, mayonnaise, grated onion and juice of lemons, salt and pepper to taste. Mix well. Cut a square of cheesecloth that will overlap mold, wet it and lay it loosely in mold. Pack shrimp in this, and place in ice box several hours before serving. Unmold and serve on bed of lettuce with crackers or melba toast.

MRS. MICHAEL GROVES (Margaret Trouche)

Shrimp Remoulade

3 cups or 2 pounds shrimp
  (boiled and picked)
1 cup olive oil
  (or salad oil)
½ cup tarragon vinegar
1¼ cups chopped celery
2½ teaspoons chopped
  green pepper
2 tablespoons chopped onion
5 tablespoons chopped
  parsley
¾ cup creole mustard, or
  mustard and horseradish
2½ teaspoons salt
½ teaspoon black pepper
¼ cup paprika

Mix all ingredients and let marinate in refrigerator for twenty-four hours, stirring often. Use as salad, or on toast or crackers.

MRS. C. NORWOOD HASTIE (Sara Simons)

Spiced Pickled Shrimp

2 pounds shrimp
Bay leaves
6 small white onions
1 cup olive oil
¼ cup tarragon vinegar
2 teaspoons salt
½ teaspoon dry mustard
1 teaspoon sugar
1 teaspoon Worcestershire
  sauce.
Cayenne
Handful of pickling spices

In a crock, put a layer of boiled shrimp, a layer of bay leaves (about 5 to a layer) and a layer of very thin sliced onions. Alternate until all shrimp are used. Make a French dressing of the other ingredients and pour over shrimp, etc. Cover and put in refrigerator for 24 hours, stirring occasionally. Serve with toothpicks in a bowl over ice for a cocktail party or as a salad with lettuce.

MRS. JACK MAYBANK (Lavinia Huguenin)

Cheese or Paté in Aspic

2 cans consommé   6 tablespoons cold water
2 envelopes gelatine   2 tablespoons sherry

Heat consommé and add gelatine, which has been dissolved in cold water. Add sherry and set aside to cool. Pour consommé mixture about an inch deep in a lightly greased, round, oblong or melon mold. Put in ice box to congeal. When set, put either cheese or liverwurst mixture in center of mold and cover top and sides with the remaining liquid. Chill. Unmold and serve with crackers or melba toast.

CHEESE CENTER

3 (3 ounce) packages cream cheese   1 tablespoon Worcestershire
½ cup Roquefort cheese   ½ teaspoon hot sauce
     2 tablespoons sherry, or brandy or chives

LIVERWURST CENTER

1 pound liverwurst   2 (3 oz.) pkgs. cream cheese
2 tablespoons Worcester-shire   2 tablespoons whiskey

1 small onion, grated

MRS. THOMAS A. HUGUENIN (Mary Vereen)

Cream Cheese Spread

2 (3 ounce) packages cream cheese   2 teaspoons Worcestershire
2 tablespoons milk or cream   ½ pint mayonnaise
     Fine minced onion
     Dash of hot sauce

Blend cheese and mayonnaise well. Thin with milk or cream until very soft. Season to taste. Put in bowl in refrigerator to chill and serve on dish surrounded with potato chips . Serves fifteen.

MRS. STUART DAWSON (May Hutson)

Brandied Cheese Balls

1 pound sharp cheese
3 tablespoons mayonnaise
2 ounces good brandy
   or bourbon

2 dashes bitters
Salt to taste
Red pepper—dash or two

Let the cheese stand at room temperature for several hours, then put through meat grinder. Cream this thoroughly with other ingredients. *Chill before rolling into small balls.* Touch on one side with paprika and top with a sprig of green. Stores in ice box until ready to use.

MRS. KATHERINE HERMAN (Katherine Sheridan)

Cheese Balls

1 cup grated sharp cheese
¼ cup fine dry
   bread crumbs
¼ teaspoon salt
¼ teaspoon paprika

¼ teaspoon Worcestershire
1 egg yolk (slightly beaten)
1 egg white
   (stiffly beaten)
Cayenne pepper

Combine cheese with bread crumbs and seasonings. Blend thoroughly. Add egg yolk and mix well. Fold in egg white. Shape into small balls about ¾ of an inch in diameter and roll in more bread crumbs. Fry in deep hot fat until golden brown. Drain on soft paper. Serve hot.

MRS. HAROLD PETITT (Corine Neely)

Chipped Beef and Cream Cheese Spread

1 jar chipped beef (2½ oz.)
2 (3 ounce) packages
   cream cheese

½ cup cream
Onion juice

Fry beef in butter until crisp. Allow to cool and crumble. Mash cheese, and thin with cream. Season to taste with onion juice and add beef. Serve with potato chips, crackers or thin toast. Serves 12.

MRS. M. B. ALEXANDER (Ferdinand Williams)

Cheese Roll

½ pound sharp cheese   Worcestershire sauce
6 packages (small)   Garlic
   cream cheese   Grated onion
Chopped nuts

Grate the American cheese and combine with softened cream cheese, preferably in electric mixer. If too stiff to blend well, add a little cream or milk. Add grated onion and Worcestershire sauce, about two teaspoons of each, and a little very finely minced garlic. Mix well and let stand, covered, in the ice box for several hours. Shape into a ball and roll in chopped pecans. Chill again and serve with crisp crackers.

MRS. PRIOLEAU BALL (Teresa Daniel)

Cheese Straws

1 pound sharp cheese, grated   ¼ pound butter, creamed
1¾ cups plain flour   ½ teaspoon salt
¼ teaspoon red pepper

Cream butter, add cheese, salt and pepper, then flour. Put in cookie press or roll thin and cut in narrow strips four inches long. Bake in 350° oven for twenty-five minutes or until light brown. Makes about 100.

MRS. HENRY ELLERBE (Margaret Lucas)

Ice Box Cheese Wafers

½ pound grated sharp   1½ cups sifted flour
   cheese   Heavy pinch cayenne pepper
¼ pound butter, creamed   ½ teaspoon salt

Cream together cheese, butter, salt and pepper—add flour. Make into roll. Wrap in waxed paper and put in ice box. Will keep a month. When needed, slice into thin wafers and bake in moderate oven. A pecan half, baked on each wafer, is decorative. 6-8 dozen.

MRS. W. H. BARNWELL (Mary Royall)

Cocktail Biscuits

1 cup sifted flour
2 teaspoons baking powder
½ level teaspoon salt
3 level tablespoons shortening

⅜ cup milk
3-4 tablespoons cooking oil
1 cup ground country ham
¼ pound grated sharp cheese

Mix dry ingredients. Cut in shortening with knife. Add liquid gradually. Roll on floured board to ⅜" thickness. Shape with small biscuit cutter. Place in shallow pan into which cooking oil has been poured ⅛" the depth of the pan. Bake in 450° oven 12-15 minutes. Variation: Add ham or cheese to dough. Yield: 18 biscuits.

MRS. TRAPIER JERVEY (Mary Trott)

Caraway Sticks

2 cups flour
1 cup shortening
1 yeast cake

1 egg white
Water
Caraway seeds

Cut shortening into flour, rub with fingers. When thoroughly mixed, crumble the yeast over it and work with a pastry blender. Let stand one hour. Roll pieces of the dough into very thin sticks. Place on cookie sheet; brush with egg white that has been mixed with a little water; place on each stick a line of carraway seeds. Let rise until double in size. Cook in 400° oven 15 minutes. Makes many dozen.

MRS. JOHN ANDREW HAMILTON (Elizabeth Verner)

Celery Rings

1 stalk celery
3 tablespoons butter
1 (3 ounce) package
    cream cheese

3 tablespoons tomato paste
Salt and Pepper

Cream butter, add cheese and tomato paste and season to taste with salt and red pepper. Stuff all pieces of celery with mixture. First put celery hearts together, then place other pieces of celery around and make the stalk to original shape. Wrap in wax paper and chill. Slice, making rings.

Mrs. Louis Y. Dawson, Jr. (Virginia Walker)

Egg Balls

4 eggs, hard boiled
⅛ pound butter
Salt and red pepper

Worcestershire sauce
Celery seed
Bread crumbs

Grate eggs and cream with butter. Season to taste with red pepper, Worcestershire sauce and celery seed. Make into balls, put in ice box to set, then roll in rich bread crumbs that have been browned in oven. Equal parts of mashed fish and a few pinches of chopped parsley may be added to creamed eggs and rolled in bread crumbs. Makes 16-18 balls.

Mrs. Charles Waring (Margaret Simonds)

A South Sea Spread

2 ripe avocados
3 teaspoons of lemon juice

1 teaspoon salt
2 tablespoons of onion juice

Mash avocados with lemon juice; add other ingredients. This is an excellent spread for large potato chips.

Mrs. Owen Geer (Louisa Farrow)

Anchovy Puffs

½ cup butter
1 (3 ounce) package
   cream cheese

1 cup flour
1 tube anchovy paste (2 oz.)
½ cup pecans (chopped)

Blend butter and cheese, add flour. Chill and roll very thin and cut with small biscuit cutter. Spread each round with anchovy paste and a few pieces of chopped pecans. Fold over, making a puff. Bake in hot oven (400°) for about ten minutes. Serve hot. Makes about 45.

MRS. LOUIS Y. DAWSON, JR. (Virginia Walker)

Chicken and Almond Sandwich Spread

1 cup chopped chicken
1 cup chopped almonds

8 tablespoons cream
Salt and pepper to taste

Mix chopped chicken with finely chopped almonds and cream. Season to taste and make into sandwiches.

MRS. JOHN BENNETT (Susan Smythe)

Chicken Liver Spread

¼ pound chicken livers
¼ cup fresh mushrooms
1 tablespoon butter

Salt and pepper
Onion and lemon juice
Monosodium glutamate

Boil livers until soft. Drain and mash. Sauté mushrooms in butter for about 4 minutes. Chop fine and add to livers. Add salt, pepper, monosodium glutomate and juices to taste. Spread on ice box rye.

MRS. KATHERINE HERMAN (Katherine Sheridan)

Shrimp Canapé au Rhum

1½ pounds shrimp
½ cup light rum
¼ pound butter

½ teaspoon onion juice
½ teaspoon dry mustard
Lemon juice to taste

Salt and pepper to taste

Marinate boiled, peeled shrimp in rum for one hour or more. Run twice through a fine meat grinder. Cream butter. Combine with shrimp, onion juice, dry mustard, lemon juice, salt and pepper. Mix thoroughly. Chill and serve on small bread squares or potato chips.

MRS. HENRY EDMUNDS (Frances Smythe)

Mock Paté de Foie Gras Canapé

1 pound chicken livers
1 teaspoon salt
1 clove garlic
½ pound butter

1 teaspoon Worcestershire
1 tablespoon brandy
1 wineglass sherry
2 drops hot sauce

Salt and pepper to taste

Boil livers with salt and garlic until tender. When cool, put livers through ricer. Cream butter, add liver and seasoning. Yield: 48 canapés.

MISS I. L. DAWSON

Crab Meat Canapé

1 pound crab meat
  (2 cups)
2 cups finely chopped celery
  (washed and dried)
2 hard boiled eggs,
  finely chopped

1½ teaspoons mace
1 teaspoon black pepper
1 tablespoon grated onion
  and juice
¾ cup mayonnaise
Salt to taste

Mound on small rounds of white bread and top with a parsley leaf, or pile in tiny paté shells. This may be varied by using rounds of toast and sprinkling top with grated American cheese and running in oven for a few minutes.

MRS. KATHERINE HERMAN (Katherine Sheridan)

Sardine Canapé

2 small cans of sardines
  (skin and bone)
3 tablespoons lemon juice
1 tablespoon tarragon
  vinegar

½ teaspoon Worcestershire
¼ teaspoon monosodium
  glutomate
2 tablespoons melted butter
Salt and pepper to taste

Spread on buttered and toasted fingers of bread. Garnish with a border of finely chopped egg whites and top with olive rings. Serves 15.

MRS. KATHERINE HERMAN (Katherine Sheridan)

Clam Canapé

2 small cans minced clams
2 (3 ounce) packages
  cream cheese

Hot sauce, lemon juice, and
  salt to taste

Drain clams. Mix all ingredients. Heat in double boiler or chafing dish. Serve with melba toast or crackers.

MRS. THOMAS A. HUGUENIN (Mary Vereen)

Ham and Chutney Canapé

1 cup Virginia ham
  (ground)
1 cup chutney

½ cup heavy cream
Parmesan cheese

Mix ham and chutney thoroughly. Moisten with cream and spread heavily on rounds of toast, about ¼ inch thick. Sprinkle with grated cheese and heat in moderate oven for a few minutes. Yield: 18.

MISS I. L. DAWSON

Bacon and Cheese Canapé

1 egg, beaten
2 cups grated sharp cheese
2 loaves bread
½ pound bacon

10 dashes hot sauce
2 teaspoons Worcestershire
  sauce
1 teaspoon salt

Mix egg, grated cheese and seasonings thoroughly. Cut crust from bread and place 1 teaspoon of mixture on each one-inch piece of bread. Cover with pieces of bacon and broil in oven until bacon is done. Serves 30.

MRS. SAMUEL LAPHAM (Lydia Thomas)

Cocktail Sauce For Shrimp
Crab or Raw Vegetables

1 cup mayonnaise
1 teaspoon lemon juice
1 teaspoon curry powder
½ teaspoon finely minced
  onion

½ teaspoon Worcestershire
  sauce
½ teaspoon red pepper
  sauce
¼ cup chili sauce

Salt and pepper to taste
Mix well and keep in ice box until ready to serve.

MRS. HORACE L. JONES (Louise Dixon)

Suggestions for Mixtures to be used in Making Canapés

1. Chopped cooked lobster, cucumber, hard-cooked eggs and almonds mixed with mayonnaise.

2. Whole broiled mushroom topped with slice of stuffed olive, served hot.

3. Deviled ham mixed with chopped hard-cooked egg and horseradish.

4. Highly seasoned cheese topped with pecan, served hot.

5. Sliced tomato topped with thin slice of smoked cheese melted under flame and served hot.

6. Slice of hard-cooked egg with anchovy center.

7. Artichoke hearts marinated in tart French dressing.

8. Peanut butter covered with chutney.

9. A layer of anchovy paste covered with a paste of shredded crab meat, cream cheese and butter, seasoned with salt and pepper.

10. Shredded tuna fish mixed with lemon juice and mayonnaise.

11. Aspic jelly with anchovies or sardines included, on toasted bits of rye bread.

12. Large olives filled with cheese, wrapped in bacon; broiled.

13. Celery stuffed with cream cheese, mayonnaise and Roquefort cheese and topped with paprika.

14. Chicken liver balls rolled in minced chipped beef.

15. Anchovies on small triangles of toast spread with lemon butter.

16. Oysters or chicken livers wrapped in bacon; broiled.

17. Apples cut finger size, wrapped with chicken livers; broiled.

18. Pastry turnovers with anchovy paste, meat spreads, mincemeat, cheese.

OLD SAINT ANDREWS CHURCH
1706

SOUPS

".... Crab got tuh walk een duh pot demself or dey ain' wut."

She-Crab Soup
A soup to remember!
The feminine gender
Of crabs is expedient—
The secret ingredient.
The flavor essential
Makes men reverential
Who taste this collation
And cry acclamation.

She-Crab Soup

"She-crab" is much more of a delicacy than "he-crab," as the eggs add a special flavor to the soup. The street vendors make a point of calling "she-crab" loudly and of charging extra for them.

1 tablespoon butter	½ teaspoon Worcestershire
1 quart milk	1 teaspoon flour
¼ pint cream (whipped)	2 cups white crab meat
Few drops onion juice	and crab eggs
⅛ teaspoon mace	½ teaspoon salt
⅛ teaspoon pepper	4 tablespoons dry sherry

Melt butter in top of double boiler and blend with flour until smooth. Add the milk gradually, stirring constantly. To this add crab meat and eggs and all seasonings except sherry. Cook slowly over hot water for 20 minutes. To serve, place one tablespoon of warmed sherry in individual soup bowls, then add soup and top with whipped cream. Sprinkle with paprika or finely chopped parsley. Secret: if unable to obtain "she-crabs," crumble yolk of hard boiled eggs in bottom of soup plates. Serves 4-6.

MRS. HENRY F. CHURCH (Rea Bryant)

Carolina or She-Crab Soup

1 pound white crab meat	2 tablespoons sherry
1 pint milk	4 blades whole mace
1 pint cream	2 pieces lemon peel
½ stick of butter	¼ cup cracker crumbs

Salt and pepper to taste

Put milk in top of double-boiler with mace and lemon peel and allow to simmer for a few minutes. Then add crab, butter and cream and cook for 15 minutes. Thicken with cracker crumbs; season with salt and pepper and allow to stand on back of stove for a few minutes to bring out the flavor. Just before serving, add sherry. This same soup can be made with shrimp, which should be ground. Serves 6.

MRS. C. STUART DAWSON (May E. Hutson)

Aunt Blanche's She-Crab Soup

As given to me by my aunt, Mrs. R. Goodwyn Rhett.

1 cup white crab meat	2 cups milk
2 tablespoons butter	½ cup cream
1 small onion, grated	¼ teaspoon Worcestershire
Salt and pepper to taste	2 teaspoons flour
¼ teaspoon mace	1 tablespoon water
3 ribs celery, grated	3 tablespoons sherry

Put crab in double boiler; add butter, onion, salt, pepper, mace and celery. Let simmer for 5 minutes. Heat milk and add to crab mixture. Stir, add cream and Worcestershire sauce. Thicken with paste made of flour and water. Add sherry. Cook over low heat for ½ hour. Serves 4.

MRS. C. O. SPARKMAN (Mary Rhett Simonds)

46

Shrimp Soup

2 plates (2½ pounds)   4 cups milk
   cooked shrimp   Salt and pepper to taste
4 tablespoons butter   1 pint cream
Sherry to taste   2 tablespoons flour

Grind shrimp and add to milk. Place in top of double-boiler and cook over hot water for ½ hour. Remove from fire and add cream, butter, flour, salt and pepper which have been rubbed to a smooth paste. Sherry added just before serving improves the flavor. Serves 8.

MRS. LAWRENCE LUCAS (Nell Hall)

Company Oyster Stew

1 quart small oysters   ½ pint heavy cream
Suggestion of grated onion   3 tablespoons butter
½ cup finely cut celery   Salt, pepper and paprika
½ cup milk   1 tablespoon dry sherry

Strain oysters, saving liquor. Add onion to oysters and heat in liquor until edges curl. Into a heavy saucepan put celery and milk; simmer about 3 minutes. Add cream and butter, bring to the boiling point. Turn off heat and slowly add oysters and liquor. Add seasonings. Keep hot, but never let boil from this point. Heated sherry may be added, but try first without. Serve in hot soup plates with oyster crackers. Good with grapefruit-avocado salad and coffee. Serves 3-4, if the main dish.

MRS. R. BARNWELL RHETT (Virginia Prettyman)

Oyster Stew

1 quart milk	½ teaspoon pepper
1 cup cream	8 saltines, crumbled
1 quart oysters	1 cup steamed, diced celery
1 tablespoon butter	A little whole mace, if
1½ teaspoons salt	desired

Heat milk, cream, butter, saltine crumbs, soft celery and seasonings in top of double-boiler. Add oysters and cook until they curl on the edges. Serves 6.

MRS. WILLIAM H. BARNWELL (Mary Royall)

Oyster Soup

3 tablespoons butter	⅛ teaspoon black pepper
¾ cup diced celery	½ teaspoon monosodium
2 tablespoons flour	glutamate
1 quart whole milk	1 blade mace
1 pint oysters	½ teaspoon onion juice
1 teaspoon salt	(optional)

Over medium heat, melt butter and cook celery until tender. Shake in flour, stirring constantly. Pour in a little milk and stir until smooth, then slowly add remainder of milk. Add dry seasonings and cook until boiling point is reached. Add oysters and oyster liquor and onion juice, if desired. Serve as soon as oysters are thoroughly hot and plump. Serves 4-6.

MRS. LOUIS T. PARKER (Josephine Walker)

Brown Oyster Stew with Benne (Sesame) Seed

4 slices bacon

1 large onion, sliced

2 tablespoons flour

1½ cups oyster liquor

2 cups oysters

2 tablespoons parched

benne (see p. 356, No. 51)

Fry the bacon and onion until brown and remove from pan. Into the hot grease shake the flour and stir vigorously until flour is brown. Remove from stove and add oyster liquor or water slowly until the mixture is smooth. Return to fire and stir until slightly thickened. Pound the benne seed, using pestle and mortar, if available, and add to sauce. Lastly, add the oysters and cook until the edges curl. Serve immediately on rice or hominy. Serves 6.

MRS. AUGUSTINE T. S .STONEY (Louisa Jenkins)

Oyster Bisque

2 quarts oysters

1 cup thinly sliced onions

2 small cloves garlic

1½ cups oyster liquor

¼ cup butter

2½ cups light cream

Salt and pepper to taste

Drain the oysters; cook till the edges curl. Chop fine and put through a sieve. Add oyster liquor to the purée. Fry onions and garlic (minced fine) in butter until transparent but not brown. Add the cream, oyster purée and liquor. Heat together with seasoning, but do not boil. Serves 14.

MRS. FRANCIS J. PELZER, JR (Mary Branch Chisolm)

Clam Bisque

1 pint clams	Sprig of parsley
1 quart soup stock	1 bay leaf
(veal or chicken)	1 cup cream
½ cup uncooked rice	Salt and pepper to taste

Boil clams in their own liquor until they are done. Chop them very fine and return to liquor. Add soup stock, rice, parsley and bay leaf. Boil until the rice is tender. Strain the soup, mashing as much of the rice and clams through the strainer as possible. Strain again. To serve, heat the soup, add the cream and seasoning and beat with an egg whip. Serves 6-8.

MRS. JOHN SIMONDS (Frances Rees)

Clam Chowder

3 dozen clams in the shell	4 cups milk
3 cups of clam broth	Salt and pepper to taste
4 slices bacon	2 tablespoons flour
4 tablespoons butter	2 medium onions

2½ cups diced raw potatoes

Scrub clams clean with hard brush. Open with clam knife, being careful not to lose any of the liquor in the shell. Strain liquor through two thicknesses of cheese cloth. Grind clams. Chip bacon and onions and fry until brown. Put ground clams, potatoes, bacon and onions in kettle and cover with just enough water to cook potatoes and clams. When done, add clam liquor, milk and seasonings. If a thick chowder is desired, make a paste of melted butter and flour and thicken to desired consistency. Add butter, salt and pepper. Serves 8-10.

MRS. CARLTON G. DAVIES (Harriet Goodacre)

Creamy Fish Chowder

6 pounds of fish
1 bay leaf
1 stalk celery (with tops)
3 cups milk
Fat from 2-inch square of
    salt pork

3 large Irish potatoes
2 cups cream
Salt to taste
3 onions

Select whiting, flounder or blackfish. The last is my choice. Buy almost 1 pound of fish per person if the chowder is to be the main dish and served in large bowls. Cut all amounts in half for ordinary portions.

Clean and scale fish, leaving on heads, tails and fins. Wash thoroughly and place in cold water to cover. Chop celery and onions very fine. Add these, bay leaf and salt to fish. Bring to a boil and simmer for 20 minutes. Remove from fire; when cool, bone and skin the fish. Strain broth. To broth, add tried out fat from diced salt pork, and potatoes, diced very small. Boil until potatoes are done. Add fish, cream and milk. Simmer for 5 minutes and serve with crackers. Serves 8-10.

MRS. JOHN McGOWAN (Elizabeth Calvin)

Sea-Food Gumbo

¼ pound butter
2 quarts water
2 pounds fresh okra
1 pint raw oysters
4 tablespoons flour

2 pounds fresh raw shrimp
Salt and pepper to taste
5 fresh tomatoes
1 pound fresh crab meat
2 pounds fresh fish

Melt butter and add flour. Make a smooth paste and stir constantly over fire until a rich brown, being careful not to burn. Add water, tomatoes and okra (chopped fine). Cook slowly for one hour. Add crab meat, oysters, shrimp (picked and de-veined) and fish (minus bones and skin). Cook 15 minutes; add seasonings. Soup should be thick. Add steamed rice to each serving. Serves 8.

MRS. CARLTON G. DAVIES (Harriet Goodacre)

New Cut Plantation Gumbo

½ pound raw ham	1 large bell pepper
½ pound raw veal	1 clove garlic
1 pound raw shrimp	2 bay leaves
1 pound fresh crab meat	Few sprigs of parsley
(dark)	A little thyme
3 medium onions	2 tablespoons filé powder
2 large cans tomatoes	3 quarts water
½ pound fresh okra	Salt and pepper to taste

Cut ham, veal, okra, onion, bell pepper and parsley into small pieces and fry in bacon drippings. When brown, add boiling water, tomatoes, thyme, garlic, (cut fine) bay leaves, salt and pepper. Cook 30 minutes, then add shrimp and crab and cook 30 minutes longer. Add filé powder, stirring well. This is better made the day before and re-heated to allow the gumbo to become well-seasoned. Serve with steamed rice. Serves 16.

MRS. ROBERT GAMBLE (Mildred Franklin)

Gumbo with Sassafras

1 four-pound hen or capon	2 large onions
2 tablespoons butter	3 dozen oysters
½ pound lean ham	1 tablespoon filé
2 teaspoons creole	(ground sassafras
herb blend	leaves)
¼ pod red pepper	1 teaspoon salt
(remove seeds)	1 quart plain water and
½ teaspoon garlic salt	liquor from oysters

Chop ham fine. Cut chicken fine. Put butter, ham and chicken in soup kettle, cover tightly and fry 10 minutes. Add onions, salt, garlic salt, red pepper, herb blend, and stir until brown; add water slowly; add oyster liquor. Cook 1½ hours or until meat is tender. When ready to serve, and still boiling, add oysters and cook 3 minutes. Mix in filé just before serving. A tablespoon of steamed hot rice may be served in each soup plate. Serves 8-10.

MRS. SIMONS VANDER HORST WARING (Louisa Johnson)

Cooter Soup

1 large or 2 small
  "yellow belly" cooters
  (preferably female)
1 large onion, chopped
Salt to taste
2 teaspoons allspice

Red pepper to taste
3 tablespoons dry sherry
4 quarts of water
1 small Irish potato, diced
12 whole cloves
2 tablespoons Worcestershire

Flour to thicken

Kill cooter by chopping off head. Let it stand inverted until thoroughly drained, then plunge into boiling water for five minutes. Crack the shell all around very carefully, so as not to cut the eggs which are lodged near surface. The edible parts are the front and hind quarters and a strip of white meat adhering to the back of the shell, the liver and the eggs. Remove all outer skin which peels very easily if water is hot enough. Wash thoroughly and allow to stand in cold water a short while, or place in refrigerator over night.

Boil cooter meat, onion and potato in the water, and cook until meat drops from bones—about 2 hours. Remove all bones and skin and cut meat up with scissors. Return meat to stock, add spices and simmer. Brown flour in skillet, mix with 1 cup of stock to smooth paste and thicken soup. Twenty minutes before serving add cooter eggs. Add sherry and garnish with thin slices of lemon. Serves 6-8.

MRS. CLARENCE STEINHART (Kitty Ford)

Brown Soup

1 beef soup-shank
2 quarts water
2 tablespoons lard
1 large onion, chopped fine
2 potatoes, diced small

Few whole spice
Salt and pepper to taste
2 hard boiled eggs, sliced
1 lemon, sliced
Sherry

Brown meat, then chopped onions, in lard. To this add water, potatoes, salt, pepper and spices. Cook slowly for several hours. Add sliced egg, or a lemon slice to each serving, or a bit a sherry, if desired. Serves 8.

MRS. I. G. BALL (Janie Johnson)

Mrs. Alston Pringle's Mock Terrapin Soup

Mrs. Alston Pringle's reputation as a fine cook was so well-established that it is still spoken of almost reverentially. In fact, a colored cook who worked in her household once remarked, "When she puts in de buttah, ah turns ma back."

3 pounds lean beef	½ teaspoon dry mustard
1 pint milk	1½ quarts water
1 tablespoon flour	¼ pound of butter
½ teaspoon mace	½ pint cream

Salt and pepper to taste

Boil meat and water until 1 quart of liquid remains. Add 1 pint of milk and ¼ pound butter. Remove meat, allow to cool, grind and return to stock. Let it cook down a little more. Add flour dissolved in cream. Add seasonings. Serves 8.

Mrs. John Simonds (Frances Rees)

Mrs. Alston Pringle's Calf's Head Soup

1 calf's head	4 quarts water
1 teaspoon salt	1 teaspoon red and
1 teaspoon allspice	black pepper
1 rib celery	1 small onion, chopped
1 tablespoon flour	Few sprigs parsley

Sherry to taste

Remove brain from calf's head, wash head thoroughly, and boil in four quarts of water until tender. Remove all bones, cut meat very fine, and return to stock. Add all seasonings and boil one hour. Thicken with browned flour and boil one-half hour longer. Add sherry just before serving. Serves 8-10.

Mrs. C. O. Sparkman (Mary Rhett Simonds)

Mrs. Alston Pringle's White Soup

1 five-pound fowl	5 quarts water
3 blades mace	6 blanched almonds
1 quart cream	3 slices bread
1 pint milk	1 tablespoon flour

Salt and pepper to taste

Cut up the fowl, add mace and water. Boil until very tender. Remove meat and bones from stock . Cut meat very fine. Beat almonds to a paste and mix with chicken. Break bread in small pieces and add to 1 quart of stock and 1 quart of cream. Add this to chicken and work into a paste, add more liquor if it needs thinning. Bring to a boil, thicken with flour, season and add milk. Serves 10-12.

MRS. C. O. SPARKMAN (Mary Rhett Simonds)

Mrs. Alston Pringle's Onion Soup

3 pounds lean beef	2 cups vermicelli
1½ quarts water	2 cups crisp, fried onions

Cover beef with water and cook until meat is very well done. Add vermicelli and let boil until it is tender; add onions. Stir swiftly until it thickens, then season to taste with salt and pepper. Serves 8.

MRS. JOHN SIMONDS (Frances Rees)

Chicken Soup

A 5-pound fowl, cut up	3 teaspoons salt
4 quarts water	3 tablespoons flour
1 stalk of celery	5 medium onions
(tops also)	5 sprigs parsley

1 teaspoon pepper

Chop onions, celery, parsley and add to chicken and water. Add salt and pepper as soon as boiling begins. Cook until meat falls from bones (at least 2 hours) then remove bones. Make a smooth paste of flour and 1 cup of broth and thicken soup. Steamed rice may be added if desired. Serves 8-10.

MRS. CARLTON G. DAVIES (Harriet Goodacre)

Grouper Cubillon

3 pounds grouper
1 quart water
2 ribs celery
1 onion, quartered
1 bay leaf
1½ teaspoons salt
6 peppercorns
Salt and pepper to taste

2 green peppers, chopped
6 medium onions, chopped
½ pound butter or ¾ cup
   olive oil
3 (No. 2) cans tomatoes
   (7½ c.)
1 clove garlic, crushed
3 bay leaves

Cut fish into small cubes, reserving heads and large bones for stock. Use them with 6 ingredients, next listed, and simmer together until stock is reduced to half. In a deep skillet, cook peppers and onions in the fat until tender. Add remaining ingredients and cook 10 minutes more. Add stock until the mixture is of chowder consistency and gently place fish on top. Let simmer, without boiling, for 10 minutes. Do not stir. When fish is cooked, mix together and serve in soup plates with French bread. (Any chowder fish may be used.) Serves 8.

MRS. SERGE POUTIATINE (Shirley Manning)

Okra Soup

1 large beef shank
4 quarts water
Salt and pepper
3 quarts okra, cut small
1 teaspoon sugar

1 (No. 2) can tomatoes (2½ c.)
1 (No. 2½) can tomatoes (3½ c.)
1 medium onion, chopped

1 extra quart water

Boil shank in 4 quarts of salted water until tender . Add okra, tomatoes, onion, sugar, salt and pepper. Cook slowly about 5 hours, adding extra water as soup cooks down. Yield: about 5 quarts.

MRS. DAVID HUGUENIN (Lavinia Inglesby)

Charleston Okra Soup

1 large beef bone (plenty of meat)	3 quarts water
2 medium onions (chopped)	1 piece breakfast bacon
3 pounds fresh okra, chopped fine	8 large, fresh tomatoes, or 2 (No. 2½) cans tomatoes (7 c.)

Salt and pepper, bay leaf

Cook meat in water slowly for two hours. Add okra, bacon, and peeled tomatoes, bay leaf, onions, salt and pepper to taste; let cook another two hours; add more water, if needed. Hot rice and buttered cornsticks are a tasty accompaniment. Serves 8-10.

Mrs. Daniel E. Huger (Louise Chisolm)

Turkey Stew

1 turkey carcass with considerable meat	1 large onion, chopped
	Salt and pepper to taste
2 tablespoons flour	Sprig of thyme

Break up turkey carcass, place in kettle with seasonings and just enough water to cover. Cook until meat falls off the bones. Remove all bones and cut meat up in very small pieces. Mix flour with ½ cup of the broth to make a smooth paste. Add to boiling soup; add cut-up meat and cook until a little thicker. Serves 6.

Mrs. F. Mitchell Johnson (Margaret Silcox)

Split Pea Soup

1 meaty ham bone	1 package green or yellow split peas
3 quarts water	
½ cup chopped celery	2 medium onions, chopped

Salt and pepper to taste

If you wish the soup to cook quickly, soak the peas in water overnight. Drain. Put peas and ham bone in water, add onions and celery. Bring to a boil and simmer slowly, stirring occasionally until peas have disintegrated and turned to mush. Add seasonings. Serves 8-10.

Mrs. William Dotterer (Sue Bolt)

Black Bean Soup

2 cups black beans	2 quarts water
1 ham bone	2 tablespoons chopped onion
2 ribs celery, chopped	2 teaspoons salt
½ teaspoon pepper	¼ teaspoon dry mustard
4 tablespoons butter	1½ tablespoons flour
3 tablespoons sherry	1 lemon, thin-sliced

Soak beans overnight. Drain. Add to water and ham bone. Cook onion in one-half the butter (2 tablespoons). Add onion and celery to beans and simmer three to four hours in covered kettle (until beans are soft). Put through fine strainer for a smooth soup. Re-heat to boiling, add salt, pepper, mustard and remaining butter, and flour. Add sherry when ready to serve and garnish with lemon. Serves 8-10.

MRS. ERIC BIANCHI (Kay Dennison)

Cream of Mushroom Soup

½ pound fresh mushrooms	¼ teaspoon paprika
4 cups water	4 tablespoons butter
½ small onion	4 tablespoons flour
Sprinkle cayenne pepper	1 cup milk

½ cup cream

(Save a few mushroom caps to add to soup).

Cover mushroom caps and stems (which have been peeled and chopped) with water. Add sliced onion and salt and boil slowly for ½ hour. Melt butter in top of double-boiler and add remainder of mushroom caps, chopped. Cook 3 minutes, add flour and milk to make a smooth, thick sauce. Add mushroom liquor and mushrooms rubbed through a sieve or puréed in blender. Just before serving add cayenne pepper, paprika and cream. Serves 6.

MRS. C. O. SPARKMAN (Mary Rhett Simonds)

Cream of Spinach Soup

2 quarts fresh spinach or   ½ teaspoon salt
   1 package frozen spinach   1 quart milk
2 tablespoons butter   ½ cup chopped onion
2 tablespoons flour   Cayenne pepper to taste

Blend melted butter and flour, add salt and cook 5 minutes. Add the milk slowly. Cook fresh or frozen spinach your favorite way. Mash spinach through a wire strainer with onion. Add to milk, with seasoning. Serve hot with or without a topping of whipped cream and paprika. Serves 6-8.

MRS. LIONEL LEGGE (Dorothy H. Porcher)

Cream of Cheese Soup

1 quart milk   4 tablespoons grated sharp
1 2-inch piece of carrot   cheese
½ onion   2 egg yolks
2 tablespoons soft butter   ¼ teaspoon mace
2 tablespoons flour   ¼ teaspoon nutmeg
                       Salt and pepper to taste

Combine milk, onion and carrots in saucepan; boil until the vegetables are tender, stirring so as not to burn the milk. Remove the vegetables and place the milk in top of a double boiler. Add the roux made from the butter and flour (combined to a thick smooth paste). Place over medium heat and stir until thickened. Add cheese and stir until well blended and smooth. Remove from heat and beat in slightly beaten egg yolks and seasonings with a whisk. Serve hot. Can be reheated over low heat in a double boiler. Serves 6.

MRS. T. LADSON WEBB, JR. (Ann Moore)

Iced Spinach Soup

1½ pounds fresh spinach or 1 package frozen spinach	1 cup chicken stock
	1 cup cream
	Salt and cayenne pepper to taste
1 cup milk	

Cook fresh or frozen spinach your favorite way. When cool, put through a fine meat grinder or in blender. Add milk, cream, and stock; season and chill thoroughly before serving. Serves 5-6.

MRS. EUGENE JOHNSON, JR. (Mary Atmar Smith)

Tradd Street Cucumber Soup

2 cucumbers	1 quart milk
Salted water	1 can consomme
¼ pound butter	Salt and pepper, to taste
4 tablespoons flour	Paprika or chives

Peel and dice cucumbers. Boil until clear in sufficient salted water to cover, then drain. Melt butter and cook cucumbers in this for ten minutes. Add flour and stir well. Add milk slowly. Cook until fairly thick, then add consomme, salt and pepper. Serve hot with paprika or cold with chopped chives. Serves 6.

MRS. MARTIN ROBERTSON (Mary Martin)

Cold Cucumber Soup

3 tablespoons butter or margarine	1½ tablespoons parsley, chopped
2 onions, chopped	2 teaspoons dry mustard
3 or 4 cucumbers, diced and unpeeled (or peeled if preferred)	2 cans chicken broth
	1 pint half and half
	Salt and ground pepper to taste
2 potatoes, diced	

Melt butter and cook onions until transparent; add broth, potatoes, parsley, mustard, salt and pepper. Cook low until potatoes are tender; then put mixture in blender with raw cucumbers and purée. Chill well before serving, and then add cream. The mixture lasts well for a week in refrigerator for small servings. A frozen package of chopped spinach, cooked and drained, adds zip to above mixture when blended. Serves 8 to 10.

MRS. HUGH LANE (Beverly Glover)

Crème Vichyssoise

6 leeks (white part only)	2 quarts chicken stock
2 medium onions	1 cup sweet cream
¼ pound butter	Salt and white pepper
¾ pound white potatoes	Chives

Chop onions and leeks fine, cook them very slowly in ¼ pound butter. Do not brown, just cook until soft, then add stock and potatoes peeled and cut in small pieces. Add salt and pepper to taste and cook until potatoes are done. Put through a very fine strainer. Add cream. Chill thoroughly. When serving, sprinkle finely chopped chives on top. Serves 6-8.

MRS. LOUIS DEB. McCRADY (Eleanor Laurens)

Crème Vichyssoise with Curry

Delicious for a "Three O'clock Dinner."

6 tablespoons butter	2 quarts chicken broth
10 leeks (white portion only)	½ teaspoon curry powder
1 pound potatoes (finely sliced)	2 cups light cream
	3 tablespoons chopped chives
	Salt and pepper to taste

Melt butter and simmer cut-up leeks in covered pot for 10 minutes. Add sliced potatoes and continue to simmer for 10 minutes more, being careful not to brown the leeks and potatoes. Add chicken broth, salt and pepper and boil gently in covered pot for 45 minutes. Mash through a fine strainer, add curry and 1 cup of cream. Boil 5 minutes more, then set aside to chill. Before serving, stir in remaining cream and half of the chives. Garnish each serving with remaining chives and serve icy cold. For an interesting variation use sour cream for the second cup—the one stirred in before serving. Serves 8.

MISS JOSEPHINE PINCKNEY

Chilled Shrimp Soup

1½ pounds	1 tablespoon butter
fresh raw shrimp	3 tablespoons sherry
1 quart milk	1 teaspoon salt

1 cup cream

Heat milk in top of double-boiler, add butter and salt. Pick and de-vein raw shrimp and grind. Add shrimp to milk and continue to cook 20 minutes. Remove shrimp from milk, setting aside a small portion to sprinkle over each serving. Mash remainder of shrimp through a strainer and return to milk. Set aside to cool, add cream and sherry and allow to become icy cold. Top each serving with a sprinkling of ground shrimp and grated parsley and serve as cold as possible. Serves 6.

MRS. MARGUERITE S. VALK (Marguerite Sinkler)

Tomato-Cheese Ice

2 tablespoons grated	1 teaspoon salt
Roquefort cheese	⅛ teaspoon pepper
1 three-ounce package	2 tablespoons lemon juice
cream cheese	2 cups tomato juice
¼ teaspoon grated onion	2 stiffly beaten egg whites
1 teaspoon Worcestershire	

Cream together grated Roquefort cheese and cream cheese. Add onion, Worcestershire sauce, salt, pepper and lemon juice. Add gradually tomato juice, blending smoothly. Pour into freezing tray and freeze until all but a portion of the center is frozen. Then remove from tray, break up in a bowl and beat smooth with a chilled rotary beater. Quickly fold in beaten egg whites, return to freezing tray and serve in sherbet glasses when frozen. This is a delicious first course. Serves 6.

MRS. WILLIAM McG. MORRISON (Caroline Sams)

Tomato Emincé

7 very large tomatoes
1 small onion, grated
1½ teaspoons salt
¼ teaspoon ground pepper

5 tablespoons mayonnaise
1 heaping tablespoon minced
   parsley
1 teaspoon curry powder

Scald, skin and chop tomatoes. Add onion, salt and pepper. Chill in freezing tray of refrigerator until very cold, but not frozen. Mix mayonnaise, parsley and curry thoroughly. Serve tomato mixture in chilled bouillon cups and top each with 2 teaspoons of the curried mayonnaise. Serves 4-5.

MRS. SERGE POUTIATINE (Shirley Manning)

Basic Cream Soups for Blenders

2 cups milk
2 tablespoons butter
2 tablespoons flour

Sliver of onion
Accent
Salt and pepper to taste

Put all ingredients in blender except butter. Then put in heavy pot, add butter and heat. Cut down on flour if using alot of vegetables.

MRS. THOMAS A. HUGUENIN (Mary Vereen)

Seasoning for Soup

2 ounces onions
5 ounces carrots
5 ounces leeks
1 ounce celery
2 quarts water

1 bouquet of herbs
   (parsley may be
   substituted)
Any herbs may be used
   except sage

2 pounds beef soup-shank

Boil down to 3½ pints.

MRS. W. TURNER LOGAN, SR. (Louise Lesesne)

CASTING FOR SHRIMP

 # SEAFOODS

" 'E hab uh hebby pan full uh mullet, en' 'e hab swimp en' crab all two, en' 'e hab hominy en' ting."

"Lady, git yo' dishpan—

"Yuh come de swimp-man!

"Swimpee! Swimpee! Raw, raw, swi-i-mp!"

"Fi-ish! Fresh Fish! I got de porgy!

"Oh, de porgy walk an' de porgy talk,

"De porgy eat wid de knife an' fork!

"Porgy! Porgy! Fresh fish!

Shrimp

The very small shrimp caught in the creeks and inlets abounding the Carolina Low-Country are most delicious. They cannot be purchased from the markets but from the negro hucksters who cry their wares through the old city's streets: "Swimpee, raw, raw swimp!" These shrimp give the following receipts that extra flavor and distinction so much enjoyed.

Most receipts call for cooked or boiled shrimp. To cook shrimp: Wash the shrimp thoroughly and boil 4 or 5 minutes in a covered pot, using just enough salted water to cover them. As soon as they cool, they are "picked" or peeled. Large shrimp are cooked longer; the black line removed and the shrimp cut into pieces. Black pepper, celery, onion, or paprika can be boiled with shrimp for added flavor. Beer is sometimes substituted for water in cooking shrimp. To pick a shrimp any local person will tell you to "pull, peel, pinch"—you pull off the heads, peel shell off the body, and pinch shrimp out of the tail.

Shrimp for Breakfast

Shrimp prepared in various ways have long been a breakfast favorite in the coastal region, and they are always served with hominy. Many of the following receipts have been handed down for generations. The simplest and easiest way of serving breakfast shrimp is to sauté them in melted butter and serve hot. Use either cooked shrimp for this or shrimp that have been peeled raw. Slices of shrimp paste are a good breakfast accompaniment with hominy. (See receipt for shrimp paste under Canapés).

Breakfast Shrimp

1½ cups small, peeled raw shrimp	Salt and pepper to taste
2 tablespoons chopped onion	1 teaspoon Worcestershire sauce
2 teaspoons chopped green pepper	1 tablespoon tomato catsup
3 tablespoons bacon grease	1½ tablespoons flour
	1 cup water or more

Fry onion and green pepper in bacon grease. When onion is golden, add shrimp; turn these several times with onion and pepper. Add enough water to make a sauce—about 1 cup. Do not cover shrimp with water or your sauce will be tasteless. Simmer 2 or 3 minutes and thicken with flour and a little water made into a paste. Add seasoning, Worcestershire sauce and catsup. Cook slowly until sauce thickens. Serve with hominy. Serves 4.

MRS. BEN SCOTT WHALEY (Emily Fishburne)

Variations A variation to the above receipt says that cooked shrimp may be floured and fried with onions browned in butter. Hot water is slowly added and shrimp allowed to simmer under cover for several minutes or until a thick gravy forms. Stir constantly.

Charleston Shrimp Pie

2 pounds shrimp
2 cups bread crumbs
2 cups tomato juice
½ teaspoon salt

3 tablespoons butter
1 tablespoon hot sauce
2 tablespoons Worcestershire
1 cup tomato catsup

Cook and peel shrimp. Mix all ingredients together and bake in casserole for 30 minutes at 350°. Serves 8.

Mrs. Owen Geer (Louisa Farrow)

Edisto Shrimp Pie

2 cups peeled cooked shrimp
2 cups bread crumbs
    (about 3 large slices)
1 cup milk
1 tablespoon chopped celery
    or parsley

2 tablespoons sherry wine
Salt and pepper to taste
1 teaspoon Worcestershire
2 tablespoons butter
Pinch of nutmeg or mace,
    if desired

Soak bread in milk, add shrimp, butter and seasonings; place in buttered baking dish and bake in moderate oven (375°) for 30 minutes. Serves 6.

Miss Margaret Read

Beaufort Stewed Shrimp

1 pound or 1 plate raw
    shrimp
½ cup water

1 heaping tablespoon butter
2 tablespoons vinegar
Salt and black pepper

Boil shrimp in salted water until tender. When cool enough, peel shrimp and put in saucepan with water, pepper, salt and butter. Let simmer for a few minutes and then add vinegar. Continue to let them simmer for another five minutes or so longer. Serve either hot or cold for breakfast with hominy. Serves 4.

Mrs. Stuart Dawson (May Elliott Hutson)

My Favorite Shrimp Pie

3 slices bread, cubed
1 cup milk
2 cups cooked shrimp
2 tablespoons melted butter

3 eggs, well beaten
1 cup chopped green pepper
    and celery, mixed
Salt and pepper to taste

Soak bread in milk and mash with fork. Add shrimp, butter, eggs and other seasonings. Turn it into buttered casserole and bake in moderately hot oven about 20 minutes. Serves 4-6.

JAMES F. BYRNES, GOVERNOR OF SOUTH CAROLINA

Sullivan's Island Shrimp

1 pound sliced bacon,
    chopped
¼ pound butter
2 cups chopped onions
2 cups chopped celery
2 (No. 2½) cans tomatoes
    (7 c.)
1 can water
1 can condensed tomato soup
1 bottle tomato catsup
1 tablespoon salt

2 cloves garlic
1 teaspoon celery seed
1 teaspoon powdered
    allspice
1 teaspoon curry powder
1 lemon, sliced thin
Hot sauce to taste
5 pounds raw dressed shrimp
1 cup crushed saltine
    crackers
1 cup sherry

Cook bacon in frying pan until crisp, remove. Add butter, onion and celery to grease in pan; sauté until tender. Transfer bacon and this mixture to large pot, add remaining ingredients (except shrimp, cracker crumbs and sherry) and cook slowly for 2 hours until mixture thickens. Add raw shrimp and cook until shrimp are done. Add cracker crumbs and sherry and serve with fluffy rice. Serves 16.

MRS. CORNELIUS HUGUENIN (Evelyn Anderson)

James Island Shrimp Pie

This receipt came originally from Mrs. Robert Lebby, Sr. of James Island, about 1860.

1 cup of raw rice	5 tablespoons tomato catsup
2 cups water	2½ tablespoons Worcester-
1 teaspoon salt	shire
¼ cup butter	Salt and pepper to taste
2 eggs	2 pounds shrimp
Pinch of mace	1 cup milk (approximately)

Cook rice in salted water until very soft and stir butter into it. Combine all ingredients with cooked shrimp, adding enough milk to make mixture the consistency of thick custard. Put in buttered casserole and bake in moderate oven until brown on top (about 30 minutes). Serves 8.

MRS. JOHN T. JENKINS (Hess Lebby)

Popham Shrimp Pie

1 quart canned tomatoes	2 or 3 pounds shrimp
½ pound shortening	6 strips bacon
1 quart cooked rice	1 teaspoon Worcestershire
½ pound onions	Red pepper, salt, paprika, mace, to taste

Fry the onions, grated fine, the tomatoes, the shrimp (which have been picked while raw) and all the seasoning in the shortening. Cook these at a very low heat. Add boiled rice (must be dry and fluffy) to the cooked sauce of shrimp and tomatoes and place in a baking dish. On top of the mixture add 6 or 8 strips of raw bacon and place the dish in oven, preheated to 375°, and cook until bacon is crisp. If preferred, the dish may be kept in oven at 250° for two hours or more so as to be ready at any time for an evening dish.

MRS. WILLIAM POPHAM (Louisa Stoney)

Old Receipt for Corn and Shrimp

2 pounds shrimp
3 eggs
3 cups sweet milk
½ cup chopped celery
¼ cup chopped onion
¼ cup chopped green
    bell pepper
1 cup chopped green (fresh)
    corn

1 teaspoon each prepared
    mustard and
    Worcestershire
½ stick butter (¼ cup)
Salt, pepper
Milk biscuits or
    lunch crackers
Cracker crumbs

Beat eggs slightly. Mix all ingredients together. (Wash shrimp and pick raw. They may be put in raw, or cooked 5 minutes in double boiler. Put in juices if they are cooked.) Season to taste. Line buttered casserole with milk biscuits or lunch crackers. Pour in mixture. Sprinkle top with buttered cracker crumbs. Bake at 300° for one hour. Serves 10.

MRS. M. L. McCRAE (Ena Mae Black)

Shrimp Casserole

½ pound sliced mushrooms
2 tablespoons butter
1 minced onion
2 tomatoes, cut up
½ cup thin cream
2 tablespoons flour

¼ cup sherry
1 tablespoon Worcestershire
3 pounds shrimp
½ cup buttered bread
    crumbs
Salt, pepper and paprika

Sauté mushrooms in butter. Add onion and tomatoes and simmer for ten minutes. Blend cream and flour and add along with sherry, Worcestershire, salt, pepper and paprika, to taste. Add shrimp, cooked and peeled, and put in large buttered casserole. Top with crumbs and bake in 350° oven until brown (20 minutes). Serves 8.

MRS. KENNETH LYNCH (Lyall Wannamaker)

Shrimp and Corn Pie

2 cups corn, grated from cob or 1 can of corn	½ cup milk 1 cup cooked shrimp
2 eggs, slightly beaten	1 teaspoon Worcestershire
1 tablespoon butter	Salt, pepper and mace to taste

To grated corn, add eggs, butter, milk, shrimp and seasoning. Bake in buttered casserole in 300° oven for 30 minutes. Serves 6. *Variation:* Some prefer to use corn cut from cob and not grated.

MRS. REES F. FRASER (Mary Maybank)

Shrimp Stuffed in Bell Peppers

6 bell peppers (medium)	3 tablespoons chopped celery
2 cups shrimp, cooked and picked	1 tablespoon chopped onion 1 tablespoon chopped
1 cup bread crumbs	bell pepper
2 eggs, beaten	1 teaspoon salt
½ cup milk	⅛ teaspoon black pepper
3 tablespoons butter	1 tablespoon Worcestershire

Cut off tops and remove seeds from peppers. Cook pepper shells in boiling water for five minutes and then put at once into cold water. Cut shrimp slightly. Combine with eggs, crumbs and milk. Sauté chopped ingredients in butter for three minutes, and add to shrimp mixture. Add seasonings and stuff into pepper shells, putting a few bread crumbs and a dot of butter on top of each Bake 30 to 40 minutes in moderate oven (375°). Serves 6.

MRS. LOUIS T. PARKER (Josephine Walker)

73

Shrimp in Guinea Squash

1 guinea squash	Dash hot sauce and mace
(eggplant) medium	1 cup finely crumbled bread
1 pound shrimp	1 teaspoon Worcestershire
2 eggs	½ teaspoon black pepper
1 teaspoon salt, scant	Toast crumbs

Small piece of butter

Cut guinea squash in half, lengthwise. Scoop out pulp, taking care not to pierce shell. Steam or boil pulp until tender, mash thoroughly. Add cooked shrimp, bread crumbs, and seasoning, then the well-beaten eggs. Pour into squash shells which have been wiped outside with oil. Sprinkle tops with toast crumbs, dot with butter. Bake in moderate oven about 30 minutes . Serves 4-6.

MRS. ARTHUR J. STONEY (Anne Montague)

Baked Shrimp Paste

3 pounds shrimp	Salt and pepper (red and
6 baking powder biscuits	black) to taste
¼ pound butter	1 teaspoon Worcestershire
½ small bell pepper	Pinch dry mustard

Boil and peel shrimp. Grind them thoroughly in a meat choper with biscuits and bell pepper. Add seasoning and Worcestershire sauce. Mix with hands until well blended. Add melted butter to this. Use hands to pat and press this mixture into a greased loaf-shaped pan. Bake at 400° for 15 minutes. Turn out when cold and cut in thin slices. (See Canapé chapter for shrimp paste). Serves 8.

MRS. THADDEUS STREET (Mary Leize Simons)

Hampton Plantation Shrimp Pilau

4 slices bacon	2 tablespoons chopped
1 cup rice (raw)	bell pepper
3 tablespoons butter	Salt and pepper to taste
½ cup celery cut small	1 teaspoon Worcestershire
2 cups shrimp (cleaned)	1 tablespoon flour

Water for rice (pg. 157)

Fry bacon until crisp. Save to use later. Add bacon grease to water in which you cook rice. In another pot, melt butter, add celery and bell pepper. Cook a few minutes; add shrimp which have been sprinkled with Worcestershire sauce and dredged with flour. Stir and simmer until flour is cooked. Season with salt and pepper. Now add cooked rice and mix until rice is "all buttery" and "shrimpy." You may want to add more butter. Into this stir the crisp bacon, crumbled. Serve hot. Serves 6.

MRS. PAUL SEABROOK (Harriott Horry Rutledge)

Shrimp Croquettes

3 tablespoons butter	1 teaspoon grated onion
5 tablespoons flour	1 teaspoon Worcestershire
1 cup milk	2 eggs
½ teaspoon salt	2 cups cooked, ground
Pepper	shrimp

Bread or cracker crumbs

Make a thick cream sauce of butter, flour and milk; add seasoning. **Remove** from stove, stir in one raw egg. Add shrimp and **refrigerate** until firm enough to shape into oblong croquettes. Roll **in fine** crumbs, then in beaten egg, and again in crumbs. Fry in **deep** fat.

Variation: Crab meat can be used instead of shrimp. Serves 6.

MRS. FREDERICK RICHARDS (Sarah Lee Watkins)

Jehossee Plantation Fried Shrimp

1 pound shrimp
2 egg whites, beaten

Salt and pepper
Cracker crumbs

Peel shrimp raw and leave tails on. Spread tails with a rolling pin. Salt and pepper shrimp, dip in egg whites, then cracker crumbs ,and egg whites again. Fry in deep fat until lightly brown. Serves 4.

MRS. JACK MAYBANK (Lavinia Huguenin)

Fried Shrimp

1 pound raw shrimp
2 eggs
2 tablespoons milk or water

Cracker meal
Fat for frying
Salt and pepper

Remove the heads and peel shrimp, leaving last segment and tail on. Dip each shrimp in egg which has been beaten and mixed with milk or water. Roll in cracker crumbs to which salt and pepper have been added. Fry in hot deep fat until golden brown. Drain and serve hot with cocktail sauce (receipt found under sauces). Serves 4.

MRS. HENRY CHISOLM (Elizabeth Edwards)

Shrimp or Lobster Cutlets

1 cup milk
1½ tablespoons flour
¼ stick of butter
Salt, hot sauce, and
   sherry, to taste

Bread crumbs
Flour for rolling cutlets
1½ pounds shrimp
   (ground) or 1 can
   lobster

1 egg (beaten)

Make thick cream sauce of milk, flour, butter, salt and hot sauce. Add shrimp, then sherry. Shape like croquettes, then mash flat. Dip lightly in flour, then egg, then bread crumbs. Fry in deep fat.

MRS. KINLOCH McDOWELL (Annie Bissell)

Buffet Supper Shrimp

2 pounds shrimp
1 cup cracker meal
1 small can evaporated milk

1 teaspoon salt
½ teaspoon red pepper
1 cup fat for frying

Boil and shell shrimp. Make a batter of cracker meal, milk, salt and pepper. Dip shrimp in batter and fry in hot fat.

DRESSING

2 hard boiled eggs,
   chopped
1 teaspoon grated onion
½ cup tomato catsup

4 teaspoons chopped celery
½ cup sweet pickles,
   chopped
½ cup mayonnaise

Mix in order given and place in refrigerator until very cold. Serve the fried shimp hot with cold dressing. Serves 6.

MRS. SAMUEL LAPHAM (Lydia Thomas)

Shrimp Curry

4 tablespoons butter
1 large onion chopped fine
½ cup apple chopped fine
½ cup celery chopped fine
1½ cups water

3 pounds shrimp, boiled and
   cleaned
2 tablespoons curry powder
1 pint cream
Salt and pepper to taste

Put butter in a frying pan. When melted, add onion, apple and celery. Simmer these, then add water. Let all simmer gently until apple and celery are tender and most of the liquid has cooked away. Stir into the mixture the seasonings. Add the cream and shrimp. Cook gently until cream is reduced to sauce consistency. Serve with plenty of well-cooked rice. Have small bowls of grated coconut, chutney, chopped almonds, and pickle relish. Serves 8.

MRS. ROBERT M. HOPE (Nellie Rivers)

Shrimp Royale

3 onions, sliced
⅔ cup diced celery
1 tablespoon flour
2 tablespoons shortening
1 teaspoon salt
2 tablespoons chili powder
1 cup water

2 cups canned tomatoes
2 tablespoons canned peas
1 tablespoon vinegar
1 teaspoon sugar
2 cups cooked shrimp
3 cups hot boiled rice
⅓ cup sherry

Cook onions and celery in the fat until brown. Add flour and seasonings. Add water slowly; cook 15 minutes. Add tomatoes, peas, vinegar, sugar and shrimp. Cook for 10 minutes, or until shrimp are thoroughly heated. Add sherry at last minute. After the rice is cooked, mould it into a ring and fill the center with the shrimp mixture. Serves 6.

MRS. JOHN BENNETT (Susan Smythe)

My Grandmother's Stewed Shrimp

2 tablespoons butter
1 tablespoon flour
2 onions, finely chopped
2 pounds peeled shrimp
6 tomatoes (or 1¾ cups
   canned tomatoes)
1 cup water
1 green pepper, diced

1 teaspoon fresh thyme
   (or ½ teaspoon dried
   thyme)
2 teaspoons chopped parsley
1 bay leaf (or ½ teaspoon
   powdered bay leaves)
½ teaspoon garlic salt
Salt and pepper to taste

Melt butter, add flour gradually, cook to a light brown. Add onions and sauté until golden. Add shrimp and mix well. Let cool slightly, add tomatoes, water, green pepper, and seasoning. Cook, stirring frequently, for 10 minutes. Serve over rice. Serves 8.

MRS. LAWRENCE LADUE (Caroline Mullally)

Brewton Inn Creole Shrimp

4 tablespoons bacon drippings
2 medium size onions
1 green pepper
1½ cups celery

1 quart can tomatoes
3 tablespoons tomato paste
Salt and pepper to taste
3 cups cooked shrimp
1 teaspoon sugar

Cut up onions, green pepper, and celery and fry in bacon drippings 15 or 20 minutes. Add quart can of tomatoes, sugar and paste . Let this mixture simmer slowly to thick consistency for 30 to 45 minutes. Add pepper and salt. Fifteen minutes before serving, add cooked shrimp. This should be served with rice. Serves 6-8.

Mrs. Herbert McNulta (Kathryn Deeds)

Shrimp Supreme

2 pounds shrimp
1 bay leaf
Red pepper (dash)
½ lemon (juice)
Salt and pepper to taste

4 tablespoons butter
4 tablespoons flour
8 tablespoons tomato catsup
1½ cups milk
4 tablespoons Worcestershire

Cream butter and flour. Add milk and make a thick cream sauce. Add Worcestershire sauce, catsup, bay leaf, red pepper and lemon juice. Salt and pepper to taste. Add cooked shrimp and allow to get very hot. Serve in a ring of rice. Serves 6.

Mrs. David Maybank (Marion Taber)

Pickled Shrimp

1 pint cooked shrimp
¾ cup cider vinegar
¼ cup water in which shrimp were boiled

1 teaspoon salt
1 tablespoon salad oil or melted butter
Pickling spices

Bring vinegar and "shrimp water" to boil, drop in shrimp and cook until liquid reaches the boiling point. Put into sterilized jars immediately. Add salt, then salad oil to exclude air—seal. Do not boil shrimp in vinegar liquid as it will toughen them. A pinch of pickling spices may be added, if desired. Yield: 1 pint.

Mrs. W. H. Barnwell (Mary M. Royall)

Sea Food Ragout

2 pounds cooked shrimp
¼ cup of butter
¾ pound of mushrooms
¾ cup of cream
¼ cup of flour
Few grains of cayenne
Salt to taste

Few drops of onion juice
¼ teaspoon pepper
1 pint oysters
¾ cup diced cooked chicken
2 tablespoons sherry
1 tablespoon finely
    chopped parsley

Parboil oysters. Make sauce of cream, flour and butter. Add seasoning, then the shrimp, mushrooms, chicken, oysters, wine and parsley. Serve hot. Serves 8.

Mrs. Rees F. Fraser (Mary Maybank)

Carolina Deviled Sea Food

1 pound shrimp
½ pound fresh flaked
    crab meat
1 pint small oysters
½ pint fresh scallops
1 bell pepper
1 or 2 eggs

Salt, red pepper and
    Worcestershire to taste
1 onion, size of an egg
1 cup celery chopped
1 cup mashed potato
1 cup canned tomatoes
Cracker crumbs

Prepare all sea food and cook until tender, adding oysters afterwards. Cut up vegetables and cook celery, onions, and pepper until tender and add to sea food with the mashed potatoes, red pepper, salt and Worcestershire to taste. Now add 1 or 2 eggs with sufficient cracker crumbs to make right consistency to fill ramekins or shells, which have been greased with a little butter. After filling, sprinkle with cracker crumbs and dot with butter. Bake about 10 minutes in a hot oven and serve with lemon as a garnish. Serves 8.

Mrs. Horace G. Smithy, Jr. (Sara Rankin)

How to Cook Crabs

Have one inch of water in the pot in which crabs are to be cooked. Add 2 or 3 tablespoons of vinegar and salt to this. Put in crabs when water boils. Steam crabs for 25 to 30 minutes. The vinegar and steam make the crabs easy to pick. Keep clean crab shells in the refrigerator before using.

Deviled Crabs

(Quickly prepared and eaten)

Mix 1 pound crab meat with 1 cup mayonnaise (a commercial brand may be used); season with juice of 1 lemon, ½ teaspoon Worcestershire sauce, 2 tablespoons chopped parsley, hot sauce, salt and pepper. Put in shells, cover with buttered crumbs, bake in 400° oven 30 minutes. Serves 6-8.

MRS. R. BARNWELL RHETT (Virginia Prettyman)

Deviled Crabs

4 tablespoons butter	2 teaspoons lemon juice
2 tablespoons flour	1 tablespoon chopped
1 cup milk	parsley
1 teaspoon prepared mustard	2 cups crab meat
½ cup bread crumbs toasted	2 hard-boiled eggs, minced

Salt and pepper to taste

Make a rich cream sauce with butter, flour and milk. Add other ingredients, putting in chunks of crab meat last. Put in shells with buttered toast crumbs on top. Bake in 400° oven for 30 minutes. This fills about 6 large crab shells.

deSAUSSURE DEHON

Variation: Mix 1 beaten egg and 1 tablespoon of Worcestershire sauce with other ingredients before adding crab meat, if desired, omitting hard boiled eggs.

Deviled Crabs

1 pound crab meat	2 hard-boiled eggs
1 can condensed	½ cup grated sharp cheese
mushroom soup	¼ cup sherry
¼ cup bread crumbs	½ stick butter, melted
1 egg (raw)	Salt and pepper to taste

Mix all together. Put in shells. Add more bread crumbs, dot with butter and grated cheese. Bake 30 minutes in moderate oven.

MRS. KINLOCH McDOWELL (Annie Bissell)

Deviled Crabs

1 pound crab meat
12 saltines (mashed)
¼ pound butter
1 tablespoon mayonnaise
2 tablespoons sherry
Pinch dry mustard
Pinch minced parsley
1 teaspoon Worcestershire
Salt, pepper to taste

Pour melted butter over cracker crumbs, saving out 4 teaspoons to put on top of the stuffed crabs. Add mayonnaise, and other seasoning, then mix in crab meat with fork to keep from breaking up. Fill 6 large backs generously, then sprinkle with cracker crumbs, pouring the remaining butter on top. Bake in 400° oven for 30 minutes. Serve piping hot.

Mrs. Thaddeus Street (Mary Leize Simons)

Crab Meat Casserole

Make this dish in an earthenware or glass shallow casserole which can be placed over a fire. Serve in the dish in which it is cooked.

1 pound fresh crab meat
2 teaspoons mild
    grated onion
4 large mushrooms,
    sliced thin
2 fresh tomatoes, peeled
    and cut in pieces
2 teaspoons parsley,
    finely minced
1 teaspoon chives, finely cut
2 large tablespoons butter
1¼ cups heavy sweet cream
1 jigger of brandy
Salt and cayene to taste

Melt butter in casserole; add sliced mushrooms and cook 5 minutes. Add onion and tomatoes and cook another 5 minutes. Then add crab meat, leaving it in as large lumps as possible. Season and heat, then add the cream, stirring gently. Let boil 1 minute, no longer, then add parsley, chives and brandy. Serve at once from the casserole into shallow soup plates into which one has put a spoon of cooked rice. Serves 4 to 6.

Mrs. H. P. Staats (Juliette Wiles)

Crab Soufflé

1 pound crab meat	½ pint milk
1 tablespoon butter	½ teaspoon salt
1 tablespoon flour	Nutmeg to taste
2 eggs	White or cayenne pepper
2 tablespoons sherry	

Melt butter and rub in flour to a paste. Add milk, salt, pepper and nutmeg. Cook in double-boiler until thick. When cool, stir in the yolks of eggs, slightly beaten. Add sherry. Now fold in the stiffly beaten whites and crab meat. Put in baking dish with crumbs on top and cook *at once* in pan of hot water in moderate oven 45 minutes. Serve immediately. Serves 6.

MRS. T. LADSON WEBB, JR. (Anne Moore)

Crab with Curried Rice

2 pounds crab meat	1½ cups sharp cheese—
1 quart thick white sauce	grated coarsely
½ cup finely cut bell pepper	2 tablespoons Worcestershire
½ cup chopped pimientos	2 tablespoons sherry
1 cup finely cut celery	Paprika, salt and pepper

Season sauce with salt, pepper, Worcestershire and sherry. Combine all ingredients or arrange in layers in casserole dish, keeping back ½ cup cheese for top of dish. Sprinkle paprika over top and bake for one hour in moderate oven.. Serves 8-10.
Serve with rice curry, prepared as follows:

2 cups rice	1 tablespoon curry powder
2 cups chicken stock	Salt

Steam for one hour.

MRS. JACK W. SIMMONS (Irene Robinson)

Crab Mousse

1 pound white crab meat	1 tablespoon powdered
½ bottle capers	mustard
½ cup chopped olives	1 tablespoon Worcestershire
(whole ones chopped)	1 envelope plain gelatine
1 cup mayonnaise	¼ cup cold water
½ cup cream or milk,	1 cup finely chopped celery
heated	Vinegar

Mix crab, celery, capers and olives. Stir in mayonnaise, Worcestershire and mustard dissolved in a little vinegar. Soften gelatine in cold water and add to hot milk or cream. Pour this in your mixture and beat well. Put in oiled mold. Good with green or vegetable salad with French dressing. Serves 6.

MRS. FRANCIS B. STEWART (Katherine Felder)

Meeting Street Crab Meat

1 pound white crab meat	½ pint cream
4 tablespoons butter	4 tablespoons sherry
4 tablespoons flour	¾ cup sharp grated cheese

Salt and pepper to taste

Make a cream sauce with the butter, flour and cream. Add salt, pepper and sherry. Remove from fire and add crab meat. Pour the mixture into a buttered casserole or individual baking dishes. Sprinkle with grated cheese and cook in a hot oven until cheese melts. Do not overcook. Serves 4. (1½ pounds of shrimp may be substituted for the crab).

MRS. THOMAS A. HUGUENIN (Mary Vereen)

Soft Shell Crabs

How to clean a soft shell crab: lift and bend back the tapering points on each end of the crab's soft shelled back. Remove the spongy substance under them. This is locally called the "dead man." (That's what you'll be if you eat it—so it's said.) Remove the eyes and the sand bag found behind the eyes. Then turn crab on its back and remove the long narrow piece which starts at lower center of shell and ends in a point—this is called the apron.

Fried Soft Shell Crabs

1 egg	1 teaspoon baking powder
½ cup milk	Fat for frying
½ cup (or little more) flour	Pinch of salt

Beat egg and milk. Add salt. Dip crabs thoroughly in egg and milk mixture, then in flour and baking powder which have been mixed. Have hot fat about ½ inch deep and cook until golden brown. Serve with tartar sauce.

MRS. JOHN SIMONDS (Frances Rees)

Charlotte's Broiled Soft Shell Crabs

(From her San Domingan Grandmother)

Lay crabs in shallow baking pan, tucking claws close to body. Put a teaspoon of butter on each crab; put under broiler for ten minutes; then in top oven for ten minutes. If lemon juice is liked, pour over ½ cup to each dozen crabs before cooking—use no seasoning. Salt in crabs and butter is sufficient. Can be served on toast and garnish with parsley and lemon slices.

MRS. W. TURNER LOGAN, SR. (Louise Lesesne)

Cream Sauce for Shrimp, Lobster or Chicken

1¾ cups milk
3 tablespoons flour
¼ pound butter
1 tablespoon green pepper, chopped
1 tablespoon pimiento, chopped
½ small onion, chopped
1 teaspoon Worcestershire sauce

Dash of red pepper
¾ teaspoon salt
2 egg yolks, beaten
¾ cup heavy cream
1 cup mushrooms, chopped
3 pounds shrimp or
3 pounds lobsters, picked, or
1 (4 pound) hen (diced, cooked meat)

Using double boiler, make a thick white sauce of the milk, flour, butter; then add green pepper, pimiento, onion, Worcestershire, red pepper and salt. Mix egg yolks and cream, then add to sauce just before stirring in mushrooms and shrimp, lobster or chicken. Make just before serving. Delicious with curried rice. Serves 8.

MRS. HENRY J. MANN (Florence Hossley)

"Maum Nancy's" Scalloped Oysters

This receipt was obtained by my father from his cook, "Maum Nancy"—a former slave.

1 cup toasted bread crumbs
½ teaspoon grated nutmeg
Pinch of mace
4 or 5 cloves (beaten)
Salt to taste

Black and red pepper to taste
1 quart oysters (drained)
1 wineglass sherry
¾ cup liquor from oysters
Butter

Mix crumbs and dry seasonings. Into a baking dish put, alternately, a layer of crumb seasonings, then one of oysters and small pieces of butter. Pour wine and oyster liquor (mixed) over each layer to moisten. Finish with a layer of crumbs, dotted with butter. Bake slowly in a moderate oven about 45 minutes. Serves 6.

MRS. WILLIAM HENRY PARKER (Elizabeth E. Robertson)

Scalloped Oysters

1 quart oysters	½ cup butter
Milk	2 salt spoons of pepper
1 pint cracker crumbs	2 salt spoons of mace

Salt to taste

Drain oysters and add to the liquor enough milk to make one pint. Salt to flavor and set where it will heat. Mix pepper and mace with cracker crumbs. Melt butter and add to crumbs. Put oysters and crumbs in baking dish in layers—crumbs first and then oysters. Pour the liquor over the top and bake in a moderate oven for 20 to 30 minutes. Serves 6-8.

MISS JANE CHRISTIE HAMMOND

Broiled Oysters

1 pint oysters	1 cup cracker crumbs (fine)
½ cup salad oil	½ teaspoon salt

¼ teaspoon pepper

Drain oysters then dry in towel. Dip in oil and then cracker crumbs to which salt and pepper have been added. Broil in hot oven (425°) until oysters are golden brown on one side. Turn each oyster and cook on other side until done. Serve at once with tomato catsup. Serves 4-6.

MRS. JOHN MITCHELL, JR. (Edith LaBruce)

Fried Oysters

1 quart oysters	Salt and pepper
2 eggs, beaten	1 cup bread crumbs,
2 tablespoons milk	cracker crumbs or
	corn meal

Drain oysters; mix eggs, milk, seasonings. Dip oysters in egg mixture and roll in crumbs. Fry in deep fat (375°F) about 2 minutes or until brown. Or fry in shallow fat about 2 minutes on one side, turn and brown on other side. Serves 6.

MRS. THOMAS E. MYERS (Elizabeth Norcross)

Mrs. C. C. Calhoun's Chafing Dish Oysters

4 tablespoons butter
½ cup thick cream
6 waffle squares

1 pint small oysters
1 wineglass sherry
Cayenne, mace, celery, salt

Melt butter in a chafing dish. Add the oysters and cook for 3 or 4 minutes. Pour the cream in slowly and carefully and bring just to the boiling point. When ready to serve add the sherry. Before ladling onto the crisp, hot waffles, dust with seasonings.

Mrs. Laurens Patterson (Martha Laurens)

Oyster Fritters

1 cup chopped, drained
    oysters
4 eggs, separated
⅛ teaspoon pepper

½ teaspoon salt
6 tablespoons flour
1 tablespoon minced
    onion (optional)

Beat egg yolks until thick and creamy. Add onions, salt and pepper, then flour (a little at a time). Fold in oysters and stiffly beaten egg whites. Drop by spoonfuls in hot fat. Serves 5.

Mrs. Robert Wilson, Jr. (Gabrielle McColl)

Corn Oysters

1 cup raw corn, grated,
    or canned corn
    (creamed style)

1 well beaten egg
¼ cup flour
1 pint large oysters

Salt and pepper to taste

Combine corn, egg and flour—season. To each tablespoon of this mixture add one oyster. Drop in deep fat or cook on a hot, well greased grill. Serves 4.

Mrs. Rees F. Fraser (Mary Maybank)

Baalam's Oysters

1 pint oysters	1 or 2 teaspoons
1 cup rich cream sauce	prepared mustard
1 teaspoon red pepper	12 or 14 crackers
sauce	½ teaspoon salt
	1 or 2 eggs, beaten

1 teaspoon Worcestershire

Add everything except crackers to cream sauce. Cover bottom of shallow casserole with crumbled crackers. Pour in mixture of sauce and oysters; cover with more crumbs and dot with butter. Bake in hot oven until crumbs look pretty and brown. Sherry may be used in place of hot seasoning and is nice for a change. Serves 6.

MRS. T. M. UZZELL (Marjorie McColl)

Oysters with Macaroni

1 pint oysters	3 tablespoons butter
1 small box macaroni	1 teaspoon salt
2 cups milk	1 teaspoon black pepper

Cracker crumbs

Boil macaroni in water and when cooked pour off water. Place 1 layer of macaroni in baking dish and then 1 layer of oysters, continuing until the oysters and macaroni have been used up. Pour milk into baking dish and put pieces of butter around sides of dish. Add salt and pepper and cover top with cracker crumbs. Bake for 30 minutes in 350° oven. Serves 8.

MRS. JAMES D. LUCAS (Janie Larsen)

Variation: Milk may be omitted and more butter added--servings will be less juicy.

Low-Country Oysters with Mushrooms

1 pound fresh mushrooms
(sliced)

1½ quarts oysters

8 tablespoons butter

2 small cans pimientos
(sliced)

4 cups cream

8 tablespoons flour

Salt and pepper to taste

Sauté mushrooms and pimientos in butter. After mushrooms have cooked a few minutes, sift flour over mixture and when it begins to thicken, add cream, salt and pepper. Let oysters simmer in their own liquor in another pan until the edges curl. Add oysters to mushroom sauce and add more cream if too dry. Serve from chafing dish or on a platter surrounded by toast triangles. Serves 8.

MRS. THOMAS A. HUGUENIN (Mary Vereen)

Oysters and Sweetbreads in Patty Shells

1 quart oysters

1 pair sweetbreads

1 level tablespoon flour

2 tablespoons butter

½ to 1 cup thick cream

1 cup oyster liquor

Salt, pepper, cayenne to taste

Blanch and chill sweetbreads; remove membrane and chop quite fine. Heat oysters in their own liquor about 3 minutes. Drain and chop fine. Rub together the flour, butter, salt, pepper and cayenne. Put oyster liquor in double boiler with butter-flour mixture. Stir constantly until thickened, then add cream. Add sweetbreads and oysters to sauce. Mixture must not be too stiff. Fill patty shells with mixture. Serves 6.

MRS. JOHN D. WING (Elizabeth Hoffman)

Curried Oysters

1 quart oysters	2 teaspoons curry powder
2 tablespoons butter	¼ pint oyster liquor
½ teaspoon onion juice	¼ pint milk
1 tablespoon flour	1 small teaspoon salt

Put butter and onion juice in pan, add flour and curry powder and when mixture bubbles, stir in oyster liquor, milk and salt. When the sauce is smooth and boils, put in oysters and cook until they are plump and the edges crimp. This will take about 4 minutes. Serves 6-8.

MRS. NATHANIEL I. BALL, JR. (Anne Barnwell)

Clams Southside

1 quart hard-shell clams (not in shell)	¼ cup butter
	Salt and pepper
1 small onion	Worcestershire to taste
½ pint heavy cream	Chopped green fresh pepper

Toast

Put clams through coarse meat chopper. Sauté finely chopped onion in butter until gold in color. Cook clams and onion in double-boiler 20 minutes. Add salt, pepper and Worcestershire, then cream. Garnish with peppers and serve on toast. Serves 4.

MRS. JOHN D. WING (Elizabeth Hoffman)

Clams and Guinea Squash (Eggplant)

1 large guinea squash	½ cup milk
1 (10½ oz.) can minced clams	3 tablespoons butter
	Salt and pepper to taste
1 cup cracker crumbs	

Peel, slice and boil guinea squash in salty water until tender. Drain and mash well; stir in 2 tablespoons butter. Drain clams and reserve the juice. Place thin layers of guinea squash, clams and cracker crumbs dotted with butter in casserole. Continue until all ingredients are used. Mix the milk with the clam juice and season with salt and pepper, then pour over the mixture in casserole. Cook uncovered in oven 350° about 30 minutes. Serves 8.

MRS. HUGH CATHCART (Marguerite McDonald)

John C. Calhoun's Lobster Newburg

4 lobsters	1½ pints cream
½ pound butter	1 tablespoon flour
1 teaspoon paprika	(or more)
½ teaspoon salt	1 wineglass sherry

Salt and pepper to taste

Cook lobsters in boiling water for half hour. Cut meat from tails and dice. Cook slowly in ¼ pound of butter on side of stove. Add paprika and salt. Let cream come to a boil, add ¼ pound butter that has been mixed with flour. Put on knife blade to test for thickness. Stir in lobster and lastly sherry and more salt and paprika, if desired. Serves 6.

MRS. LOUIS D. SIMONDS (Mary Rhett)

My Great-Grandmother's Lobster Newburg

Meat of 4-pound lobster	½ pint cream
4 tablespoons butter	2 teaspoons salt
2 tablespoons brandy	¼ teaspoon red pepper
2 tablespoons sherry	¼ teaspoon nutmeg

4 egg yolks

Cut meat of lobster into small, delicate pieces. Put the butter in a frying pan. When hot, put in lobster. Cook slowly for 5 minutes. Then add salt, pepper, and nutmeg, stirring constantly, adding the cream with the beaten egg yolks. Add brandy and sherry at the last as mass begins to thicken. Serve on puff paste or toast.

Variation: Shrimp or crab meat may be substituted. Serves 6-8.

MRS. J. ROSS HANAHAN, JR. (Muriel Viglini)

Otranto Pine Bark Stew

"As told me by my Father"

Arise early and go on the Lake and catch about eighteen Big-Mouth Bass, Bream or Red Breast.

Have "Patsie" make an outdoor fire of pine bark—then have her slice about one dozen Irish potatoes and about one dozen small onions.

Place a large deep iron saucepan over the fire and fry one pound of bacon. Remove bacon and leave grease in bottom of saucepan. Place a layer of sliced potatoes and then a layer of sliced onion in saucepan (using 1/3 of potatoes and 1/3 of onions). Cover with boiling salted water. Let simmer for 10 minutes, then place a layer of whole fish on top. Sprinkle about 1 tablespoon curry powder on fish. Then place a second layer of potatoes, onion and fish and add boiling salted water to cover. Top with third layer of potatoes and onions. Place top on saucepan and cook very slowly all morning. It is done when the top layer of potatoes is soft.

SAUCE

Melt ½ pound of butter in saucepan. Add about ½ bottle of Worcestershire sauce, ½ bottle tomato catsup, 1 tablespoon curry power, ½ teaspoon red pepper, and ½ teaspoon black pepper. Add to this several cups of the extract from stew and mix well. Pour sauce over Pine Bark Stew and place bacon on top and serve with rice. Serves 12.

LOUIS Y. DAWSON, JR. (President of Otranto Club)

Soused Fish

"This is from an old book of Maria Bachman, the wife of my great-grandfather, the Rev. John Bachman. It was she who painted many of the backgrounds for Audubon's famous paintings."

Sprinkle any fish with salt and pepper as if you were going to fry it. Then boil the fish in vinegar instead of water. Season with cloves, mace, pepper and Worcestershire sauce. Put fish and sauce into mould. The bones will all become soft, and the whole will turn out in a form like jelly.

MRS. LIONEL K. LEGGE (Dorothy Porcher)

Channel Bass

(Any fillet of fish can be used)

"Until Mrs. S. James O'Hear gave me this receipt, I had always thought channel bass a rather uninteresting fish to eat, but now I no longer give my catch away."

2 or 3 pound bass	1 tablespoon dry white wine
¼ pound butter	Salt, pepper, and paprika
Lemon juice	Parmesan cheese

Fillet fish and salt and pepper them. Put butter in shallow baking dish in hot oven (400° to 500°) until it is browned. This gives the distinctive flavor. Place fillets flesh side down in sizzling hot butter and return to oven for 10 or 15 minutes. Turn with spatula and baste with juice. Sprinkle each piece with lemon juice and dry white wine, Parmesan cheese and paprika. Return to oven until done—approximately 5 minutes. Run under broiler and broil quickly. Baste fish with sauce and serve in the sauce. This receipt is good for any fish fillet. Serves 4.

MRS. CHARLES W. WARING (Margaret Simonds)

Fillet of Sole Marguery

1 large sole or flounder	1 pound cooked shrimp
⅔ cup white wine	½ pound fresh mushrooms
1 tablespoon flour	2 tablespoons butter
2 cups heavy cream	Salt

Fillet sole or flounder; place in buttered pan, sprinkle with salt and pour ⅓ cup white wine over fish. Bake 20 minutes, basting often. Remove fillets to platter. Thicken stock, in which fish has been baking, with flour. When well blended, add cream, shrimp, mushrooms (chopped fine and sauté in butter). Now add remaining wine. Pour this over fillets; garnish with parsley and serve piping hot. Serves 4-6.

MRS. ROBERT SMALL (Louise Johnson)

Pompano with Shrimp Sauce

6 pompano fillets
2 cups thick white sauce
½ cup chopped shrimp
Salt to taste

½ clove garlic, minced
4 tablespoons onion, minced
4 tablespoons green pepper, chopped

Season sauce with shrimp, garlic, onion, pepper and salt. Spread fillets with sauce. Place each one on a square of parchment or cooking paper. Wrap so that no steam will escape and bake in 350° oven for 45 minutes. Serve directly from paper. Flounder or bass fillets may be substituted for pompano.

MRS. WILLIAM GRANBY DODDS (Louise Hutson)

Pompano à la Gherardi

"An original creation of Henry's and named for Admiral Gherardi."

1 pompano
Salt and pepper
Small shrimp

4 ounces stuffing
Bacon strips
Chopped olives

Select a firm whole pompano. Remove head and split down flat side, removing center bone structure in order to provide pocket. Salt and pepper fish then stuff with the following, topping pocket opening with whole shrimp, chopped olives and bacon strips. Place in covered vessel and bake for 15 minutes.

STUFFING

2 pounds cooked shrimp
1 pound white crab meat
1 loaf bread
1 bunch green onions

½ cup sherry
1 cup butter
½ bunch parsley
2 eggs

Salt and pepper to taste

Mince above ingredients and mix well. Cook slowly to prevent scorching. Stuff pompano. (Above stuffing receipt sufficient for 12 small pompano).

WALTER L. SHAFFER (Henry's Restaurant)

Boneless Baked Shad

3 or 4 pound shad   1 tablespoon vinegar
1 quart water   Salt and pepper to taste
4 or 5 strips bacon

Boil shad in water and vinegar with seasonings for 20 minutes. Drain off water; put in a heavy, tightly covered roaster and cook in oven slowly (200°) for 5 or 6 hours. Add roe about 30 minutes before fish is done. Put strips of bacon across the shad and place under broiler for bacon to brown. This is delicious. When done, the bones are completely dissolved. Serves 6.

MRS. JENNINGS W. P. FOSTER (Mary Leiper)

Planked Shad

Scale and clean a 4 or 5-pound shad, preferably a roe shad. Remove head and fins and with very sharp knife cut along backbone on either side, making two fillets. Backbone portion with flesh adhering may be reserved for frying. Salt and pepper fillets. Grease well a large oak plank about 18 inches long (can be purchased in hardware stores) and place fillets skin side down on plank. Dot with butter and broil under medium flame until done (20 to 30 minutes). When done, fish flakes easily when touched with fork. Add more butter just before removing from oven. Finely chopped parsley may be sprinkled over fish or parsley sprigs and lemon slices used as a garnish. Whipped and creamed Irish potatoes may be also used as edge around plank just before removing from oven. The roe may be broiled separately and added to the plank if desired. Serve with sauce tartare. Serves 6, generously.

MRS. JOHN A. HERTZ (Adele B. Mathewes)

Boiled Sheepshead or Blackfish with Egg Sauce

1 large or 2 medium sheepshead or blackfish (4 pounds)	1 bay leaf
	2 large slices onion
	¼ cup celery

Sauce:

2½ tablespoons butter	¼ cup chopped parsley
1 tablespoon flour	2 hard boiled eggs
Lemon slices	Salt and pepper to taste

Clean and scale, leaving fish whole; salt and pepper thoroughly. Place fish in heavy covered roaster or baking pan with about ½ inch of water, bay leaf, onion and celery. Simmer gently in medium oven or on top of stove until fish is thoroughly cooked. Now make a thickened sauce as follows: melt the butter in saucepan, add flour, stir smooth and add liquid in which fish was cooked. (There should be about 1½ cups.) Return to roaster and add parsley and baste fish with sauce for a few minutes. Carefully remove fish whole to large deep platter. Slice hard boiled eggs over fish and pour sauce over whole. Garnish with parsley and lemon. Serve with hot rice. Serves 6.

MISS JEANNIE T. CASON

Barbecued Fish

One, 3 or 4-pound fish	1 cup tomato catsup
2 tablespoons chopped onions	1 tablespoon fat or bacon grease
2 tablespoons vinegar	⅓ cup lemon juice
2 tablespoons brown sugar	½ teaspoon salt
3 tablespoons Worcestershire	Dash pepper

Place fish in greased shallow pan, sprinkle with salt and pepper. Lightly brown onions in fat, add remaining ingredients . Simmer 5 minutes then pour over fish. Bake in hot oven (425°) 35 to 40 minutes. Baste fish with sauce while cooking. Serves 6.

MISS VIRGINIA MITCHELL

The Bluff Plantation Cooter Pie

1 medium sized cooter (terrapin)
½ cup stewed tomatoes
1 cup milk
1 cup liquor from stew pot
2 tablespoons butter
1 tablespoon whiskey
1 tablespoon sherry
2 hard-boiled eggs, cut up
2 slices toasted bread (crumbed)
Worcestershire sauce
Celery salt
Mace
Red pepper
Black pepper to taste

Drop live cooter in the pot of boiling water. Cook 45 minutes. Open shell with a saw and take out meat, fat, liver and eggs. Be careful not to break the gall. Remove meat from the feet and legs. Put all this in a pot with a little water and salt and stew until tender, usually about one hour. Then cut up meat, liver and eggs and add stewed tomatoes, milk, liquor from stew pot, butter, whiskey, sherry, eggs (cut up), bread crumbs and seasonings. Put in shell which has been thoroughly cleaned, cover with cracker crumbs, dot with butter and bake in 375° oven about 45 minutes. Serves 6.

MRS. HENRY H. FICKEN (Julia Ball)

Fish Mousse

1 pound halibut or any fish
Salt and pepper to taste
1 teaspoon lemon juice
⅓ cup cream
3 egg whites, stiffly beaten

Boil fish until tender. Drain and put through a sieve. Season and add lemon juice. Beat cream to a stiff froth and add to the fish; then fold in egg whites. Put in a buttered mold and cook in hot water in a moderate oven for 20 minutes. Turn out and serve with any preferred sauce around it. Serves 6.

MISS EUGENIA FROST

Shrimp Cocktail Sauce

The famous Brewton Inn receipt which gourmets the world over have long sought.

4 egg yolks (raw)　　　½ teaspoon hot sauce
1 quart salad oil　　　　Juice of 2 lemons
1 teaspoon salt　　　　1 tablespoon vinegar
　　　　　1 bottle tomato catsup

Beat egg yolks. Make a sauce in a separate bowl of the salt, hot sauce, lemon juice and vinegar. Gradually add oil and sauce to eggs. Mix well and add catsup. Will keep several weeks in refrigerator.

MRS. KINLOCH MCDOWELL (Annie Bissell)

D. P. L.'s Cocktail Sauce

(for shrimp or crabs)

1 cup good mayonnaise　　3 tablespoons chili sauce
1 tablespoon lemon juice　2 tablespoons horseradish
3 tablespoons tomato catsup　2 tablespoons whipped
　　　　　　　　　　　　　　　cream

Mix ingredients. Add hot sauce, mace, celery salt, cayenne, and nutmeg to taste.

MRS. LIONEL K. LEGGE (Dorothy H. Porcher)

Tartare Sauce

1 cup mayonnaise　　　　1 tablespoon chopped capers
3 tablespoons chopped pickle　2 tablespoons chopped
1 tablespoon chopped　　　stuffed olives
　　parsley　　　　　　1 teaspoon chopped onion

Mix all ingredients and chill. Serve with soft shelled or deviled crabs and fish.

MRS. F. MITCHELL JOHNSON (Margaret Silcox)

Onion Sherry

Slice onions, put in jar or bottle and cover with cooking sherry. Receptacle can be refilled twice. For creamed shrimp, crab, fish or chicken. Keep well corked.

MRS. W. TURNER LOGAN, SR. (Louise Lesesne)

Shrimp Sauce

1½ cups olive oil
½ cup vinegar
1 teaspoon onion juice
Salt, pepper and paprika
    to taste

Powdered mustard "to
    desired temperature"
1 or 2 cloves of garlic
Few drops of hot sauce

Make two or three days ahead of time and shake well before using. Keeps well in refrigerator.

MRS. D. R. STEVENSON (Kate Waring)

Oyster Cocktail Sauce

4 tablespoons tomato catsup
    or chili sauce
2 teaspoons lemon juice
1½ teaspoons Worcester-
    shire

Salt
Few grains red pepper
1½ teaspoons grated
    horseradish (optional)

Mix and pour over oysters just before serving. Serves 4.

MRS. W. H. BARNWELL (Mary M. Royall)

Horseradish Sauce

2 tablespoons grated
    horseradish
1 tablespoon vinegar

¼ teaspoon salt
¼ teaspoon pepper
4 tablespoons whipped
    cream

Mix horseradish with vinegar, add seasonings and stir in cream, whipped stiff.

MRS. J. ROSS HANAHAN, JR. (Muriel Viglini)

SWORD GATES 1849

MEATS

Ef dey ain' bin no meat 'pun de table, de dinnuh ain' wut!

Sing a song of ground beef, baked in a pie;
Sing a song of chicken, ready to fry;
Sing a song of veal-loaf, jellied and cold;
Sing a song of lamb bits, baked in a mold.
Serve with a gravy, or sauce with a zing.
When the dish is served, the guests begin to sing.

Beef à la Mode

"My father's method, which he brought back from France, where he was educated."

6 pounds beef off the round or a haunch of venison	Ground: cloves, whole black pepper and 2 teaspoons whole allspice
1 pound bacon (cut up)	Bay leaf
3 large onions (chopped)	Red pepper
1 cup shortening (approx.)	Salt and pepper
1 quart apple cider vinegar	

Use a very carefully selected cut of beef off the round, no bone (costs now about one million dollars). Put this, the night before, in an earthen bowl with vinegar and enough water to cover after having stuffed it with bacon, onions, spices and a bit of bay leaves—no salt. It is stuffed by piercing meat with sharp knife and ramming down the mixed seasonings. These gashes are cut in the top of the beef as well as both sides. When the beef is fairly bursting and as swollen as a pouter pigeon, then all is well. Bind cord around the meat to keep seasonings in. Next morning the meat is lifted out, rubbed with salt and pepper, covered heavily with shortening and coated with flour. Sear on top of the stove until a rich brown. Pour off all the liquid except one cup, adding one cup of water to this. Cook in a covered roaster in a 300 degree oven 20 minutes to the pound. The gravy can be thickened, and Browning added, if necessary, after the meat is taken out. It is good eaten hot and served with rice or Hoppin' John or sliced cold, for weeks (but it will not last that long). My daughter tells me she has used chuck meat, instead of the more expensive round. Serves about 25.

ELIZABETH O'NEILL VERNER

Spaghetti with Beef

1 pound ground round steak	1 large box spaghetti
5 slices bacon, cut in small pieces	1 large onion, chopped
	1 large bell pepper, chopped
1 medium can mushrooms (stems and pieces)	1 small bottle stuffed olives, chopped
4 tablespoons olive oil	Salt
2 tablespoons tomato catsup	Paprika
3 cups grated cheese	Cayenne Pepper

1 quart can tomatoes

Put bacon in frying pan, cook with onions and bell pepper until slightly brown. Add olive oil and ground meat. Cook until meat begins to brown. Add rest of ingredients, tomatoes, chopped olives, tomato sauce, salt, pepper and mushrooms. Cook until it thickens; then pour over cooked spaghetti. Cover with grated cheese. Serves 6-8.

MRS. J. WALKER COLEMAN (Felicia Chisolm)

Meat Loaf on Top of Stove

1 pound ground beef	1 teaspoon tomato catsup
Season to taste	½ teaspoon Worcestershire sauce
1 bay leaf	

Small grated onion

Mix, shape in loaf, put in heavy-bottomed pot. Cover, cook on medium heat about 45 minutes, basting often with juice from meat. When brown, thicken gravy with 1 tablespoon flour. Serves 6.

MRS. A. T. SMYTHE (Harriott Buist)

Corned Beef or Pork

5 pounds good round of beef or leg of pork	1 tumbler (cup) salt
	1 tablespoon brown sugar

1 tablespoon saltpeter

Rub salt, sugar and saltpeter thoroughly into the meat. Leave in this pickle 7 days. Add no liquid. Turn meat from time to time. After 7 days, wash meat with cold water; place in pot and cover with water. Boil covered about 3 hours or until tender. Do not brown the beef, but dress the pork as a ham, with brown sugar and cloves, and run in the oven to brown. Serves 10.

MISS ELLEN PARKER

Beef Strogonoff

2 pounds lean round steak	2 cups sour cream
3 small onions	½ pound fresh mushrooms
1 or 2 tablespoons tomato paste	or 1 large can
	Soy sauce to taste
Consommé or beef stock	Salt, pepper and flour

Cut beef in thinnest possible slices. Pound in flour, salt and pepper. Cut into strips about 3 inches by ½ inch. Dice onions and fry slowly until soft and just turning yellow. Then add meat and sauté until well seared. Add tomato paste and enough consommé or beef stock to just cover. Add soy sauce to taste. Simmer until tender. Transfer to top of double-boiler and add sour cream and mushrooms. Re-heat in double-boiler when ready to serve. Serve on rice or red rice. Serves 6.

MRS. JOHN E. FLORANCE (Mary Elizabeth Warley)

105

Baked Calf's Head

1 calf's head	1 pinch of nutmeg
2 sprigs parsley	3 hard-boiled eggs
1 pinch of thyme	1 cup of bread crumbs

Pepper and salt to taste

Soak calf's head overnight in salt water. Boil with parsley, thyme, and nutmeg until thoroughly done. Cool and cut it up into small pieces. Make brown gravy, put bread crumbs and chopped-up hard-boiled eggs in it. Mix chopped calf's head thoroughly with the gravy. Put mixture into greased baking dish, cover lightly with cracker crumbs, and bake in oven 350° until browned, about 35 minutes. Serves 6.

WILMER HOFFMAN

Flanders Tongue

2 fresh tongues	½ teaspoon thyme
1 quart stock	1 pound mushrooms
6 crushed peppercorns	2 tablespoons butter
4 cloves	4 teaspoons flour
4 bay leaves	½ cup tarragon vinegar
1 teaspoon nutmeg	½ cup sherry

Boil tongues in salted water until tender. Skin, cool and slice fairly thin. Add peppercorns, cloves, bay leaves nutmeg and thyme to stock. Boil 5 minutes and strain. Sauté mushrooms in butter. Remove from grease and add flour to brown. Add tongue stock. When thickened, add tongue and mushrooms. Add vinegar and simmer for half an hour. Before serving, add ½ cup sherry. Serve with mashed potatoes . Serves 10-12.

MRS. CHARLES W. WARING (Margaret Simonds)

Creamed Sweetbreads with Sherry

2 pairs sweetbreads	4 tablespoons of good sherry
1 teaspoon lemon juice	2 egg yolks
½ cup small mushroom buttons	4 tablespoons of butter or margarine
1 teaspoon finely chopped spring onion, tops and all	1 cup of whipping cream Salt, pepper, paprika, and a dash of curry powder

Parboil the sweetbreads. Then cover with ice cold water for thirty minutes, and remove loose membranes. A few drops of lemon juice in the cold water will keep the sweetbreads snowy white. Cut the sweetbreads into medium slices. Season with salt and pepper and sauté for three minutes in the butter. Add the drained mushrooms and sauté five minutes longer. Add the minced onions and sherry and let the whole simmer for fifteen minutes. Blend together the egg yolk, ¼ teaspoon of lemon juice and two tablespoons cream. Remove the sweetbreads from the fire and stir in the egg yolk mixture very slowly, stirring gently from bottom of pan. Place in oven-proof dish. Whip the remaining cream, flavored with salt, paprika and dash of curry. Spread over sweetbreads. Set under flame of broiling oven for a minute to glaze. Serves 4.

MRS. WALTER METTS (Jane Stauffer)

Corned Tongue

1 large tongue	1 light tablespoon brown sugar
2 tablespoons salt	Saltpeter size of a pea
1 pint hot water	

Melt saltpeter and sugar in hot water. Salt tongue and place in the bottom of a crock and cover when water is cool. Turn tongue over after a day or two. Boil slowly. Serve cold. Keeps indefinitely. Serves 6.

MRS. LIONEL K. LEGGE (Dorothy Porcher)

Roast Pork

In the days of good Queen Bess, "Master Skylark" undoubtedly enjoyed this dish.

1 leg pork, 8 to 10 pounds or smaller	1 quart can tomatoes
1 cup brown sugar	3 sliced onions
1 tablespoon salt	1 tablespoon hot sauce
1 tablespoon black pepper	1 cup tomato catsup
	1 cup water

Rub into pork the brown sugar, salt and black pepper. Add to the pan for basting: the tomatoes, onions, hot sauce, catsup, water. Roast slowly about 3½ hours, preferably in a double roaster, in a 350° oven, 30 minutes per pound. Serves 8 to 10.

MRS. JOHN BENNETT (Susan Smythe)

Pork Supreme

3 strips of bacon	1 cup of diced onion
1 pound of lean pork which has been coarsely ground	1 cup of diced celery
	2 teaspoons of ground ginger
1 egg plant (diced)	½ cup of soy sauce
1 cup of diced green pepper	1 can of bean sprouts
½ cup of pecans	

Fry bacon, remove from pan and add pork, stirring constantly until it is well cooked, but not brown. Add diced vegetables and two cups of water. Mix well. Add ginger and soy sauce . Cook until tender, then add bean sprouts and pecans and cook for five minutes. Serve over steamed rice. This receipt calls for NO salt. Serves 6.

MRS. W. T. HARTMAN (Betty Blaydes)

Sweet and Sour Pork

"During World War II my husband, Colonel Louis Y. Dawson, Jr., was stationed in China. He had the pleasure of attending a dinner given by Madame Kung (one of the Soong sisters). He enjoyed so much the "Sweet and Sour Pork," which was served, that he asked a friend, General Ho Shi Li, to obtain the receipt for him."

1 pound lean pork	Pea flour (plain flour will
Salt	**do)**
Pepper	Peanut oil (vegetable oil)
1 teaspoon soy sauce	Carrots, 1 cup finely
Seanium oil (vegetable	chopped
oil)	½ cup of diced green
	bell peppers

Cut one pound of lean pork into pieces about ¼" thick, 1" long and ½" wide. Add salt and pepper to taste, and soy sauce. Fry the pieces of pork in seanium oil. When well done, roll the pork in pea flour, and broil for five minutes in boiling peanut oil. Remove the pork and broil the carrots and bell peppers for one minute in the boiling peanut oil. Mix the pork, carrots and bell peppers and serve with the hot Sweet and Sour Sauce. Serves 6.

SWEET AND SOUR SAUCE

1 cup sugar	1 teaspoon lemon juice
¾ cup white vinegar	1 teaspoon catsup
1 teaspoon salt	1 teaspoon garlic, finely
1 teaspoon soy sauce	chopped

MRS. LOUIS Y. DAWSON, JR. (Virginia Walker)

"Cheaper by the Dozen" Spare Ribs

3 or 4 pounds spare ribs

2 onions (sliced)

2 teaspoons vinegar

2 teaspoons Worcestershire
    sauce

1 teaspoon salt

1 teaspoon paprika

½ teaspoon red pepper

½ teaspoon black pepper

1 teaspoon chili powder

¾ cup catsup

¾ cup water

Select meaty spare ribs. Cut into servings or leave uncut. Sprinkle with salt and pepper. Place in roaster and cover with onions. Combine remaining ingredients and pour over meat. Cover and bake in moderate oven (350 degrees) about 1½ hours. Baste occasionally, turning spareribs once or twice. Remove cover last 15 minutes to brown ribs. Serves 6.

MRS. FRANK B. GILBRETH, JR. (Elizabeth Cauthen)

Baked Ham Slices

2 slices tenderized ham,
    1½" thick

2 cups fruit juice (apricot,
    pineapple or orange)

1 cup sherry

½ cup honey

Apricot halves

Mustard

Peanut butter

Spread ham slices with prepared mustard and peanut butter and put 1 slice on top of other. Pour 2 cups fruit juice over ham. Bake ½ hour at 325°. Add wine. Bake another hour. Place apricot halves (or cherries) on top and pour on ½ cup honey and bake 20 minutes longer. Serves 10.

MRS. CHARLES E. PRIOLEAU (Anne Little)

Baked Ham

"This is contributed by a friend of the Junior League from Georgia and is often served at Colonial Dames Meetings at the Powder Magazine in Charleston. It is superlative for Country—not Smithfield ham—but good for any standard ham."

The ham is baked in a dough blanket, made as follows:

4 cups flour	2 tablespoons dried mustard
1 cup brown sugar	1 teaspoon black pepper
2 tablespoons ground cloves	Peach pickle juice or
2 tablespoons powdered	apple cider
cinnamon	

Cut rind off ham. Combine dry ingredients and add enough juice to make a dough which can be rolled. Cover fat part of ham with the dough, put in a cold oven and bake at 325°, about 20 or 25 minutes per pound—four or five hours for a 15 pound ham—basting every 30 minutes. Take dough off and finish with brown sugar or any favorite way of browning ham.

MRS. M. B. ALEXANDER (Ferdinand Williams)

Ham Loaf

1½ pounds lean pork, cooked and ground	1 can tomato soup
1½ pounds ham, cooked and ground	1½ cups milk
	2 eggs
	1 cup cracker crumbs

Pepper

Combine and put in loaf pan, pour 1 can tomato soup over loaf. Bake at 350° for 1½ hours. Serve with mustard sauce. Serves 6.

MRS. ADRIAN R. MARRON (Polly Ficken)

111

Hog's Head Cheese

"This receipt has been handed down through generations of the Huger family and is a favorite with old Charlestonians. It is a best seller at the St. Michael's bazaar. The traditional Christmas and New Year's Day breakfast is Hog's Head Cheese and hominy. It is also delicious with crackers."

½ hog's head	Salt to taste
2 tablespoons allspice	Hot pepper, catsup or
¼ cup vinegar	hot sauce to taste

Have butcher clean head and feet. Cover head and feet with water and boil until meat falls off bones. Remove head and feet from the liquid. Mince meat fine, removing all small bones and fat. Place liquid in refrigerator overnight. Next morning, skim off grease. Boil liquid until just enough to cover meat. Add meat, vinegar and seasonings (consistency of thin pudding after meat added.) Pour in molds. This will harden into a jelly which can be sliced. Serves 18 or more. Good with hominy or served on crackers as hors d'oeuvres.

MRS. M. B. ALEXANDER (Ferdinand Williams)

Fillet of Veal

4 or 5-pound veal roast cut from the middle round	2 small onions, chopped fine
	Lard
1 pound white side meat (salt pork) diced	Pepper
	Flour

Tie string around meat using skewers, if necessary, before preparing. Cut small holes in veal halfway through meat, using small paring knife. Fill these holes with bacon, onions, and pepper, which have been combined. Repeat process on other side of meat. Cover top side with a thick layer of lard. Dredge with flour. Put about ¾ cup of water in bottom of roaster, after adding meat. Cook in 325 degree oven, 25 to 30 minutes per pound. Add more water when needed. Baste frequently. A haunch of venison may be prepared the same as above. Serves 10.

MRS. DAVID HUGUENIN (Lavinia Inglesby)

Kidney Stew

2 veal kidneys, or 3,
   if very small
2 medium sized onions
2 rounded tablespoons butter
2 level tablespoons flour

Seasoning to taste (salt,
   pepper, Worcestershire,
   hot sauce, chives, herbs,
   if desired)
1 jigger wine (sherry or
   burgundy), optional

Wash kidneys and simmer very slowly until tender in several cups of water with salt and pepper to suit individual taste. A small onion, or a piece of one, and a bit of celery can be used, also. The kidneys should simmer at least an hour or more. Remove kidneys when tender and save the broth. There should be at least two cups of broth. Cut up kidneys in small pieces and put aside. Mince the onions and sauté a few minutes in one tablespoon of butter, browning very, very lightly. Add to the onions the other tablespoon of butter and when melted add the cut-up kidneys and sauté together but do not let kidneys brown. Dredge lightly with the flour in proportion to the amount of liquid, about one tablespoon of flour to one cup of broth. Let the onions, kidneys (*lightly* dredged with flour), cook one or two minutes together and add broth (not too hot) from the kidneys very slowly so the kidney stew will not lump. Cook stew very slowly. Add Worcestershire and hot sauce, minced chives and a jigger of cooking sherry, if served as a luncheon or supper dish. Delicious with waffles. Serves 4 to 6.

Miss Jane Christie Hammond

Liver Terrapin

1 pound veal liver
1 tablespoon butter
1 teaspoon dry mustard

2 tablespoons browned flour
3 hard boiled eggs
Sherry to taste

Salt and pepper to taste

Parboil the liver, keeping the liquor for gravy. Cut liver into small pieces and return to saucepan with the liquor. Season with salt, pepper, and butter. Mix mustard and flour and add. Chop eggs, and add these, along with sherry to taste. Serves 4.

MRS. ALEXANDER MARTIN (Elizabeth Stevens)

Roast of Lamb, with Anchovies

1 leg of lamb
1 small can anchovies
1 can consommé
1 can pimentos

Wide noodles
Parsley
Salt, pepper, butter
Garlic

Have butcher pierce small holes in surface of lamb, as for larding. Rub with garlic, *lightly* salt and pepper and stuff holes with chopped anchovies. Sear the lamb in plenty of butter, add consommé and roast slowly, basting often (300° oven, 30 to 35 minutes per pound). Boil noodles, not over 9 minutes, drain, dress in melted butter, garnish with pimiento and parsley and serve around lamb. Serves 8.

MRS. JOSEPH HENRY MOORE (Sally Horton)

Baked Lamb Steaks

1 leg of lamb	½ pint heavy cream
1 large Bermuda onion	Parmesan cheese

Butter, salt and pepper

Cut steaks off leg ¾ to 1 inch thick. Pepper steaks on both sides. Butter bottom of baking dish. Place slice of onion about ⅛ inch thick on top of each steak. Pour 1 tablespoon heavy cream over each onion. Sprinkle heavily with Parmesan cheese. Bake for 40 minutes in 325° oven. Remove to platter. Add water and salt in bottom of pan to make gravy. Add gravy to platter. Serves 8.

PETER GETHING

Hobotee

2 pounds cooked meat	1 dessertspoon sugar
2 onions	Juice of lemon or 2 tables-
Large slice of bread	spoons vinegar
1 cup milk	6-8 almonds, chopped, or
2 eggs	½ cup coconut
2 tablespoons curry powder	2 tablespoons cooking oil

Mince the meat, soak bread in milk and squeeze dry. Fry chopped onion in oil and when nicely browned sprinkle in curry powder and cook for a few minutes, being careful not to burn. Mix all ingredients with minced meat and bread, adding 1 egg. Whisk up other egg with milk, and after putting curry mixture into greased cups, pour some of this over it, sticking a slice of lemon or bay leaf into each little cup. Bake for 30 minutes and serve (in cups) with rice and chutney. May be baked in a casserole and any left over meat may be used instead of fresh. Cook in moderate oven. Serves 8.

MRS. RICHARD C. MULLIN (Hasell Townsend)

115

Mrs. Norman Scott's Curry

1 chicken (boiled or baked)	1 can evaporated milk
2 onions (finely grated)	½ pound butter
1 tablespoon (large)	1 clove garlic
curry powder	4 chicken bouillon cubes

2 tablespoons flour

Fry finely grated onion in butter and add the whole clove of garlic and remove it when the clove is brown. Add flour, curry, then milk. When this begins to thicken, add chicken gravy or broth and the bouillon cubes dissolved in 2 cups warm water. Place cut-up chicken in the sauce and simmer for at least an hour, thickening and thinning sauce at cook's discretion. Turkey or shrimp may be used instead of chicken. A 6-pound chicken serves 8.

CONDIMENTS FOR CURRY

1 pound of bacon, fried and crumbled in small bits; 1 pint chutney; crisp fried onion rings; 4 hard-boiled eggs, with whites and yolks put separately through ricer; 1 box grated coconut, browned till dry in oven; 1 can lichee nuts, cut in half; chopped peanuts. Optional: Bombay duck; 4 green peppers cut small, small bits of fried banana; and good pickle.

All these condiments are arranged in small separate dishes and the guests serve themselves with their own desired mixture on top of mound of boiled rice, which has been liberally covered with curry sauce and meat.

MRS. WILLIAM POPHAM (Louisa Stoney)

Hampton Plantation Smothered Chicken

Cut chicken in pieces. Place gizzard, neck and tips of wings in saucepan. Cover well with water. Add chopped celery, onion and salt. Simmer about 20 minutes. Then put grease in frying pan, using a good tablespoon or more. When hot, not too hot, add chicken, which has been salted and rolled in flour. Cover and cook about 25 minutes over medium flame. Turn pieces several times. Pour off grease, add the simmered gravy, cover closely and cook on very low fire for 5-10 minutes. Serves 4 to 6.

MISS CAROLINE RUTLEDGE

Fried Chicken

| 1 fryer (1½ to 2½ lbs.) | ½ teaspoon salt |
| 1 cup flour | ¼ teaspoon pepper |

Fat for frying

Dress and disjoint fryer. Chill in ice box overnight, if possible. Sift flour and mix with salt and pepper. Put flour mixture in paper bag and add several pieces of chicken to this at a time, to coat chicken with flour. Have about 2 inches of grease in large hot frying pan. When all chicken is in, cover for 5-7 minutes. Uncover and turn chicken when underside is golden brown. Cover again for 5-7 minutes, then remove top and cook until bottom side is brown. Reduce heat and cook 20 minutes longer. Turn chicken only once.

FRIED CHICKEN GRAVY

Pour off most of the fat, leaving the brown crumbs. Add a little flour and brown. Add hot water and stir until smooth and thickened. Season with salt and pepper.

MRS. HARRY SALMONS (Rosamond Waring)

Ida's Broiled Chicken

2 to 2½-pound chicken   2 tablespoons butter
Salt, pepper   1 tablespoon flour

Place chicken breast down in shallow covered pan. Dot with butter, salt and pepper. Cover. Cook 15 minutes in oven 375-400°. Remove cover. Reverse chicken. Broil under low light for about 15 minutes, basting often. If desired, thicken gravy with 1 tablespoon flour and ½ cup stock. This gravy should be a light brown and have very good flavor. Serves 4.

Mrs. A. T. Smythe (Harriott Buist)

Chicken Hemingway

2-pound broiler,   2 tablespoons bacon grease
   split in half   2 tablespoons olive oil
Salt   2 tablespoons lemon juice
2 tablespoons butter   2 tablespoons grated onion
1½ cups sherry   1 teaspoon salt

Boil last 6 ingredients, cool and pour over salted broiler cut side up and soak for several hours or overnight. Cook 15 minutes in 350° oven, browning slightly, then under broiler flame, basting with sauce frequently at all times. Serves 4.

Mrs. Joseph Henry Moore (Sally Horton)

Chicken with Brandy

1 chicken (cut for frying)   2 heaping teaspoons curry
¼ pound butter   2 cupfuls fresh cream
4 medium sized diced onions   3 ounces brandy or rum
Salt and pepper to taste

Brown onions in butter, add chicken, sprinkle with salt and pepper and cook slowly for 35 minutes. Just before serving remove chicken from pan; mix and add cream, spirits and curry, bring to boil in same pan and pour over chicken. Serve with rice. Serves 4.

Mrs. G. Simms McDowell (Henrietta Phillips)

Faber's Pilau

"Samuel Faber, who has always been with our family and officiates as doorman at the St. Cecilia Balls, is a superior cook besides being a leader among his people, particularly among the farmers of Charleston county."

One 6 or 7-pound rooster

Neck

Giblets

Liver

One large onion, chopped
fine

2 tablespoons salt

2 No. 2 cans tomatoes

1 tablespoon whole black
pepper

2 or 3 twigs of thyme

¼ pound of margarine

3 cups rice

3 tablespoons flour

Take a six or seven-pound rooster, wash, put in roasting pan on top of stove. Cover two-thirds of rooster with hot water. Put neck, giblets and liver in water, also. Add onion, salt, thyme and tomatoes put through a colander. Cover and boil hard. After one hour, add whole black peppers, and margarine. Turn down to simmer. Baste and turn fowl occasionally. After 2½ hours of cooking, take out 2½ cups of liquid. Put in separate pot, bring to boil, then into that washed, unsalted rice and cook. After 3½ hours cooking, remove rooster from roasting pan, thicken liquid in pan with flour, after that is thoroughly mixed, return rooster to roasting pan for thorough heating before serving. Serve with rice spread on big platter and rooster in nest of rice. Serves 10. When using hens for this pilau, cut down cooking time and do not put in margarine if hens are fat.

MRS. ALBERT SIMONS (Harriet Stoney)

Mrs. S. G. Stoney's Chicken in Corn

½ pound butter
1 jointed frying-size
   chicken

12 ears small tender
   green corn—raw
Salt and pepper

Fry the chicken lightly and flavour with pepper and salt. Place chicken and part of butter in glass baking dish, and grate the corn over it. Put the rest of the butter on the corn with more salt and pepper and bake in a slow (300°) oven till a nice brown. Do not let it get too dry. More butter may be added if necessary. Serves 4.

MRS. W. S. POPHAM (Louisa Stoney)

Chicken Tetrazzini

6 or 8 large mushrooms
4 tablespoons butter
½ cup good sherry
2 tablespoons flour
2 cups hot milk
Salt and pepper to taste
Sprinkling of nutmeg

1 cup thick cream
2 egg yolks
5 cups diced cooked chicken
1 nine-ounce package
   thin spaghetti
1 cup grated Parmesan
   cheese

Sauté mushrooms in 2 tablespoons butter. Add sherry and cook for a few minutes. Make a cream sauce of 2 tablespoons butter and 2 tablespoons flour. Rub these together and add hot milk. Cook in a double-boiler, stirring constantly until smooth and of a good body—about 20 minutes. Season with salt and pepper and nutmeg. Beat the yolks of the eggs into the cream and add to the sauce. Continue to stir. After 5 minutes, add chicken. Season to taste. Add mushrooms. Cook spaghetti. Butter a shallow casserole and put the cooked spaghetti in the bottom. Cover with the creamed chicken mixture. Sprinkle cheese over top and put under broiler until golden brown and bubbling. Serves 6-8.

MRS. HENRY P. STAATS (Juliette Wiles)

Hunter's Chicken

1 fryer, weighing in the vicinity of three pounds
Cooking oil
2 shallots, thinly sliced, or four tablespoons chopped onion
½ clove of garlic, thinly sliced

1½ pounds tomatoes, peeled, seeded and chopped
½ to ¾ cup dry wine
2 tablespoons tomato purée
Salt and pepper to taste
Bay leaf
1 tablespoon each butter and minced parsley

½ pound mushrooms

Disjoint fryer and brown in hot oil (enough to cover bottom of pan). When brown, remove from pan and sauté shallots, garlic and mushrooms in the oil, adding more if necessary. Put the chicken back in the pan and add remaining ingredients, except butter and parsley. Cook covered, over simmering heat, until chicken is tender, about 35 minutes. Arrange chicken on platter, add butter and parsley to sauce in pan and pour over bird. Serve over rice or plain potatoes. Serves 4.

MRS. THADDEUS STREET, JR. (Margie Lee)

Chicken Specialty

1 large chicken, or 2 frying chickens, disjointed (4-5 lbs.)
Seasoned flour
Salad oil
3 large onions, sliced

1 garlic clove, minced
1 green pepper, diced
1 No. 3 can tomatoes
1 cup beer
1 tablespoon salt
¼ cup seedless raisins

4 cups cooked rice

Dust chicken with seasoned flour; brown on all sides in salad oil. Remove chicken; add onions, garlic and green pepper to fat in pan; cook until soft, but not brown. Return chicken to pan; add tomatoes, beer and salt. Cover; simmer 1 hour or until tender. Add raisins; cook 10 minutes longer. Serve with paprika or red rice. Serves 6-8.

MRS. GEORGE PALMER (Frances Kirk)

My Grandmother's Chicken Croquettes

1 quart chopped, cooked
   chicken
Salt
Black pepper
Red pepper to taste
1 quart milk
½ onion, sliced very thin
Rind of 1 lemon
3 eggs

1 tablespoon parsley, chopped
¼ whole nutmeg, grated
½ pound butter
1 tablespoon (rounded)
   cornstarch
3 tablespoons flour
3 tablespoons milk

Bread crumbs

Put the onion and lemon rind into 1 quart of milk and let it come almost to a boil. Break into a bowl the eggs, minus the yolk of one, add parsley, nutmeg and red pepper. Into a large saucepan put butter, cornstarch, and flour. Cream these. As soon as milk comes nearly to a boil, remove onion and lemon rind; pour over creamed butter and flour, stirring all the time. Add eggs, parsley, and seasoning, and when thickened, add the meat. Taste for seasoning, and pour on flat dish to cool. Mold into croquettes using large pointed wine-glass. Dip into yolk of egg which was put aside. Mix egg yolk with milk; dip croquettes into mixture and roll in bread crumbs. Fry in deep hot fat. Serves 10.

MISS NATHALIE DOTTERER

White Fricassee Chicken

1 large hen
2 hard-boiled eggs
1 onion

1 bay leaf
4 tablespoons flour
Salt and pepper to taste

Cut hen as for frying. Place in pot covered with cold water. Boil slowly until tender. Make sauce from liquor after removing chicken from pot. Add to liquor, flour, eggs (mashed with fork), onion chopped fine, bay leaf, and salt and pepper. Place chicken on platter, garnishing with a slice of hard-boiled egg on top of each piece. Serve sauce separately. Serves 6.

MRS. WILLIAM V. HUTCHINSON (Eva Austin)

Carolina Barbecued Chicken

Juice of 1 lemon   Salt to taste
Vinegar   Black and red pepper to taste
Water   ¼ pound butter
                1 broiling-size chicken

Measure lemon juice, add equal amount of vinegar; measure lemon juice and vinegar, add equal amount of water. Add seasonings, then melted butter. Split chicken in half; cover with above liquid ingredients; place breast side down in oven bottom under flame; set broiler at 300°. Baste frequently, turning chicken after 1 hour, cooking about 2 hours altogether. Turn broiler higher last ½ hour to brown chicken. Serves 2.

MRS. ALSTON RAMSAY (Hazel Hunter)

Chicken Country Captain

1 bunch parsley (chopped)   Salt and pepper to taste
4 green peppers (chopped)   1 clove garlic (chopped)
2 large onions (chopped)   2 fryers, cut in pieces
Cooking oil   Paprika and flour
1 (No. 2½) can tomatoes   ½ box currants
        (3½ c.)   Cooked rice
1 teaspoon mace   ½ pound blanched almonds
2 teaspoons curry powder

Fry parsley, green peppers and onions in cooking oil slowly for 15 minutes. Put this mixture in roaster and add tomatoes, spices, salt and pepper. Simmer 15 minutes, then add garlic. Dredge chicken in a mixture of flour, salt, pepper and paprika. Fry till brown. Lay chicken in the sauce and simmer at 275° in a covered roaster for 1½ to 2 hours. Add currants ½ hour before serving. Arrange rice on a large platter, pour sauce over this and place pieces of chicken on top. Sprinkle toasted almonds on chicken. Serves 8.

MRS. E. H. deSAUSSURE (Eleanor Charlton)

Chicken Soufflé

Part I

6 tablespoons butter	Salt and pepper to taste
6 tablespoons flour	½ cup minced mushrooms
2 cups milk	1½ cups diced chicken

Make heavy cream sauce of above ingredients except the chicken, adding this when sauce has been cooked. Allow to cool.

PART II

3 tablespoons butter	Salt and pepper to taste
3 tablespoons flour	4 egg yolks (beaten)
1 cup milk	4 egg whites (beaten)

Make a second cream sauce of the butter, flour, milk, salt and pepper. Pour slowly on beaten yolks. Fold in stiffly beaten egg whites. Put mixture of Part I in bottom of buttered baking dish, then pour soufflé mixture on top. Set baking dish in pan of hot water. Bake in 325° oven 40 minutes. (A 10½-ounce can of condensed cream of mushroom soup may be substituted for the mushroom sauce of Part I, but it is not as good). Serves 6.

MISS CAROLINE ALSTON

Chicken Ring

1 hen (5 pounds)	3 chopped hard boiled eggs
¼ pound almonds	Cream sauce
Salt and pepper to taste	

Boil hen until meat falls from bones, then grind with almonds in meat grinder. Add 3 chopped hard boiled eggs and mix with enough cream sauce to hold it together. Fill a buttered ring mold and steam 1 hour. Serves 8.

MRS. JOSEPH HENRY MOORE (Sally Horton)

124

Chicken Mousse with Cream

1 cup chicken, cut fine	Cayenne pepper
1 cup well seasoned stock	1 tablespoon gelatine
2 egg yolks, well beaten	1 cup whipped cream
Celery salt	3 egg whites

Salt to taste

Combine first 5 ingredients, bring to a simmer, just enough to cook yolks. Cool. Then add gelatine (which has soaked in ¼ cup cold water and dissolved in a little hot water), the whipped cream, eggs (beaten dry) and salt. Beat well. Pour into wet mold to congeal. Unmold, serve on lettuce with mayonnaise. Serves 4.

MRS. ANDREW JACKSON GEER (Mary Owen)

Chicken Mousse

1 large fowl	1 quart chicken stock
(about 5 pounds)	1 green pepper
1 small stalk of celery	Hot sauce, salt and onion
2 packages gelatine	juice to taste

Boil fowl until tender. Run meat and celery through smallest grinder. Put stock back on stove with onion juice, pepper, (chopped), salt and hot sauce. Dissolve gelatine in ½ cup cold water, and add to stock while hot. Season highly. Strain stock and mix with ground chicken. Put in moulds. Makes 12 individual moulds.

MRS. NORWOOD HASTIE (Sara Simons)

Jellied Chicken Loaf

1 rooster or hen	Salt, red and black
(4 or 5 pounds)	pepper to taste
8 hard cooked eggs	1 stalk celery

2 packages plain gelatine

Boil chicken in slightly salted water until it is ready to fall apart. Take it from pot, and separate white and dark meat. Cut each pile of meat into very small bits. Slice 2 eggs, lengthwise. Chop up other six, season lightly with salt and pepper. Cut one stalk celery into small pieces. Line bottom of loaf pan with sliced eggs. Then place one layer of dark meat, one layer of celery, one layer of white meat, and one layer of chopped eggs. Repeat this until all ingredients are used. In the meantime, add seasoning, more salt if needed, red pepper, a little black pepper to stock, and turn on low light until this comes to a boil. Dissolve gelatine in ½ cup cold water. Next, pour boiling stock over gelatine . Then pour this over solids in loaf pan, making sure that liquid permeates all layers. Press down tightly with large spoon and when cool put in ice box four or five hours. Turn out on platter decorated with lettuce, ripe or stuffed olives, and strips of red pimientos. Slice and serve on lettuce with mayonnaise. Serves 8.

Mrs. Ashley Halsey (Eleanor Loeb)

Ham Mousse

2 eggs	¼ pound butter
½ cup finely chopped	1 can consommé
green pepper	1 tablespoon gelatine
½ cup finely chopped	2 cups ground ham
celery	1 tablespoon mustard

Separate eggs, beat yolks well, put with mustard, consommé and butter in double-boiler. Cook slowly until consistency of custard. Stir in ham, celery, pepper and gelatine, which has first been softened in ¼ cup water. Let cool, then fold in stiffly beaten egg whites. Put in wet mold. May be garnished with hard-boiled egg (sliced), green pepper, etc. Good with either tomato jelly or green salad. The basic receipt is good for shrimp or lobster instead of ham. Serves 8. Mrs. Francis B. Stewart (Katherine Felder)

Pressed Chicken

Two 5-pound hens
1½ cups finely chopped
  celery
1 small jar stuffed olives,
  chopped
¼ pound chopped almonds
4 chopped hard boiled eggs
1 quart stock

Several pieces of celery
1 small onion (chopped)
4 tablespoons gelatine
1 tablespoon chopped
  green pepper
Salt, pepper and cayenne
  to taste
1 lemon (juice)

Boil hens in water to cover until meat falls off bones, with several pieces of celery and the onion. Boil stock down, skimming off fat, until it makes 1 quart of stock. Soak gelatine in ¾ cup of water and add to hot stock, stir, add lemon juice. Cut chicken up coarsely, removing skin and gristle. Mix all ingredients and chill in refrigerator in mold. Slice and serve with mayonnaise and lettuce. Serves 12. MRS. JOSEPH HENRY MOORE (Sally Horton)

Jellied Daube Glacé

3 pounds of round or
  rump of beef
2 pound of veal steak
2 well-cleaned pig's feet
5½ quarts of water
Salt and pepper to taste

½ clove garlic, bay leaf,
  sprig of thyme
1 onion, minced fine
2 whole cloves, pounded
½ cup of cooking sherry
1 tablespoon Dah's Browning
  (Page 128)

Put beef (bone removed) in sauce pan, cover with 1½ quarts cold water, bring to a boil slowly, reduce the heat and keep simmering 4 hours. In another pan, put veal steaks and pig's feet with four quarts of water, garlic, bay leaf, thyme, onion, cloves, salt and pepper. Keep boiling until the meat falls from the bones. Mince the meat. Strain the liquor, remove bones, add sherry and browning. Place the whole beef, which has been simmering for four hours, in a deep bowl. Pour the beef stock and minced meat over the beef. Put in a cool place to harden. It will be completely set in about six hours. Turn out on platter, slice thin with a sharp knife. Delicious with hominy for supper or breakfast. Makes 50 thin slices. MRS. WALTER METTS (Jane Stauffer)

Veal Paté

2 pounds lean veal; free from strings and chopped fine

1 pound fat salt pork, chopped fine

1 (large) can mushrooms; put through chopper, cut fine

2 baking powder biscuits rolled into crumbs (or equivalent amount of coarse cracker meal)

1 egg, salt, pepper and nutmeg to taste

Mix thoroughly, mould into oval loaf form, place in baking pan (*not* greased), sprinkle with biscuit crumbs; put a little water in pan. Bake in a moderate oven until cooked through, basting from time to time with the water. When necessary, add a little more *hot* water. Venison, beef or other meats may be used instead of the veal. Serves 12.

FOR THE JELLY

1 box gelatine

1 pint cold water

1 pint hot water

1 tablespoon beef extract

Salt

Pepper

Dissolve gelatine in cold water, let stand for five minutes. Add hot water, beef extract, salt and pepper. (When paté is cold and jelly nearly so, pour jelly over plate and chill.

MISS MARY A. SPARKMAN

Dah's Browning

(For Making Gravy)

"Dah is a colloquial expression for a colored nursemaid, who, in this case, was Fields Parker."

Heat iron skillet very hot, then put in ½ pound white sugar, stir constantly over fire until a dark brown. Pour in ½ pint of boiling water and stir until dissolved. Use a long-handled spoon and pour water in slowly, as it foams and splashes. Bottle when cold. Keeps indefinitely.

MRS. W. TURNER LOGAN, SR. (Louise Lesesne)

Black Magic with Gravies

Remember the redoubtable cook on Blue Brook Plantation in Julia Peterkin's novel, "Black April"? I am sure her gravies were of a thinness, brownness and piquancy evolved in an earlier time when meats and fowl were roasted on a turning spit before a blazing fire, their precious juices caught in the tin trough of the spit. Here is a formula I like to think she followed and which applies to beef, pork, lamb, turkey or chicken gravy:

4 Tbsp. drippings, 3 Tbsp. flour, 2½ cups liquid, seasonings.

Here's how. When meat or fowl is done, remove from roasting pan and pour off all fat, being careful not to lose any of the brown sediment. Place pan over top-stove heat, measure back the fat, stir in flour to make a smooth roux; then, SLOWLY, add liquid, stirring all the while and scraping bottom of pan for brown coloring. Let boil up, cut off heat, add salt and pepper to taste. Commercial seasonings, liquid or powder, may be added if desired.

Water is the liquid used for meat gravy. For fowl, simmer neck and giblets in three cups water with two ribs minced celery. Use this stock, with celery and enough water to make three cups liquid, for gravy. Add giblets and two hard-boiled eggs, chopped. A trick which insures richer, browner gravy and a prettier bird is to cover entire outside of turkey or chicken with a thick paste of melted butter, (margarine) and flour. Place fowl in open roasting pan in 500° oven and bring to a deep, golden brown, then reduce temperature to 325° and finish cooking, covered, basting now and then. When done, liquid in pan will be full of dark-brown crumbs which will much improve the gravy.

This buttery paste works wonders on broilers, allowing ½ chicken per serving. Split front and back, rub in salt and pepper, cover with paste and brown as above. Reduce heat, add a little diced celery with ½ cup of water, and cook, covered, 45 minutes longer. When making gravy, add one small can cut mushrooms, with liquor. Serve on big chop dish, surrounding a mound of dry rice, and garnish with pickled peaches.

Try thinly-sliced onions to cover beef roast while cooking, then add to gravy; try capers with lamb; try a pinch of sage for pork. Try minced parsley, oregano, thyme—experiment and enjoy it.

Mrs. Dean M. Dockstader (Mary Ralls)

129

Bread Stuffing

FOR FISH OR FOWL

3 cups soft bread crumbs
½ medium onion, well-
    chopped
⅓ cup oil

½ teaspoon salt
⅛ teaspoon pepper
¼ teaspoon poultry
    seasoning

Mix crumbs, onion and seasonings. Add oil and toss well. This makes about 3½ cups. Oysters may be added, if desired.

MISS MARGARET WALKER

Turkey Stuffing

3 pounds chestnuts
1½ pounds fillet of
    tender veal

1 pound mushrooms
1 pan cooked cornbread
2 tablespoons butter

Boil, peel and mash chestnuts. Cook veal until tender and grind. Slice and sauté mushrooms in butter. Mix all these ingredients with cornbread, using a little milk if necessary. Truffles may be added. Stuffs a 15-pound turkey.

MRS. HARRISON RANDOLPH (Louise Wagener)

Sausage Stuffing for Turkey

½ cup butter
1 onion chopped
1 cup cracker crumbs

1 pound sausage meat
1 cup milk
2 tablespoons sherry

Salt and pepper

Let onion brown in butter. Add other ingredients and cook a few minutes.

MRS. KINLOCH McDOWELL (Annie Bissell)

Peanut Dressing

1 cup shelled, parched
  peanuts (or peanut
  butter)
2 cups ground-up
  cornbread

2 tablespoons melted butter
1 egg yolk
Broth from turkey
Salt and pepper

Grind peanuts; add crumbs, melted butter and egg yolk. Moisten with a little broth made by cooking the giblets and neck. Season with salt and pepper. This makes enough stuffing for the neck end of a turkey. Variation: 1 lb. ground salted peanuts, without other ingredients.

WALKER FAMILY RECEIPT

(OTHER STUFFINGS IN GAME CHAPTER)
Steak Sauce

¼ pound butter
1 tablespoon catsup
1 tablespoon Worcestershire
  sauce

1 teaspoon paprika
½ teaspoon dry mustard
2 teaspoons vinegar or
  lemon juice

Place pan over low heat and stir until butter is blended with condiments. Be careful not to let curdle. Pour over steak before serving.

MRS. ADRIAN R. MARRON (Polly Ficken)

Tartar Sauce

1 bunch parsley (chopped)
Small bottle of stuffed
  olives (chopped)

1 teaspoon grated onion
1 cup mayonnaise
Touch of garlic

Mix and serve on seafood or steak.

MRS. ELLIOTT HUTSON, JR. (Mary B. Means)

Egg Sauce for Boiled Fowl

1 pint chicken stock	1 tablespoon flour
3 or 4 eggs	1 tablespoon butter

Hard boil eggs. Rub egg yolks, flour and butter together. Add hot stock slowly and let boil very slowly for about five minutes. Take from fire, and add whites of eggs mashed with a fork. Serve.

MRS. GABRIEL CANNON (Jennie Heyward)

Tomato and Chicken Sauce
or Gravy for Fried Chicken

Trimmings from 2 or 3 chickens (necks, backs, gizzards, tips of wings)	Pepper
	Salt
	Bacon grease
	Minced onion
1 quart can tomatoes	Pinch of sugar

Salt and pepper the trimmings. Dip in flour and fry in bacon grease. Mash tomatoes through a colander. Add 1 quart of water, onion, pepper, salt, and pinch of sugar. Also add chicken and bacon grease and boil slowly for two hours or more. (If no bacon grease is on hand and bacon has been fried to obtain same, then add strip bacon to above before boiling.)

MRS. THADDEUS STREET (Mary Leize Simons)

Hot Apple Sauce with Rum

1 (No. 2) can apple sauce
    (2½ c.)
1 (No. 1) can sliced
    pineapple (1⅓ c.)
1 tablespoon lemon juice
1 tablespoon (or more)
    cornstarch

Dash of cinnamon, cloves,
    nutmeg
2 tablespoons rum
¼ cup toasted slivered
    almonds

Heat apple sauce and drained pineapple (cut in small pieces). In a separate pan mix pineapple and lemon juice, add cornstarch and cook until it thickens. Add spices and rum. Just before serving, sprinkle with almonds. Serves 4.

MRS. W. JERVEY RAVENEL (Kathryn Martin)

Apple Rings for Garnishing Pork

Using 1 cup sugar, ¾ cup water, ⅓ lemon (sliced) and ½ teaspoon red food coloring to every 3 apples: wash and cut apples crosswise into rings, leaving skin and core. Boil sugar and water till syrup spins a thread; add coloring, then fruit. Skim out rings separately after 10 minutes, and serve cold. Yield: 12 rings.

MRS. LOUIS T. PARKER (Josephine Walker)

Barbecue Sauce

¼ cup Worcestershire sauce   ¼ cup water
¼ cup brown sugar   1 large teaspoon chili
¼ cup vinegar   powder
       ¼ cup tomato catsup

Boil until thick, pour over meat ½ hour before being done, basting constantly.

Mrs. M. B. Alexander (Ferdinand Williams)

Curry Sauce

1 onion   1 tablespoon flour
1 apple   1 tablespoon butter
1 cup tomato juice   1 tablespoon curry
       1 cup cream

Chop onion and apple fine, and fry in butter. Add tomato juice and cook slowly. Mix flour, butter and curry and add to mixture. Then add cream. Strain and serve over shrimp and rice, or chicken and rice. Chutney and French fried onions should be served with it.

Miss Caroline S. Porcher

Ham Gravy

3 tablespoons butter   1¾ cups water
⅓ cup flour   Sherry to taste
2 teaspoons concentrated
     beef extract

Melt butter. Add flour and extract. Mix thoroughly. Slowly add water. Cook until smooth and thick. Add sherry to taste.

Mrs. Mary H. Bailey (Mary Huguenin)

Honey Glaze

1 cup honey   Grated peel of ½ orange

Mix ingredients and spread on ham about forty-five (45) minutes before removing from oven.

Jelly Glaze

1½ cups red jelly   ½ cup hot water

Mix ingredients and spread on ham about thirty (30) minutes before removing from oven—Score the ham and stud with cloves.

Orange Glaze

1 cup brown sugar   Grated peel of one orange
Juice of one orange   Grated peel of ½ lemon

Mix ingredients and spread on ham about thirty (30) minutes before removing from the oven.

Mrs. Louis Y. Dawson, Jr. (Virginia Walker)

Raisin Sauce for Ham

1 cup raisins   ¼ teaspoon salt
1 cup water   Pinch of pepper
5 whole cloves   1 tablespoon butter
¾ cup brown sugar   1 tablespoon vinegar
1 teaspoon corn starch   ¼ teaspoon Worcestershire
                                                 sauce

Cover raisins with water, add cloves and simmer for ten minutes. Add the sugar, cornstarch, salt and pepper which have already been mixed together. Stir until slightly thickened, then add the remaining ingredients.

Mrs. Kenneth Lynch (Lyall Wannamaker)

Mustard Sauce

1 tablespoon flour	½ cup powdered mustard
¼ cup butter	⅓ cup sugar
½ cup vinegar	1 bouillon cube
½ cup boiling water	2 eggs, well beaten

Cream together flour and butter. Add vinegar, boiling water, mustard, sugar, bouillon cube, eggs. Cook 10 minutes in double boiler. Serve hot or cold with ham loaf.

MRS. ADRIAN R. MARRON (Polly Ficken)

Ham Paste

1 pound prunes	2 tablespoons ground cloves
1 cup water	2 teaspoons ginger
Small can of shredded pineapple (not too wet)	2 teaspoons cinnamon
	1 tablespoon molasses
1 cup brown sugar	1 teaspoon mustard

Soak prunes in water over night. Take out stones and pour off water in morning. Put all ingredients in wooden mixing bowl and make a paste. Apply this to the cooked ham after it is skinned. Then put in oven for about a half-hour or until nicely glazed.

MRS. WILLIAM S. POPHAM (Louisa Stoney)

Stuffed Oranges

6 oranges	½ cup shredded coconut
½ cup stewed dates	1 egg white
½ cup chopped nuts	½ cup powdered sugar

Cut a slice from end of each orange and carefully remove pulp. Discard all tough membrane. Clean and chop dates. Mix dates, nuts, orange pulp and coconut together. Reflll orange shells. Beat egg white until stiff, add sugar gradually. Continue beating. Pile on top of oranges. Brown. Serve hot. Serve around ham or other meat.

MRS. KINLOCH McDOWELL (Annie Bissell)

GAME

"One time uh huntuh-man git up soon de mawnin', load 'e gun, en' gone out fuh hunt . . . 'E tell 'e wife . . . "Uh fuh cock me gun, en' me yeye en' me yez . . . . Den uh fuh sneak. Ef you ebbuh see cat creep 'pun bu'd, da' duh me! Uh nebbuh fuh mek no soun'.'"

Unluckily, I can not bear
To shoot a duck or dove or deer
Myself; but, when my friends bring game,
I heartily partake of same,
And raptly study how to do
A partridge pie or cooter stew!

Roast Wild Turkey

Prepare for roasting, wipe clean with damp cloth. Stuff with any desired stuffing. Put strips of fat bacon on the breast. Truss and roast uncovered in a moderately slow oven (325-350°) until tender, basting frequently. Allow 20-25 minutes per pound for total roasting time. To make gravy, remove turkey to a hot platter when done, and thicken the liquid in the pan on top of the stove with a flour and water mixture (2 tablespoons flour to 1 cup water).

MRS. W. W. HUMPHREYS (Martha Lynch)

Chestnut Stuffing for Wild Turkey

3 cups chestnuts
2 tablespoons butter
1 cup cracker crumbs

Cream
Salt and pepper to taste

Cook chestnuts until very tender and put through colander. Add butter, salt and pepper, then cracker crumbs. Moisten to desired consistency with sweet cream. If more dressing is required, make up in same proportion.

MRS. KIRK LYNCH (Juanita Kirk)

137

Corn Bread Stuffing

2 cups corn meal
1 cup flour
2 large tablespoons
  shortening
1 teaspoon salt
1 teaspoon baking powder
1 cup milk

2 eggs
1 cup chopped celery
1 cup chopped onion
2 slices toast (crumbled)
Salt and pepper to taste
2 cups (approx.) turkey
  stock

Mix corn meal, flour, shortening, salt, baking powder, milk and eggs. Bake at 350° for ¾ hour. Crumble bread when cold. Add celery, onion, toast, seasonings and moisten with stock to desired consistency.

Mrs. Frank Ford, Jr. (Elizabeth Coker)

Oyster Mushroom Stuffing

2 cups grated bread
  crumbs
¾ cup chopped celery
  leaves
3 tablespoons diced bacon
1 quart oysters,
  cut in pieces

¼ pound mushroom caps,
  halved and sauté
2 teaspoons salt
⅛ teaspoon paprika
1 tablespoon Worcestershire
  sauce
2 tablespoons walnut catsup

Mix ingredients by tossing lightly with a fork; pack loosely in cavity.

Miss Margaret B. Walker

Orange Stuffing for Wild Ducks

3 cups toasted bread cubes
1½ cups hot water
2 teaspoons grated
  orange rind
⅔ cup orange pulp

2 cups diced celery
¼ cup melted butter
1 beaten egg
½ teaspoon salt, pepper
  to taste

Soak bread cubes in hot water for 15 minutes. Add other ingredients. Mix well and stuff in ducks.

Mrs. John Simonds (Frances Rees)

Lavington Plantation Roasted Wild Duck

Prepare ducks for roasting. Stuff with Irish potato dressing or any other desired dressing. Dust with flour, salt and pepper and place several strips of bacon or thin slices of fat pork over the breast. Place in roaster and add one cup of water . Cook uncovered in a hot oven (400°) for about one hour. Baste frequently.

IRISH POTATO DRESSING

To 1 cup of mashed potato, add 1 tablespoon of finely chopped onion, 2 tablespoons of finely chopped celery, salt and pepper.

MRS. DAVID MAYBANK (Marion Taber)

Wild Duck with Mushrooms

One duck
1 onion, sliced
½ cup butter or drippings,
Salt and pepper
2 cups water

1 cup fresh mushrooms, sliced
2 tablespoons flour
⅛ teaspoon powdered thyme
1 bay leaf

Prepare and disjoint duck, brown with onion and fat. Add salt and pepper and 2 cups water and 1 bay leaf. Cook 1½ hours slowly. Sauté mushrooms, add flour and thyme. Add to duck and continue to cook 30 minutes. Serve on chop plate and border with wild rice or sausage and rice pilau.

MRS. HERBERT RAVENEL SASS (Marion Hutson)

139

Wild Duck Roasted

Method 1:

Dress, clean, stuff with sliced apple or whole peeled onion. Sprinkle with salt and pepper, cover breast with two very thin slices of fat pork, and truss. Place breast side up in roaster, and bake 15 to 30 minutes according to size in a very hot oven (500°) basting every 5 minutes with fat from pan. Remove apple or onion. Serve with a tart jelly or game sauce made by warming a glass of currant jelly in half as much port wine.

Method 2:

Ducks may be stuffed as above, or with wild rice dressing made by boiling wild rice and seasoning with salt, pepper and chopped onion; or any favorite dressing may be used. Salt and pepper the outside of the ducks and place them breast side up in a roaster. Cover the bottom of the roaster with water and cover tightly. Roast at 450° for the first 15 minutes then reduce heat to 350°. Baste every 15 minutes with the liquid in the pan. When almost tender, remove cover from pan (for last 15 minutes or so) to allow skin to brown.

LAWRENCE A. WALKER

Mrs. B. A. Hagood's Quail and Oysters

Quail	Corn meal
3 oysters per quail	Flour
Melted butter	Butter

Salt and pepper to taste

Wipe birds inside and out with damp cloth. Dip oysters in melted butter, then in corn meal and place inside bird. Make flour and butter into a paste and rub breasts well with the paste. Put birds in baking dish with a strip of bacon across each bird. Bake 30 minutes, basting well with butter. Serve on toast.

MRS. JAMES HAGOOD (Antoinette Camp)

Mrs. H. C. Mazyck's Partridge Pie

12 partridges (doves, snipe, etc.)
1 bunch minced parsley
1 onion, chopped fine
3 whole cloves
Salt and pepper to taste

½ pound salt pork, diced
2 tablespoons browned flour
Butter size of an egg
1 pint potatoes, diced small

Rich pie crust

Split birds in half, put in saucepan with about 2 quarts of water. When it boils, skim off all scum that rises, then add salt and pepper, parsley, onion, cloves and salt pork. Let all boil until tender, using care that there be enough water to cover the birds. Thicken with flour and let boil up. Stir in butter. Remove from fire and let cool. Line sides of a buttered pudding dish with the crust. Lay in birds, then some of the potatoes ,then birds and so on until the dish is full. Pour over the gravy. Put on the top crust with a split cut in the center and bake in hot oven 15-20 minutes. Serves 12.

MRS. ROBERT L. KERR (Louise Mazyck Frierson)

Deep Fried Quail

Clean quail thoroughly. Salt and flour each bird then place a lump of butter and a few grains of basil in the cavity. Fry in deep fat, fast at first until birds are brown all over, then slower for about 20 minutes. Do not cover. Place on brown paper to drain and serve while hot.

MRS. KARL MONTGOMERY (Rose Jenkins)

Roasted Quail

Clean quail thoroughly. Salt lightly, and place lump of butter inside each bird. Rub birds with mixture of flour and butter. Place in baking pan and bake in slow oven for about 1 hour, basting frequently with a little water, melted butter and sherry wine, to which ¼ teaspoon of marjoram or tarragon has been added.

MRS. KARL MONTGOMERY (Rose Jenkins)

Halidon Hill Potted Birds

Wipe birds inside and out with a damp cloth, then stuff lightly. Salt, pepper and flour birds. Melt about 2½ kitchen spoons of lard in an iron pot or skillet. Brown birds, then add a little water and cook (covered) very slowly on back of stove until tender. Add additional water when necessary.

STUFFING
(for 6 birds)

6 slices toasted stale bread

¼ small onion, minced

4 slices breakfast bacon

Salt and pepper to taste

¾ cup hot water

Fry bacon and chip fine. Add onion and cook until golden, then add bread, broken into small pieces, salt, pepper and hot water. Stir well.

MRS. THOMAS A. HUGUENIN (Mary Vereen)

Potted Doves

6 doves

6 slices bacon

1 cup catsup

1 small onion, sliced

3 tablespoons Worcestershire

1 tablespoon butter

Red pepper or hot sauce

Salt and pepper

Steam birds for 20 minutes on top of stove with a little water. Then add seasoning and catsup, and lay the bacon on top of the birds. Cook covered for about 1½ hours or until very tender. Remove cover and brown in oven.

MRS. DAVID MAYBANK (Marion Taber)

Quail in Milk and Celery

1 pint sweet milk
¼ pound butter
2 pieces chopped celery
1 cup sherry

2 slices onion
1 teaspoon salt
½ teaspoon black pepper
1 dozen quail

Pour ingredients mixed together over quail. Cover vessel and cook slowly on top of stove 2 hours or until tender. Add milk, if necessary.   MISS VIRGINIA MITCHELL

Smothered Marsh Hens

Parboil eight skinned birds in salt water just long enough to take out the blood and keep the shape. Drain and put in deep frying pan on top of stove. Add the following gravy:

2 cups chicken stock or
   1 can chicken soup
6 tablespoons of browned
   flour

6 tablespoons of bacon
   grease
Salt and pepper

Cover and cook about 1 hour, then uncover and slip under the broiler flame for 15 minutes.

MRS. JOHN LAURENS (May Rose)

Marsh Hens

3 marsh hens
3 tablespoons shortening or
   bacon grease

2 onions, sliced
¾ cup flour
1½ cups water

Salt and pepper

Soak skinned birds in cold salted water from 2 to 3 hours. Fry onions in shortening until golden brown. Salt, pepper, and flour the birds, then fry them with the onions until they are browned. Add water, cover, and let simmer slowly until tender. Stir occasionally. Serve in the gravy. Serves six.

MRS. W. H. BARNWELL (Mary M. Royall)

Venison

The loin gives the best roasts or steaks (sirloin or porterhouse). The chuck and rump are good for pot roasts and ground meat.

The round will make good steak unless the animal is particularly tough and then it may be used as Swiss steaks or ground up.

If the leg is small, it may be roasted all in one piece like a leg of lamb.

The shank, neck flank and spareribs can be best used for soups, stews, and ground meat. The neck will be tender if the tendons are removed and will make good roast.

The characteristic venison flavor is concentrated largely in the fat and the removal of the bulk of the fat will make it less "gamey."

LAWRENCE A. WALKER

Venison Roast

1 haunch of venison   1 onion, chopped
½ to 1 pound of bacon   Salt and pepper to taste

Wash in tepid water, dry thoroughly with cloth. Make dressing with bacon, onion, salt and pepper. Cut slits in meat and stuff with dressing. Cover with strips of bacon. Use 1 cup hot water using more when needed. Cover and cook until done in slow oven allowing 25 minutes per pound, basting frequently.

MRS. ELLIOT HUTSON, JR. (Mary B. Means)

"The Laurels" Roast of Venison

1 haunch of venison   1 bottle of port wine
   (hung for 4 or 5 days,   1 large jar crabapple
   or in ice box 1 week)   jelly, melted

Cook venison as for rare roast beef. Baste venison while cooking with sauce made of the wine and jelly. Serve with sauce poured over the venison.

MRS. SIMONS VANDER HORST WARING (Louisa Johnson)

Venison Cutlets

2 pounds venison steak Flour
2 tablespoons butter Salt and pepper
½ cup sour cream Celery salt
Worcestershire sauce Bay leaf

Cut venison into individual cutlets and roll in well seasoned flour. Melt butter in heavy skillet and brown cutlets on both sides over medium heat. When nicely browned, pour sour cream over cutlets and season with salt and pepper, Worcestershire sauce, celery salt and bay leaf. Cover skillet and cook about an hour over low heat or until tender. Serves 6-8.

PETER GETHING

Venison Meat Loaf

(For neck, flank and shoulder)

1 pound ground venison ½ cup dried bread crumbs
⅓ pound ground pork 1 cup milk
1 egg 1½ teaspoons salt
½ tablespoon minced onion

After mixing the meats thoroughly, add egg, milk, bread crumbs and seasonings. Place in greased pan and bake for 1 hour in a medium oven (350°). Serves 4.

MRS. W. W. HUMPHREYS (Martha Lynch)

Potted Venison

3 cups cooked venison Red and black pepper and
 (ground) salt
1 cup butter or shortening Pan gravy
1 onion, chopped

Allow butter to soften and mix well with venison. Add gravy, if not sufficiently moist. Add freely, onion and seasoning to taste. Mix thoroughly again. Put mixture in a biscuit pan and bake in a moderate oven until lightly browned. Allow to cool, then cut into squares. Serve with hominy for breakfast.

MRS. C. STUART DAWSON (May Elliott Hutson)

Mrs. W. W. Elliott's Venison à la Blaise

4 cups chopped venison   1 heaping tablespoon butter

1 large onion   1 cup tomato catsup

Salt, black and red pepper

Cut left-over venison into small pieces and put in saucepan with finely chopped onion, black and red pepper, salt and butter. Add tomato catsup (preferably home made). Let boil slowly until sauce is thick. If more seasoning is desired a pinch of ground cloves and mace may be added. Serves 6-8.

MRS. C. STUART DAWSON (May Elliott Hutson)

Venison Savory Meat

From The Centennial Receipt Book by a Southern Lady (Miss Joe Waring) published in 1876.

Chop fine, some cold cooked venison, moisten it well with a large spoonful of butter, and the yolk of an egg. Season it with thyme, pepper, salt, and a little allspice; beat fine, mix well together, put in a pan and bake.

Venison Balls

From The Centennial Receipt Book

Prepare the venison in the same way as for savory meat, leaving out the butter, and adding a little bacon or cold ham chopped fine with an onion. Make into balls; fry in lard.

MRS. DAVID MAYBANK (Marion Taber)

Mrs. Samuel G. Stoney's "Back River Paté"

"An old French Huguenot dish which has been in our family for years."

Left-over venison   Butter (⅓ the amount of
                                         the venison used)

Coarse black pepper and salt

Put left-over venison and all scraps from bones through finest blade of the meat grinder twice. Add butter. Work pepper into this and add salt to taste. Place in pyrex dish and pound down with a wooden mallet until it is a solid mass. Cook slowly.at about 325° until a golden brown. Chill. Take out and cut in thin slices. Keeps indefinitely in ice box. Serve with hominy or salad.

MRS. WILLIAM S. POPHAM (Louisa Stoney)

Broiled Venison Steak

Cut haunch of young buck into steaks. Sprinkle with black pepper and lightly flour. Dot with butter. Cook under flame or in sizzling hot iron frying pan. Sprinkle with salt as you turn. Cook 10 to 15 minutes. Add enough water to pan for gravy and serve sizzling hot with rice, or wild rice.

MRS. LIONEL LEGGE (Dorothy Porcher)

Opossum

Opossum should be cleaned as soon as possible after shooting. It should be hung for 48 hours and is then ready to be skinned and cooked. The meat is light colored and tender. Excess fat may be removed, but there is no strong flavor or odor contained in the fat.

MRS. W. W. HUMPHREYS (Martha Lynch)

Roast 'possum

1 opossum
1 onion, chopped
1 tablespoon fat
¼ teaspoon Worcestershire
  sauce

1 cup bread crumbs
1 hard-boiled egg
1 teaspoon salt
Water

Rub opossum with salt and pepper. Brown onion in fat. Add opossum liver and cook until tender. Add bread crumbs, Worcestershire sauce, egg, salt and water. Mix thoroughly and stuff opossum. Truss like a fowl. Put in roasting pan with bacon across back and pour 1 quart of water into pan. Roast uncovered in moderate oven (350°) until tender. (About 2½ hours). Serve with sweet potatoes.

R. O. DION

Rabbit Pie

Rabbits should be decapitated and dressed immediately after shooting. After skinning, wipe the carcass with a cloth dipped in scalding water to remove loose hair. Cut rabbit into serving pieces. Soak in equal parts of vinegar and water for 12-24 hours. Drain and wipe dry. Sprinkle with salt and pepper and dredge with flour. Sear quickly in frying pan. Add water to cover and simmer slowly in covered pot for 1½ hours. Add 2 onions, 2 medium sized carrots and 2 or 3 potatoes, all cut in pieces. Cook until vegetables are done. Thicken with flour. Cook in a greased baking dish in a hot oven until bubbling. Cover with biscuit dough and return to oven to bake until dough is done.

MISS MARGARET B. WALKER

Hasenpfeffer

1 rabbit	3 cloves
Vinegar and water	1 bay leaf
1 sliced onion	1 cup thick sour cream
Butter	Salt and pepper

Disjoint rabbit, wash and place in crock or jar with enough vinegar and water in equal parts to cover. Add onion, a few cloves, bay leaf, salt and pepper to taste. Let the meat soak for 2 days. Then wipe dry and brown in hot butter, turning frequently. Slowly add some of the solution used for soaking the meat to the depth of ¼ of an an inch. Cover tightly and simmer until done (about 30 minutes). Do not boil. Just before serving stir sour cream into sauce.

MRS. R. O. DION (Eleanor Walker)

Squirrel

Squirrel is one of the finest and tenderest of all wild meats. Its flavor is mild, rarely gamey. There is no need for soaking, and seldom any need for parboiling. They should be cleaned as soon as possible after shooting, but skinning may wait until they are to be cooked.

MISS MARGARET WALKER

Broiled Squirrel

Clean squirrels and rub with salt and pepper. Brush with fat and place on hot broiling rack. Broil 40 minutes, turning frequently and basting with drippings every 10 minutes. Serve with gravy from drippings and season with 1 to 2 tablespoons of lemon juice.

MRS. W. W. HUMPHREYS (Martha Lynch)

HARVESTING RICE

HOMINY & RICE CHEESE & EGGS

Man, w'en 'e hongry, 'e teck sum egg or cheese an' ting an' eat till e' full. But 'ooman boun' fuh meck wuck an' trouble. 'E duh cook!

> Never call it "Hominy Grits"
> Or you will give Charlestonians fits!
> When it comes from the mill, it's "grist";
> After you cook it well, I wist,
> You serve *"hominy"!* Do not skimp;
> Serve butter with it and lots of shrimp.

Hominy

Hominy has long been a favorite in the Carolina Low-Country. This corn preparation, boiled with water and salt, was served in almost every household for breakfast—not as a cereal with sugar and cream, but mixed with butter and eaten with a relish such as bacon, eggs or fish cakes. It was not frequently used for dinner, but was often on the supper table, either cooked in the same manner, or, more often, in the form of fried hominy, baked hominy or "Awendaw." These concoctions were usually made from the hominy left "in the pot" after breakfast and were served for the evening meal with ham, shrimp, crab, or the like. Hominy is still used a great deal in Charleston and its vicinity, and may be prepared in any of the following ways:

Boiled Hominy

1 cup grist   4½ cups water

1 rounded teaspoon salt

Formerly, the grist which could be procured in fine, medium, or coarse grind, according to preference, had to be washed in several waters. It was often soaked overnight or for several hours in a pot and then boiled in that utensil with the same water. When it began to cook, it was allowed to boil hard, uncovered, being stirred constantly to keep from scorching. It was then covered and cooked on a slower heat, stirred from time to time for the last ½ hour. The hominy was sometimes beaten up with butter before being served. Today, the packaged "grits" may be added directly to boiling water and cooked for a shorter time, but should still be stirred frequently until done. (Hot water may be added if it becomes thicker than desired.) Serves 4.

MRS. LOUIS T. PARKER (Josephine Walker)

Pressure Cooked Hominy

A modern way of cooking an old favorite.

1 cup grist   1 teaspoon salt
3½ cups water   ¼ stick butter or
                               margarine (optional)

This may be started with either hot or cold water. It should be allowed to boil hard, uncovered, and stirred fequently for about 5 minutes. It can then be covered and cooked at lowest possible temperature 30 to 45 minutes. When cover is removed, according to pressure cooker directions, the hominy should be well stirred with a wooden spoon. The butter may be beaten in for extra goodness. When cooked in this way, the necessity of frequent stirring during cooking is eliminated and the result is a smooth and creamy hominy. Serves 4.

MRS. LOUIS T. PARKER (Josephine Walker)

Baked Hominy

2 cups cooked hominy,   ⅔ cup milk

    preferably hot   ⅓ stick butter

2 eggs

Beat butter into hot hominy (if using cold hominy, melt butter before adding). Beat eggs until light, add milk to eggs, then stir this mixture into hominy. Put in oven dish and set in pan of water. Bake in moderate oven (375°) for about an hour. (A little more butter and another egg may be added for extra richness.) Serves 6.

MRS. LOUIS T. PARKER (Josephine Walker)

Fried Hominy

1 tall glass cold hominy   ¼ cup of fine cracker

1 egg, beaten   meal

1 tablespoon milk or water   ¼ teaspoon salt

4 tablespoons shortening

Pour cooked hominy, while hot, into a thick tall glass, first rinsed in cold water, and put it into refrigerator to chill. When cold, turn it out and cut into slices about ⅓ inch thick. In meantime, put shortening into heavy skillet to heat. Dip each piece of hominy into egg which has been beaten with milk or water, and then in cracker meal to which salt has been added. Fry in hot fat over medium heat until golden brown on both sides (turning once). (This is often served with bacon for breakfast and seldom sweetened with syrup in this section of the country). Serves 4 to 6.

MRS. LOUIS T. PARKER (Josephine Walker)

Mrs. Ralph Izard's "Awendaw"

1½ cups hominy, cooked	1½ cups milk
1 heaping tablespoon butter	¾ cup corn meal
3 eggs	½ teaspoon salt

While hominy is still hot, add butter and eggs beaten very light. Then gradually add milk and when well mixed, add corn meal and salt. The batter should be like thick custard. Pour in deep greased pan, bake in moderate oven. (375°). Serves 6-8.

MISS EMMA GAILLARD WITSELL

Grainy Hominy

2 cups raw grist   Salt to taste

Wash grist and drain carefully; place in double-boiler, cook for 2 hours, stirring frequently with a fork. Add salt after 1½ hours of cooking time. When done, hominy should be white and flaky with every grain apart. This is an old plantation dish and is served with gravy. It is delicious. Serves 4-6.

MRS. STUART DAWSON (May Hutson)

Hominy Surprise

2 cups grist   1 tablespoon salt

8 cups water

Cook grist until thick (about 30 or 40 minutes). Pour into large mixing bowl and add:

2 raw eggs	1 tablespoon Worcestershire
1 cup grated sharp cheese	1 cup milk
1 tablespoon (or less) black pepper	1 tablespoon butter

Mix thoroughly and pour into baking dish, reserving enough cheese to cover top. Sprinkle with paprika. Bake 1 hour, or longer, in moderate oven. This is good with cold sliced ham. Serves 8.

MRS. JACK W. SIMMONS (Irene Robinson)

156

Rice

Charleston was the birthplace of rice in America. The first seed was brought to the province of Carolina about 1685. This rice had been raised in Madagascar, and a ship sailing from that island put into the port of Charles Town when in distress. The captain of the ship, John Thurber, made the acquaintance of Dr. Henry Woodward, one of the leading citizens. He gave Dr. Woodward a small quantity of rice, less than a bushel. This started the rice industry, which flourished for over two centuries. These seeds were cultivated, due to soil and climate, to the highest perfection, and became world famous as Carolina Gold Rice. Some of the following receipts have been in constant use for over a century and a half, passing from generation to generation.

Southern Rice

1 cup rice   1¾ cups water
(washed thoroughly)   1 teaspoon salt

Combine all ingredients and boil hard, uncovered, until water is absorbed (about 15 minutes). Steam about 45 minutes: either in same pot, tightly covered, and placed over very low heat or put into a colander (covered) over boiling water, forking when necessary. Serves 4.

Mrs. Louis T. Parker (Josephine Walker)

Steamed Rice

1½ cups rice   1 teaspoon salt
1¼ cups water

Wash 1½ cups rice thoroughly in cold water. Place in rice steamer or double-boiler. Add enough water to come to top of rice, but not cover it . Add salt; cover and cook over hot water for 40 minutes or until done. After first 30 minutes of cooking, remove lid and fluff up rice with a fork so that each grain is allowed to stand up and keep its shape. Replace lid and finish cooking. Approximate yield: 4 to 6 servings. Serve with meat gravy. If served with fish dinner, use egg sauce, capers sauce, or appropriate substitute.

Mrs. Francis L. Parker (Elizabeth Middleton)

157

Red Rice

1 can tomato paste	2-3 teaspoons sugar
1½-2 cans water	4 strips bacon (cubed)
2 onions (chopped fine)	8 tablespoons bacon grease
3 teaspoons salt	Good dash of pepper

2 cups raw rice

Fry bacon, remove from pan; sauté onions in grease; add tomato paste, water, salt, sugar and pepper. Cook uncovered slowly (about 10 minutes) until mixture measures 2 cups, then add it to rice in top section of steamer. Add the ½ cup additional grease; steam for ½ hour, then add bacon, crumbled, and stir with a fork. Cook 30-45 minutes longer. Serves 6-8.

MRS. CHARLES GIBBS (Wilmot Welch)

Okra Pilau (Limping Susan)

3 or 4 slices of bacon, chopped	1 cup washed rice
	Salt and pepper to taste
1 pint okra	1 cup water

Fry bacon with okra cut in rings. When okra is tender, add rice and water, salt and pepper. Put in rice steamer and cook until dry . . . about 1½ hours. Serves 4-6.

MRS. W. H. BARNWELL (Mary Royall)

Adele's Tomato Pilau

2 slices bacon (chipped)	¼ teaspoon sugar
1 onion, chopped fine	1½ teaspoons salt
1 (No. 3) can tomatoes	¼ teaspoon black pepper

2½ cups rice

Cook bacon in frying pan until brown, add onion and sauté lightly with pan covered; add tomatoes, sugar, salt, pepper. Cook over low heat ½ hour, stirring frequently. Add rice and cook 5-10 minutes. Transfer to steamer; cook 45 minutes; 10 minutes before serving, stir with fork; uncover steamer to dry rice. Serves 8-10.

MRS. REES F. FRASER (Mary Maybank)

Tomato Okra Pilau

3 slices bacon	2 quarts water
1 small onion	1 teaspoon salt
2 cups stewed tomatoes	2 cups rice
2 cups thinly sliced okra	Pepper to taste

Cook chopped bacon in deep frying pan until brown; remove bacon and fry onion in bacon fat until brown. Add tomatoes and okra and let them cook until tender, stirring occasionally; add salt and pepper. Cook rice in 2 quarts of water with 1 teaspoon salt added; after 12 minutes, drain and mix with tomato mixture and put in top of double-boiler. Let steam for 15 or 20 minutes; add bacon just before serving. Serves 8.

MRS. RIVERS T. JENKINS (Lewis Murchison)

Hopping John

Hopping John, made of cow peas and rice, is eaten in the stateliest of Charleston houses and in the humblest cabins and always on New Year's Day. "Hoppin' John eaten then will bring good luck" is an old tradition.

1 cup raw cow peas	1 cup raw rice
(dried field peas)	4 slices bacon fried with
4 cups water	1 medium onion, chopped
2 teaspoons salt	

Boil peas in salted water until tender. Add peas and 1 cup of the pea liquid to rice, bacon with grease and onion. Put in rice steamer or double-boiler and cook for 1 hour or until rice is thoroughly done. Serves 8.

MRS. W. H. BARNWELL (Mary Royall)

Curried Rice

2 cups rice   1 teaspoon salt
2 tablespoons curry powder   1½ cups chicken stock

Pick rice, but do not wash. Place all ingredients in rice steam-er for 1½ hours, stirring several times with 2-tined fork. For chicken stock, canned consommé may be used, but I prefer to use stock obtained from boiling 1 pound chicken necks with sea-sonings such as celery, onion, and bay leaf. Bits of chicken may be cut from the chicken necks and added to the curried rice after it is done.

To cook in double-boiler instead of rice steamer, use 2 cups of chicken stock, other ingredients the same . Serves 8.

Mrs. Matthew Barkley (Helen Lebby)

Baked Rice

½ pint rice   1 pint milk
1 dessertspoonful butter   1 egg

Cook rice dry and fluffy; put in a quart baking-dish with butter and milk, a beaten egg and salt. Bake ½ hour in moderate oven. Serves 4.

Mrs. Frank Cain (Parham Atkins)

Fried Rice

4 slices bacon   1 teaspoon soy sauce
1 medium onion   2 cups cooked rice

Fry bacon until crisp in heavy skillet. Remove bacon; fry chopped onion until brown. Add rice, stirring constantly until browned; add crumbled bacon and season with 1 teaspoon of soy sauce. Green peppers, celery, pimento, or chopped mushrooms may be added if desired. Serves 4.

Mrs. Matthew Barkley (Helen Lebby)

Rice Croquettes

1½ cups rice   A little butter
½ cup wheat flour   2 eggs
              ½ teaspoon salt

To 1½ cups of soft boiled rice, add ½ cup wheat flour, ½ teaspoon salt, 2 eggs and a little butter. Mix well and mould into shapes. Fry in boiling lard.

FROM MRS. S. G. STONEY's *"Carolina Rice Cook Book"*

Rice Omelet

1 cup rice, boiled in milk   3 eggs
⅛ teaspoon salt   3 tablespoons milk

Cover rice with milk and cook in a steamer until tender. Add 3 tablespoons of milk and the salt to thoroughly beaten egg yolks. Add rice. Fold in stiffly beaten egg whites. Cook until set in a hot buttered frying pan. Lift up with spatula occasionally until moisture is taken up. Set in oven for about 5 minutes until mixture rises, take out and fold over. Pour cheese sauce over omelet. Serves 4.

MRS. RALPH MILLS (Elizabeth Stevens)

Rice, Cheese and Olives

½ cup rice   1 egg, beaten
½ pound sharp cheese   ¼ teaspoon salt
1 cup milk   Pepper
              Stuffed olives

Wash and boil rice; melt cheese in milk, add egg, salt and pepper; fold in rice. Put a layer of rice mixture in buttered caserole, over this put a layer of sliced stuffed olives. Alternate the layers of rice and olives and cover with buttered crumbs. Bake in moderate oven. Serves 4.

MRS. RALPH MILLS (Elizabeth Stevens)

Picnic Pride Rice

Delicious for picnics with cold meat or hash.

1½ cups rice	½ cup chopped peanuts
1 cup water	½ cup chopped raisins
2 bouillon cubes	½ cup cut-up celery
2 tablespoons bacon grease	Salt and pepper to taste

1 teaspoon concentrated beef extract

Wash rice. Cook in steamer with water in which bouillon cubes are dissolved, and bacon grease, salt and pepper added. When half cooked, or when rice has soaked up all the water, add peanuts (which have been mashed with a rolling pin), raisins and celery. A ham skin may be cooked with the rice, if desired. Cook about 1½ hours or until done. Serves 6 eaters - 8 munchers!

Mrs. HENRY EDMUNDS (Frances Smythe)

Rice Ring

Cook 2 cups raw rice according to directions in this chapter or cook in a rice steamer. Pack in a greased 1½ quart ring mold, then set in a pan of hot water and simmer for 10 minutes, or until rice is hot. Unmold on a hot platter. Serves 8.

Mrs. D. A. GEER (Nancy Kollock)

Browned Rice

1½ cups rice	3½ cups water
2 tablespoons butter	1½ teaspoons salt

⅛ teaspoon pepper

Sort, but do not wash rice. Place dry rice in frying pan with butter and stir over moderate fire until golden brown. Add water and seasonings and let come to a boil. Put in covered casserole and let bake in a 350° oven 30 or 40 minutes, or until dry and flaky. Add more butter or ham drippings and dash of paprika and serve HOT. Serves 4.

Mrs. PRIOLEAU BALL (Teresa Daniel)

Wild Rice Casserole

1 cup wild rice	Salt and pepper to taste
1 10-ounce can condensed	1 tablespoon butter
consommé	½ pound mushrooms

Wash rice carefully, pick over and remove chaff. Place in a broad shallow casserole and cover with can of consommé—let stand 3 hours. Then bake, covered, in oven (350°.F) for about 45 minutes, adding a little water if rice becomes too dry. Add 1 tablespoon butter and ½ pound small mushrooms which have been sautéed in a little butter. Lightly mix with a fork. Uncover rice at the last and let dry out a little; lower oven to 300° F. No crust should form but all liquid should be absorbed. This is a delicious buffet supper dish. Serves 4.

Mrs. Henry P. Staats (Juliette Wiles)

Cheese Croquettes

2 tablespoons cornstarch	2 tablespoons butter
1 cup cream	1 cup sharp cheese
½ teaspoon mustard	2 eggs (yolks)
Salt to taste	1 tablespoon Parmesan
Pinch of cayenne	cheese

Bread crumbs

Cook cornstarch in hot butter. Add hot cream, gradually. When thick and smooth, season with salt, cayenne, mustard and grated Parmesan cheese. Then stir in sharp cheese, diced; when melted, add yolks. Turn into shallow pan; when cold, cut into small oblong pieces. Cover with crumbs and egg. Dip in egg and crumbs again. Fry in smoking hot deep fat. Drain and serve hot. Serves 5.

Mrs. T. Ladson Webb (Anne Moore)

Cheese Pudding

10 slices bread
½ pound cheese
2 cups milk

1 teaspoon salt
3 eggs
Butter

Take ten slices of bread, crusts removed, butter well and cut in cubes. Put in baking dish, alternating with grated cheese, then pour over the following: milk, salt, eggs, beaten. Let stand several hours before baking. Bake in 275° oven for about 45 minutes. Serves 6.

MRS. BACHMAN S. SMITH (Irene Gaillard)

Cheese Puffit

1 cup left-over cooked ham
1 teaspoon chopped onion
   (optional)
2 tablespoons lard
2 slices soft bread
   ½ inch thick
¼ pound yellow cheese

2 eggs, separated
¼ teaspoon paprika
½ teaspoon salt
1⅓ cups hot milk
1 tablespoon lard (extra)
1 tablespoon parsley,
   minced

Put ham and onion through grinder. Pan-fry gently 3 minutes with the lard. Put in greased baking-dish. Crumble bread (crust too) into small pieces, sliver cheese into small thin slices or grate coarsely. Combine bread, cheese, beaten egg yolks and heated milk; add extra tablespoon lard, salt and paprika. Let stand 20 minutes or until ready to bake. Add parsley, then fold in stiffly beaten egg whites. Pour into baking-dish over ham. Bake in slow oven (325°) 45 minutes, or until silver knife inserted in center comes out clean. This soufflé does not fall if left in warm oven with door open for a short time. Serves about 6.

MRS. ARTHUR STONEY (Anne Montague)

St. Michael's Alley Cheese Soufflé

1 tablespoon of flour   ¼ pound sharp cheese
1 tablespoon of butter   1 cup milk
3 eggs   ½ teaspoon baking powder
½ teaspoon salt   Dash of cayenne

Make sauce of flour and melted butter; add milk, beaten yolks, then cheese. Cook until smooth and thick. Beat whites stiff, adding baking powder—mix all together—pour into a well-greased baking dish; bake ½ hour in a moderate oven. Cornstarch may be substituted for flour. Serves 4.

MISS MARGARET FELL LYON

Macaroni Pie

½ pound macaroni, broken   Salt and pepper to taste
1 heaping tablespoon butter   ½ teaspoon dry mustard
1½ cups sharp cheese, cubed   3 eggs
1 pint milk

Cook macaroni in rapidly boiling water for ten minutes. Drain. Stir butter and cheese—leaving about ½ cup cheese to sprinkle over top of pie—into the hot macaroni; add salt, pepper, and mustard. Beat eggs into mixture, add milk and mix well. Put in greased baking dish, sprinkle top with cheese and dot with butter. Bake in 350° oven about 40 minutes. Serves 6.

MRS. RIVERS JENKINS (Lewis Murchison)

Cheese Sauce

4 tablespoons butter   ¼ teaspoon salt
4 tablespoons flour   ⅛ teaspoon pepper
1 cup milk   ½ cup grated cheese

Melt butter in top of double-boiler, blend in flour until smooth. Add milk gradually and stir until thick. Add other ingredients, stirring constantly. Serves 4.

MRS. RALPH MILLS (Elizabeth Stevens)

Basic Omelet

6 eggs   1½ cups milk

Salt and pepper to taste

Preheat oven to 350°. Beat yolks of eggs with milk; beat the whites and pour yolks and milk into them. Pour into greased heavy skillet and cook in oven until firm and golden (12-20 minutes). Serves 6.

Mrs. Thomas N. Carruthers (Ellen Douglas Everett)

Creamed Stuffed Eggs

8 hard-boiled eggs   4 tablespoons pecans
1 cup cooked chicken   1 cup white sauce, made
½ teaspoon onion juice   with chicken broth
                    Salt and pepper

Cut eggs in half, remove yolks and mash. Grind chicken and pecans and add to egg yolks with onion juice, salt and pepper, and enough white sauce to moisten. Fill egg whites with this mixture; place in casserole, stuffed side up, and pour over remaining sauce. Bake covered in oven 375°. Serve on toast with mushroom sauce.

MUSHROOM SAUCE

½ cup mushrooms   1 cup chicken stock or
3 tablespoons butter   1 can chicken soup
2 tablespoons flour   Paprika
⅓ cup cream   Salt and pepper

Slice mushrooms thin and sauté in melted butter. Blend in flour. Heat chicken stock and cream and add to mushroom mixture. Season with salt, pepper and paprika. Serves 6.

Mrs. Ralph Mills (Elizabeth Stevens)

Plantation Egg Pie

4 slices white bread
1 quart milk
1 teaspoon dry mustard
1 tablespoon butter

1 teaspoon salt
8 eggs (4 hard-boiled,
    4 raw)
Black, cayenne peppers,
    to taste

Soak the bread in milk and mustard. Add raw eggs and salt.
Slice hard-boiled eggs; add butter and sliced eggs. Season with
black pepper and bake in deep pan about 45 minutes at 350°.
Serves 6-8.

MRS. LIONEL LEGGE (Dorothy Porcher)

Aunt Julie Gadsden's Egg Soufflé

1 cup milk
1 tablespoon flour

1 tablespoon butter
3-5 eggs

Salt to taste

Make a cream sauce of the milk, butter and flour. When cold,
add the egg yolks then the stiffly beaten egg whites. Salt to taste
and bake in greased casserole for 10 minutes in 325° oven, then increase the heat slightly and bake for 20 minutes longer. Serves 4.

MRS. T. WILBUR THORNHILL (Ama Van Noy Smith)

Eggs with Anchovy

6 hard-boiled eggs,
    coarsely chopped
2 tablespoons butter
Pinch of cayenne

1 tablespoon flour
1 cup milk
1 tablespoon anchovy paste
Salt to taste

Cook butter and flour together until they bubble. Add milk
and stir until smooth. Put in anchovy and cayenne and 1 minute
later the eggs. Simmer 3 minutes and serve on toast. Serves 4.

MRS. NATHANIEL I. BALL, JR. (Anne Barnwell)

THE WINTER VEGETABLE GARDEN

VEGETABLES

"I's got okra, tomata an' sweet puhtatuh!
Soo-oup! Carrot! Carrot!
Fresh Cabbage! Veg-e-tubble!
Veg-e-tubble man!"

In tangles, wild asparagus grows.
Its rightful name nobody knows
Who isn't Charleston's son or daughter
Or never tasted Goose Creek water.
Mature, it's tough as chicken wire;
When young, no spinach can aspire
To equal tender "Chainey Briar!"

"Chainey Briar" (Wild Asparagus)

2 bunches of chainey briar   1 tablespoon butter

Salt and pepper to taste

Scrape the chainey briar. Put in boiling water, with the salt, and cook as fresh asparagus. Serve with drawn butter and pepper. Serves 5.

MRS. JOHN T. JENKINS (Hess Lebby)

Asparagus Casserole

1 can asparagus   ½ cup split blanched
1 cup grated sharp cheese   almonds
Salt and pepper to taste   1½ cups heavy cream
Worcestershire to taste   sauce

Cut asparagus in thirds, flavor cream sauce with Worcestershire sauce, salt and pepper. Put all ingredients together in layers in a casserole dish and bake for 40 minutes at 325°. Serves 4.

MRS. JOSEPH HENRY MOORE (Sally Horton)

Asparagus and Egg Casserole

1 large can asparagus spears	½ cup grated Cheddar
4 hard-boiled eggs—	cheese
sliced	½ cup buttered bread
1 cup medium white sauce	crumbs

Salt and pepper

Arrange half of the asparagus in bottom of greased 1½ quart casserole. Top with slices of egg, pepper, and salt, and sprinkle with cheese. Spoon in half of white sauce. Repeat in alternate layers. Top with bread crumbs and bake in moderate oven (350°) about 30 minutes. Serves 6.

Mrs. Arthur W. Allison, Jr. (Elizabeth Mastin)

Asparagus au Gratin

1 package frozen asparagus	1 cup grated cheese
5 hard-boiled eggs—	2 cups white sauce
deviled	½ teaspoon Worcestershire
5 slices buttered toast	sauce

Cook asparagus by directions on package. Add cheese and Worcestershire sauce to white sauce. Place some asparagus on hot buttered toast. Place one half deviled egg on either side of the asparagus and cover with cheese sauce. Serves 5.

Mrs. Gerald Thomas (Lottie Johnson)

Creamed Artichokes

1 pound of artichokes	Salt to taste
(Jerusalem)	2 cups of water
washed and scraped	1 cup cream sauce

Cook in boiling salted water until tender. Serve with cream sauce. Serves 4.

Mrs. David A. Geer (Nancy Kollock)

New Cut Plantation String Beans

1 pound stringless beans
6 green onions (chopped)
Salt and pepper
4 slices bacon (minced)

Fry bacon crisp in heavy pan, then remove bacon. Cook onions in fat. When onions are slightly wilted, add beans, stir well, cook one minute. Add one tablespoon water, cover, cook three minutes, then uncover. Beans should be bright green . Stir over burner until done to suit taste—about two or three minutes . Season to taste with salt and pepper, and add crisp bacon just before serving. Serves 4.

MRS. ROBERT GAMBLE (Mildred Franklin)

String Beans with Almonds

1 package frozen French-cut
   string beans
1 small can mushrooms
2 tablespoons almonds
   (blanched)
2 tablespoons butter

Cook string beans by directions on package. Sliver almonds; brown in butter, on low light. Add mushrooms and liquor. When mushrooms brown, add drained beans. Serve immediately. Serves 4 to 6.

MRS. GERALD THOMAS (Lottie Johnson)

Best Beets

2 cups beets
¾ tablespoon flour
½ cup sugar
¼ teaspoon salt
½ cup cider vinegar
2 tablespoons butter

Cook whole beets until tender . . . if baby beets, leave whole, otherwise slice. Then cover with the following sauce: Mix flour with sugar and salt. Pour on vinegar and stir until dissolved. Let come to a boil, stirring constantly. Cook for 5 minutes and add butter. Pour the sauce over beets and serve hot. Serves 4.

MRS. HENRY P. STAATS (Juliette Wiles)

Orange Sauce for Beets

1 cup orange juice
⅓ cup sugar
1 tablespoon butter

2 level tablespoons
   cornstarch
Salt to taste

Combine sugar, salt and cornstarch, blending well. Add juice and butter. Cook in top of double boiler 5 minutes. Serve over sliced boiled beets.

MRS. ALLAN DUNNING (Isabel Goodloe)

Corn Pie

5 ears of corn (grated)
1 pint sweet milk
   (heated)
2 eggs

2 tablespoons butter
1 tablespoon corn meal
   (optional)
Salt and pepper to taste

Beat eggs, add to corn. Then add milk, melted butter, salt, pepper, and corn meal. Bake in greased casserole in moderate oven for 1 hour and 25 minutes or until firm. Set pan in boiling water to prevent over-cooking. Serves 6.

MRS. VAN NOY THORNHILL (Jane Lucas)

Middleburg Plantation Corn Pudding

1 pint scraped corn
4 well-beaten eggs

2 cups cream
1 tablespoon butter

Pepper and salt to taste

Bake in buttered dish. Place in pan of hot water 30 to 40 minutes in moderate oven. Serves 6.

MRS. CHARLES GIBBS (Wilmot Welch)

Corn Fritters

6 fresh ears of corn
   grated (or 1 can cream-
   style corn)
3 eggs, separated

1 scant cup of flour
1 teaspoon paprika
1 tablespoon sugar
2 teaspoons baking powder

1 teaspoon salt

Beat egg yolks. Add corn, flour and seasonings, fold in stiffly beaten egg whites, then baking powder. Drop in deep hot grease. Serves 6.

MRS. KINLOCH MCDOWELL (Annie Bissell)

Corn Soufflé

2 cups corn (raw)
2 eggs, separated
2 cups scalded milk

1½ tablespoons butter
   (melted)
Salt and pepper to taste

Grate enough raw corn (including juice) for 2 cups. Add thickly beaten yolks, butter and seasonings; add scalded milk; then stiffly beaten egg whites. Bake in buttered dish in 375° oven until firm, (50-60 minutes). Serves 4-6.

MRS. EDWARD MANIGAULT (Mary Hamilton)

Boiled Red Cabbage

2 large heads red cabbage
2-4 tablespoons butter
1-3 tablespoons molasses
½ cup red wine

2-3 apples, peeled and
   sliced
1 onion, grated
Juice of one lemon

Salt to taste

Melt butter in iron skillet. Add shredded cabbage and molasses. Brown over slow fire, stirring constantly. Add apples, onion, lemon juice and salt. Simmer covered 1 to 2½ hours, stirring occasionally. Add wine after cooking 1½ hours. Serve with wild duck. Serves 6-8.

MRS. T. W. THORNHILL (Ama Van Noy Smith)

Cabbage au Gratin

1 small cabbage, shredded   1 cup cream sauce
½ cup grated cheese

Boil cabbage and drain. Place in casserole in layers; first the cabbage, then the cream sauce, then the grated cheese, until all are used up. Be sure there is a layer of cheese on the top. Run in 400° oven until bubbly, about 15 minutes. Serves 4.

MRS. J. S. STEVENS (Caroline Simonds)

Succotash

This is a very old dish, first served by the Indians to white settlers in America.

½ cup sieva (or   2 tablespoons butter
   butter) beans   1½ cups water
½ cup raw corn   1 teaspoon salt
⅛ teaspoon pepper

Boil sieva beans in salted water until almost done, add tender raw corn, cut from cob, and cook until both are tender. Drain, add butter, seasoning and serve. Serves 4.

MRS. LOUIS T. PARKER (Josephine Walker)

Cypress Gardens' Eggplant and Cauliflower

1 eggplant, fried   1 cup hollandaise sauce
1 cauliflower, boiled   (page 188)
Tarragon, dry or grated

To fry eggplant: peel, then cut in ¼ inch slices; soak in salted water 30 minutes, drain and wipe dry; add salt and pepper; dredge with flour; dip in mixture of 1 beaten egg and 1½ tablespoons water; roll in bread crumbs; fry in hot fat until deep brown; drain on brown paper.

Using one slice of fried eggplant per person, arrange small flowerets of cauliflower in a mound on eggplant. Cover this with hollandaise sauce to which a little tarragon has been added. Use as a first course, followed by cold meat and a salad. Serves 4-6.

MRS. BENJAMIN KITTREDGE, JR. (Carola Kip)

Hot Slaw

1 medium sized cabbage
  (2 pounds)
6 strips of bacon
½ teaspoon celery seed

¼ cup brown sugar
½ teaspoon dry mustard
¼ cup vinegar
½ teaspoon salt

Shred cabbage as for cole slaw and set aside. Cut bacon in pieces and cook to crispness in large frying pan; when done, remove bacon bits, leaving grease. To this add sugar, celery seed, mustard, salt, and vinegar. When this mixture is very hot add the cabbage, turning it over until well mixed but not cooked. Add bacon bits. Serves 4. (Excellent with hot or cold beef).

Mrs. R. Bentham Simons (E. Marion Small)

Stuffed Cabbage Leaves

A number of large
  cabbage leaves
1 small onion
2½ tablespoons fat
¼ pound of rice

2 cups bouillon
1 pound finely chopped
  beef
1 can tomato soup
Salt and pepper

Pour boiling water over cabbage leaves, leave 5 minutes then drain. Fry beef in fat. Fry finely chopped onion. Boil rice until tender, drain. Mix beef, onion, rice, and season with salt and pepper. Put tablespoon of this mixture in each leaf, wrap up like short thick sausage. Stew in bouillon until tender. Drain. Place in casserole and cover with can of tomato soup and reheat in oven. Serves 6.

Mrs. John H. Davis (Elizabeth Malloch)

Baked Guinea Squash (Eggplant)

1 large (or 2 medium) squash

½ teaspoon salt

2 eggs

2 tablespoons peanut butter

½ cup blanched slivered almonds

1 tablespoon chopped onions

Pepper

Crackers

Boil squash in salted water until tender. Remove skin, mash squash in bowl. Add eggs, salt, pepper, onions, peanut butter and almonds. Mix and put in pyrex. Cover with crackers, crushed by hand, and some almonds. Bake about 20 minutes in 350° oven. Serves 6.

MRS. LIONEL K. LEGGE (Dorothy Porcher)

Stuffed Eggplant

1 large eggplant

1 tablespoon butter

2 tablespoons grated bread crumbs

½ cup minced ham

½ onion, minced

Salt and pepper

Cut eggplant in two. Scrape out inside and put in saucepan with minced ham. Cover with water and boil until soft. Drain and add crumbs, butter, onion, salt and pepper to taste. Fill each half of hull with mixture. Add small lump of butter and bake for 15 minutes, or if preferred, omit ham, using more bread crumbs and mixing with beaten yolks of two eggs. Serves 4.

MRS. FRANK CAIN (Parham Atkins)

Eggplant au Gratin

4 small eggplants	1 pound sharp cheese
2 large onions	2 eggs
Cracker crumbs and butter	Salt and pepper

Peel and boil eggplants in salted water until soft; strain off water and mash. Fry sliced onions in butter. Beat eggs. Grate cheese, combine ingredients. Salt and pepper to taste. Place in greased casserole, cover with crumbs, dot with butter. Bake in moderate oven for 45 minutes. Serves 8 to 10.

Mrs. Gerald Thomas (Lottie Johnson)

Scalloped Cucumbers

Several slices of bread	Salt
3 large cucumbers	Pepper
Milk	Butter

Into a buttered baking dish crumble a slice of bread. Add thick large slices of cucumber, pepper, salt and butter. Repeat until dish is full. Make hole in middle with a knife and pour milk until it shows around edge. Sprinkle on top bread crumbs stirred with melted butter. Bake ½ hour in moderate oven. Serves 6.

Mrs. Charles S. Dwight (Lucille Lebby)

Baked Squash

6 large yellow squash	Bread crumbs
2 slices bacon (fried	2 tablespoons butter
crisp)	Minced green pepper
1 onion	Salt and pepper

Cut squash in half lengthwise (Do not remove skin). Boil in salted water 10 to 15 minutes, drain, scoop out, leaving ¼ inch shell. Mash scooped out part and season with chopped onion, minced pepper, salt and pepper. Add crumbled bacon and butter. Fill shells, sprinkle with buttered crumbs. Bake 20 minutes at 375°. Serves 6.

Mrs. Gerald Thomas (Lottie Johnson)

Charleston Gumbo

Good on your rice the day there is no gravy.

1 quart okra
1 pint can tomatoes
2 slices of bacon

½ small onion chopped
Salt, pepper and
    Worcestershire to taste

Broil bacon, add tomatoes, chopped okra and onion, salt, pepper and Worcestershire. Let simmer for two hours. Serves 6.

MRS. JOHN T. JENKINS (Hess Lebby)

Gumbo

1 quart okra
2 No. 2 cans tomatoes (5 c.)
3 slices bacon

2 large onions
Salt, pepper and thyme
    to taste

Grind okra and onions coarsely in meat grinder. Cook bacon and remove from pan. Add okra and onions to bacon grease and cook until all juice is cooked out, then add tomatoes, salt, pepper and thyme. Let this simmer for 3 or 4 hours, add a little water if necessary. When cooked, serve with rice with bacon crumbled on top. Shrimp or seafood of any kind may be added to make a seafood gumbo. The seafood should be cooked then added after the gumbo is finished. Serves 6.

MRS. CHARLES H. BURN (Nina McAdoo)

Lowndes Street Potatoes au Gratin

5-6 potatoes
2 cups cream sauce
½ pound grated sharp cheese

Cover whole peeled potatoes with boiling salted water and cook about 35 minutes. To make cream sauce: use 4 tablespoons butter, 4 tablespoons flour, 2 cups milk, salt and pepper. Add half of cheese to sauce. Slice and place layer of potatoes in casserole, cover with part of sauce, continue thus until all potatoes and sauce are used. Cover top with remaining cheese and bake in 375° oven 15 to 20 minutes. Serves 6.

MRS. C. STUART DAWSON (May Hutson)

Scalloped Irish Potatoes and Onions

4 or 5 large potatoes   1½ cups milk
2 large onions   Salt and pepper
4 tablespoons butter

Into a baking dish put a layer of thin sliced potatoes, salt, pepper, and dots of butter. Then add a layer of thin sliced onions. Cover these with dots of butter, salt and pepper. Repeat until all potatoes and onions are used. Pour enough milk over potatoes and onions to cover them. Cook in a moderate oven until potatoes are well browned. These proportions may be varied according to the size of the casserole. Serves 6. (Cook immediately, so potatoes won't darken).

MRS. JACK MAYBANK (Lavinia Huguenin)

Potato Apples

4 medium Irish potatoes   Paprika
2 egg yolks   Salt and pepper to taste
Cloves   Butter to taste

Shape well seasoned mashed potatoes into small apples, using clove in place of stem. Brush one side with egg yolks diluted with a little water and dust with paprika. Brown in hot oven and serve around sliced meat or ham.

MISS EUGENIA FROST

Candied Sweet Potatoes

3 large sweet potatoes   ½ cup water
1 cup brown sugar   4 tablespoons butter
6 pieces orange peel   Cinnamon

Boil whole potatoes until tender. Take off skin and slice thin. Put in buttered pyrex dish a layer of potatoes sprinkled with sugar and cinnamon and butter; when dish is filled sprinkle top layer of potatoes with sugar, butter, cinnamon and orange peel. Add water and bake until brown and well candied. About 30 minutes at 350° Serves 4.

MRS. J. T. JENKINS (Hess Lebby)

"Likker Pudding"

2½ cups milk
3 medium sized yams
2 cups sugar
2 teaspoons cinnamon
3 eggs
¼ stick butter
½ cup blanched, slivered
almonds
½ cup whiskey or rum

Put milk into 2-quart casserole. Grate yams, adding to milk as you grate to prevent potatoes from turning dark. Beat eggs well and add sugar gradually. Add cinnamon and almonds and mix well with potatoes. Dot generously with butter and bake in a 300° oven for two hours. Just before serving, pour the whiskey or rum over the pudding. Delicious with turkey. Serves 6. May be used without "likker."

MRS. W. T. HARTMAN (Betty Blaydes)

French-Fried Onions

6 large Spanish or
Bermuda onions
1 pint of milk
Vegetable fat or lard
Flour
Salt and pepper

Peel onions and cut into ¼ inch slices, cover rings with milk and let stand for thirty minutes. Drain and dredge with flour seasoned with salt and pepper. Put some of the rings in a wire basket, shake basket gently to remove any surplus flour. Plunge the basket in deep fat 370°F. and let the rings brown delicately, shaking basket occasionally to prevent onion rings from sticking together. Lift basket out, drain for a minute. Then turn onions into a paper lined pan to keep hot, while the remaining onions are fried. Be sure the fat is hot before each cooking. Delicious with steak or roast.

MRS. WALTER METTS (Jane Stauffer)

Spinach Soufflé

1 tablespoon butter	4 egg yolks
1 tablespoon chopped onions	4 egg whites (beaten)
2 tablespoons grated cheese	¾ teaspoon salt
1½ tablespoons flour	Pepper
1 cup milk	2 cups cooked, chopped spinach

Brown onions in butter. Stir in flour, add milk slowly. Add spinach, cheese, seasonings. Heat, remove from fire. Mix in unbeaten yolks. Cool, fold in whites. Pour into greased baking dish and set dish in pan of water in a moderate oven. Bake until mixture rises and sets. (about 30 minutes). Serves 8.

MRS. DAVID MAYBANK (Marion Taber)

Spinach Ring

1½ cups cooked, chopped spinach	Salt and pepper to taste
	½ cup milk
2 tablespoons butter	3 eggs
2 tablespoons flour	1 tablespoon grated onion

Make a white sauce of the butter, flour, and milk. Cook until thick, stirring constantly. Pour over the beaten egg yolks. Add salt and pepper. Add spinach, grated onion, then cool. Fold in the stiffly beaten whites of eggs. Grease a ring pan well and set in a shallow pan of water to bake in a 350° oven. Bake about 30 minutes. Turn out carefully on a platter and fill the center with creamed eggs, mushrooms or carrots. Serves 8.

MRS. HENRY P. STAATS (Juliette Wiles)

Spinach Casserole

1 cup chopped, cooked
    spinach
3 tablespoons butter
3 tablespoons flour

1 cup milk
Salt to taste
3 egg yolks, beaten
3 egg whites, beaten stiff

Make cream sauce with butter, flour, milk, and salt. Add cooked spinach when cool. Stir in yolks, fold in egg whites; pour in buttered casserole. Place in pan of hot water and bake at 350° for 30 minutes. Nice served with cheese or mushroom sauce. Serves 6.

MRS. D. TROWBRIDGE ELLIMAN (Mildred Leisy)

Spinach au Gratin

2 pounds fresh spinach
4 tablespoons melted butter
2 tablespoons flour

1½ cups sharp cheese
    (grated)
4 hard-boiled eggs
    (chopped)

Salt and cayenne to taste

Wash spinach thoroughly, then place moist spinach in a saucepan without adding additional water. Cover and cook for 7 minutes or until tender. Drain well. Mix 2 tablespoons butter and the flour and add spinach. Season well with salt and cayenne. Add the other tablespoons melted butter, chopped eggs and 1 cup grated cheese. Mix well. Put in buttered casserole and cover with ½ cup grated cheese. Brown for 25 minutes at 350°. Serves 6.

MRS. THOMAS A. HUGUENIN (Mary Vereen)

Spinach in Cream

3 pounds young tender
    spinach
1 heaping tablespoon butter
1 tablespoon flour

1 tablespoon finely grated
    onion
¼ cup heavy whipping
    cream

Salt and pepper to taste

Prepare spinach by washing carefully and discarding all tough stems. Throw spinach into a kettle of boiling water and boil 3 minutes—no longer. Remove from fire and drain; in a heavy pan put butter. Shake on it the flour. Blend well. Add spinach, onion, cream, salt and pepper. Heat thoroughly and serve immediately. This is equally good if thick sour cream is used in place of the whipping cream. Serves 8.

MRS. HENRY P. STAATS (Juliette Wiles)

Mushroom Casserole

⅓ cup butter
1 teaspoon finely minced
    parsley
1 teaspoon finely minced
    chives
1 teaspoon finely minced
    shallots
1 teaspoon onion juice
1 teaspoon salt

¼ teaspoon cayenne pepper
1 nutmeg grated
    (medium size)
1 pinch dried tarragon
1 cup heavy sweet cream
Salt and pepper to taste
18 large mushrooms
    (washed and stemmed)

Cream seasonings thoroughly into butter. Spread a part of this butter mixture on the bottom of a casserole, arrange on mixture 18 large mushroom caps, open side up. Dot each cap with some of the remaining butter mixture until all is used. Add the cream and salt and pepper. Bake in a very hot oven (450°) for 10 minutes. Then serve at once in casserole in which they are cooked. Serves 6.

MRS. HENRY P. STAATS (Juliette Wiles)

Whole Broiled Tomatoes

6 whole fresh tomatoes   6 teaspoons of brown
6 teaspoons of vinegar   sugar
6 whole cloves

Leave skins on tomatoes and cut out center. Put 1 teaspoonful of vinegar, and brown sugar ,and 1 clove in each (more cloves can be added to make tomatoes more spicy). Put tomatoes in a pyrex dish and cook for 4 hours in slow oven. They should turn a little black. Delicious! Serves 6.

MRS. WILLIAM B. FRANKLIN (Ellen Fordney)

Fried Tomatoes

2 firm tomatoes (medium   ¼ cup cracker meal
     size)   ½ teaspoon salt
1 egg   ¼ teaspoon black pepper
3 tablespoons shortening

Slice tomatoes, dip in beaten egg and then in cracker meal to which salt and pepper have been added. Cook in hot fat until golden brown on both sides, turning once. Serve hot. Serves 4.

MRS. LOUIS T. PARKER (Josephine Walker)

Glazed Tomatoes

1 No. 2½ can tomatoes   1 cup sugar
   (raw tomatoes used   ½ cup vinegar
   originally) (3½ c.)

Place all in an iron skillet. Bring to a boil. Let simmer for one hour stirring occasionally. Serve in vegetable dish. Delicious served as an accompaniment to snap beans. Serves 4.

MRS. ANDREW GEER (Mary Owen)

Tanyah (or Elephant's Ear)

Pare the tanyah root as you would a turnip. Cook in saucepan **with cold** water and bring to a boil. Pour the water off, add more **cold water** and a little salt, and cook until tender. Slice and serve **hot with** drawn butter.

FROM "THE RURAL CAROLINIAN," 1874

Green Peas

1 pint shelled peas
1 head of lettuce (shredded)
1 sprig of mint and parsley
    tied together
3 onions (white part of
    green onions sliced fine)

2 tablespoons cream
1 lump butter
1 teaspoon sugar
½ teaspoon salt

Cook peas in small amount of water until tender, with the above ingredients, except cream and butter. Remove mint and parsley. If too much liquid, drain and cook down to ½ pint. Add cream and butter before serving. Serves 4.

MRS. JOHN BENNETT (Susan Smythe)

Carrot Ring Mold

1 pint scraped, chopped
    carrots
2 well beaten eggs

½ teaspoon salt
¼ teaspoon black pepper
2 level teaspoons sugar

½ cup cream

Boil carrots in sweetened water until tender, then mash as well as possible. Add other ingredients and pour into a buttered ring mold. Place mold in a pan of hot water and bake in a moderate oven about 30 minutes. Can be served with creamed peas adding ½ cup of finely cut blanched almonds to peas. Serves 6.

MRS. WALTER A. DAVIS (Genevieve Lockwood)

Meatless Spaghetti Sauce

2 large onions	4 teaspoons olive oil
3 ribs celery	2 leaves basil
1 pepper	2 pieces parsley
1 small eggplant	1 No. 2½ can of tomatoes
½ teaspoon sugar	(3½ c.)
Dash of cinnamon	1 can of tomato paste
	Salt and pepper

Chop above ingredients. Brown onions and pepper in olive oil or bacon fat. Add other fresh vegetables and cook down. Add tomatoes and tomato paste with an equal amount of water. Season with salt and pepper, sugar, cinnamon. Cook for several hours, the longer the better.

J. S. MATURO

Hollandaise Sauce

This hollandaise sauce never fails. It may be kept and reheated.

4 egg yolks	¼ teaspoon salt
2 tablespoons lemon juice	Dash of cayenne
½ cup butter	¼ cup boiling water

Divide the butter into three parts. Beat the egg yolks and lemon juice together. Add one piece of butter and cook in a double boiler, stirring constantly until the mixture begins to thicken. Remove from stove, add a second piece of butter and stir rapidly. Then add the remaining butter and continue to stir until the mixture is completely blended. Add the salt, cayenne and boiling water. Return to double-boiler and stir until the sauce thickens. (Note: Cook sauce over small amount of water in bottom of double boiler and do not let the water boil.)

MRS. RALPH MILLS (Elizabeth Stevens)

VIEW ON CHURCH STREET

HOT BREADS

".... gal fetch um one big plate pile' up wid baddle cake. Him pit two-t'ree 'pun 'e plate en' kibbuhr'um wid muhlassis, en' staa't fuh eat."

The muffins and rolls melt in your mouth;
The waffles and biscuits hit the spot.
Oh, hear the table-call of the South:
"Take two! And butter them while they're hot!"

Biscuits

1 cup all purpose flour	½ teaspoon salt
1 heaping teaspoon baking powder	2 heaping tablespoons shortening
½ cup milk (scant)	

Sift flour, then measure, add baking powder and salt, sift into bowl. Cut in shortening with a fork until fine meal; add milk slowly until right consistency, not too sticky. Take a good forkful of dough, roll between floured hands quickly to oblong shape two inches long. Prick with fork. Put on ungreased sheet in oven 500°F. for 12 to 15 minutes. Makes a dozen biscuits.

MRS. JOHN LAURENS (May Rose)

Middleton Gardens' Benne (Sesame) Seed Biscuits

2 cups flour	½ cup roasted benne seed (see p. 356, No. 51)
½ cup shortening	1 teaspoon baking powder
½ teaspoon salt	
½ cup cold milk	

Cream shortening and flour, baking powder and salt. Add milk. Mix in benne seed. Then cream again thoroughly. Roll out on floured bread board very thin. Cut out with small biscuit cutter. Bake in 350° oven 7 to 9 min. Sprinkle with salt while hot.

MRS. J. J. PRINGLE SMITH (Heningham Ellett)

Cheese Daisies

¾ cup butter or oleo
1½ cups sharp cheese,
   grated

¼ cup Parmesan cheese
⅛ teaspoon red pepper
1 teaspoon salt

1½ cups flour

Cream shortening and cheese together. Sift pepper and salt with flour, and add. Chill for ½ hour before rolling out. Cut with small biscuit cutter. Bake at 350° for about 12 minutes. Yield: 24.

Mrs. WILLIAM ELLISON (Ruth Welton)

Mrs. Alston Pringle's Beaten Biscuits

6 cups flour
⅔ cup butter

1 teaspoon sugar
2 cups cold water

1 teaspoon salt

Mix all ingredients and knead for 15 minutes. Then beat with puttle or wooden mallet for 20 minutes or until dough is soft and very smooth. Roll ½ inch thick and cut with biscuit cutter. Pierce biscuits with a fork. Bake in 325° oven for 30 minutes.

Mrs. C. O. SPARKMAN (Mary Rhett Simonds)

Grandma's French Biscuits

3 cups plain flour
½ cup butter
¼ cup lard
2 eggs

½ cup milk
1½ teaspoons baking
   powder
½ tablespoon sugar

½ teaspoon salt

Sift flour, baking powder, sugar and salt on a biscuit board. Add lard and butter and mash thoroughly together. Beat eggs in large bowl, add milk, then stir in flour mixture. Mix to a good consistency. Knead as little as possible. Roll out on biscuit board and cut thick. Then put in baking pan. Bake in hot oven (450°) for 15 to 17 minutes. Yield: approximately 30.

Mrs. THOMAS R. WARING (Laura Witte)

Bread

1 package dry yeast	4 tablespoons cooking oil
¾ cup lukewarm water	2 eggs
3 tablespoons sugar	1 tablespoon salt
1 can (14½ oz.) evaporated milk	6-7 (approx.) cups flour
	Cooking oil (small amount)

Dissolve yeast in water in large bowl of electric mixer. Add sugar, beat 5 minutes, add milk, then cooking oil, then eggs. Continue beating at high speed. (Go dust the dining room or make a couple of beds—fifteen minutes is not too long at this stage). Add salt. Add flour in following manner: with the beater going very slowly, add flour a little at a time; let the speed increase and beat for 5 minutes after adding 1½ cups; then continue adding until dough becomes too stiff for beater. Remove from beaters and add remaining flour and stir with wooden spoon. When little pockets no longer form in the dough, pat a little cooking oil on top and place in ice box! There it will rise like mad for several hours until it reaches the top of the bowl. Rolls, coffee cake or bread can now be made.

LOAF BREAD

Divide dough into 2 parts and put in oiled loaf pans. Let rise until it nearly reaches the top of the pans. Bake in 250° oven for one hour; the smell of it makes your family feel home is really the place it's cracked up to be.

ROLLS

Dip your fingers in oil. Pick up small balls of dough, put them in muffin tins, 3 at a time. Let rise. Bake in hot oven until brown.

COFFEE CAKE

Put half the dough on a well floured board. Knead more flour into it until it becomes elastic and easy to handle. Roll, with rolling pin, as thin as possible. Dot with butter, brown sugar, cinnamon, raisins, nuts. Roll up, place on a cookie sheet, shape into a crescent, slash the top and sprinkle with cinnamon and brown sugar rubbed together. Let rise. Bake in moderately hot oven about 25 minutes.

Mrs. John Andrew Hamilton (Elizabeth Verner)

Loaf Bread

1 cake yeast	2 tablespoons salt
¼ cup lukewarm water	1 tablespoon shortening
2 cups milk	6 cups sifted enriched
2 tablespoons sugar	flour

4 tablespoons wheatgerm

Soften yeast in lukewarm water. Scald milk and cool to lukewarm. Add sugar, salt, and two cups flour. Mix thoroughly. Stir in softened yeast, then melted shortening. Add remaining flour and wheatgerm to form soft dough. Turn out on lightly floured board and knead until dough is smooth and satiny (about 8 minutes). Form into smooth ball, place in lightly greased bowl, cover and let rise in warm place (80° to 85°F.) until doubled in bulk. Punch down. Let rise again. When light, punch down and divide into equal portions. Shape each into ball, cover well and let rest for five to ten minutes. Shape into loaves. Place in greased pans. Cover and let rise until doubled. Bake in moderately hot oven (400° to 425°F.) forty-five minutes. Yield: Two one-pound loaves.

MRS. CLEMENTS RIPLEY (Katherine Ball)

Banana Bread

1¾ cups sifted flour	⅓ cup shortening
2 teaspoons baking powder	⅔ cup sugar
¼ teaspoon baking soda	2 eggs, well beaten
½ teaspoon salt	1 cup mashed ripe
	bananas

Sift flour, baking powder, soda and salt. Cream shortening well, add sugar and beat. Add eggs and beat again. Add flour and bananas alternately. Cook in bread pan (8½ by 4½ by 3). Moderate oven (350°) about 70 minutes.

MRS. ROBERT WILSON, JR. (Gabrielle McColl)

Cinnamon Flip

A good sweet bread for supper

1 heaping cup of sugar	1 cup of milk
1 rounded mixing spoon of shortening	1 egg
	2 teaspoons baking powder

1½ cups flour

Cream sugar and shortening; add milk, egg, flour, and baking powder. Grease 9 by 12 baking pan; add mixture, smoothed even with spatula. Sift a sprinkling of flour lightly over top, dot generously with brown sugar, butter and cinnamon. Bake 40 minutes in moderate oven. Serve hot or cold. Makes 15 large servings.

MRS. WALTER METTS (Jane Stauffer)

Church Street Nut Bread

2 cups flour, sifted	4 tablespoons of shortening
4 slight teaspoons baking powder	1 cup sugar
	Pinch of salt
1 egg	½ cup raisins
1 cup milk	½ cup nuts

Mix shortening, sugar and egg. Add milk and flour combined with baking powder and salt, alternately. Then add raisins and nuts. Bake for 45 minutes at 350° in loaf pan.

MRS. W. DEWAR GORDON (Phoebe Gadsden)

Short'nin' Bread

1½ cups flour	¼ cup light brown sugar

¼ pound butter (soft)

Cream the butter and sugar. Add the flour and mix thoroughly. Roll out quickly (on floured board) about ½ inch thick. Cut shapes with small biscuit cutter. Bake on lightly greased and floured shallow pan at 350° for about 20 minutes.

MRS. HENRY F. CHURCH (Rea Bryant)

Crisp Corn Sticks

1 cup corn meal	4 tablespoons cooking oil
¼ teaspoon salt	1 cup buttermilk
¼ teaspoon soda	2 tablespoons white corn
	syrup

Sift corn meal, add salt and soda and mix. Add oil, stir. Add buttermilk and syrup. Stir well, fill thoroughly greased iron corn-stick pans and bake at 400° F., for half hour. Makes 9 sticks, easy to add to for large family.

MISS SUSAN LOWNDES ALLSTON

Corn Bread Muffins

1 cup corn meal	1 teaspoon salt
1 cup bread flour	1 teaspoon baking powder
2 tablespoons sugar	2 tablespoons melted butter
1¼ cups milk	or fat

2 well-beaten eggs

Sift dry ingredients; beat in separate bowl milk, shortening and egg—add to dry ingredients. Beat lightly until thoroughly mixed. Partly fill *hot* muffin tins. Bake in quick oven 450° for 15 to 20 minutes. Yield: 2½ dozen small muffins.

MRS. R. C. MULLEN (Hasell Townsend)

Spoon Corn Bread

1 scant cup corn meal	1 teaspoon salt
3 cups milk	3 level teaspoons baking
3 eggs, well beaten	powder

1 rounded tablespoon butter

Stir meal into 2 cups milk, let come to a boil, stirring constantly, making a mush. Then add balance of milk, well beaten eggs, salt, baking powder and butter, melted. Turn at once into a quart size, well greased, glass baking dish. Bake in 400° oven about 32 minutes or until done. Serves 6.

MRS. JOHN LAURENS (May Rose)

Corn Bread Sticks

1 egg	½ cup wheat flour
1½ tablespoons shortening	1 cup corn meal
1 teaspoon sugar	1 cup clabber (or sour
1 teaspoon salt	milk)
1½ teaspoons baking powder	

Beat egg, sugar and shortening together. Sift flour and meal together with salt and baking powder, then gradually add to other mixture, alternating with the clabber. Pour into iron cornstick pans and bake at 400° for 20 minutes. Makes one dozen.

Mrs. Clarence Steinhart (Kitty Ford)

Old Time Hominy Bread

1 cup cooked hominy	1 large tablespoon
1 cup raw washed hominy	shortening
1 egg	½ teaspoon salt

Combine cooked hominy, egg, shortening, and salt, rubbing until smooth. Add raw hominy that has been washed and drained fairly dry. Bake in moderate oven (350°) for about 30 minutes or until nicely browned. This can be baked either in a sheet or muffin rings. Serves 6.

Miss Henriette Witte

Batter (Spoon) Bread

1 cup corn meal	2 cups milk (apprx.)
1 teaspoon salt	1 or 2 eggs
1 heaping teaspoon baking	1 cup boiling water (apprx.)
powder	1 tablespoon melted butter
1 tablespoon melted lard	

Mix meal, salt and baking powder. Add egg, beaten lightly, sweet milk and enough boiling water to make a very thin batter, then add butter and lard. Put in well-greased baking dish and cook 30 to 40 minutes in moderate oven. (375°). Serves 6.

Mrs. Alex Mikell (Minnie Robertson)

197

Philpy

½ cup milk
½ cup flour
½ teaspoon salt

¾ cup soft, cooked rice
2 teaspoons melted butter
1 egg, well beaten

Add milk slowly to flour and salt, beating to avoid lumping. Mash rice until fairly smooth. Combine with flour mixture; add butter and egg; bake in a greased layer cake tin in a 450° oven for 30 minutes. When done, slice, split open and butter generously. Serves 4-6.

Mrs. Alston Ramsey (Hazel Hunter)

Garlic Bread

Mince 1 clove garlic and add to ¼ pound butter (melted). Cut loaf of French bread in ½ inch slices, leaving loaf intact at bottom. Brush slices and top of loaf with garlic butter; heat in 350° oven 15 minutes. Serves 6-8.

Mrs. Thomas A. Huguenin (Mary Vereen)

"Melmore" Sally Lunn

½ cake compressed yeast
¼ cup new milk, scalded
   and cooled to lukewarm
2 eggs
2 tablespoons sugar

1¾ cups new milk
4 cups bread flour
1 teaspoon salt
2 tablespoons butter
   softened, but not hot

Soften yeast in the lukewarm milk. Beat eggs, add sugar, milk and yeast mixture. Sift in flour and salt and beat until perfectly smooth. Add butter and beat again. Let rise until almost double in bulk. Beat down with a spoon, and this time pour in a well buttered cake pan, one with center funnel is prettiest. Let rise to almost double in bulk, and bake in moderate oven for 1 hour, covering after the first ½ hour. Turn from the pan and serve hot. (4 hours for the entire process). Serves 8-10.

Mrs. Arthur J. Stoney (Anne Montague)

Mother's Sally Lunn

2 cups flour (plain)	½ teaspoon salt
½ cup sugar	2 eggs beaten separately
3 teaspoons baking powder	¾ cup milk

2 tablespoons melted butter

Add sugar to beaten egg yolks. Mix other dry ingredients and mix alternately with milk into egg and sugar mixture, then add melted butter. Beat egg whites until stiff (not dry) fold in. Bake in well-greased oblong or square pan or muffin tins. For the loaf allow 40 min. in moderate oven (350°).

MISS IDA RAVENEL

Flour Muffins

1 tablespoon lard	2 cups flour, sifted
1 dessertspoon butter	Pinch salt
1 teaspoon sugar	1 teaspoon baking powder
2 eggs	Milk

Cream together lard, butter and sugar, add eggs well beaten, then dry ingredients, with enough milk to make a stiff batter. Put in well-greased muffin tins. Bake in hot oven 425°F. for 20 to 25 minutes. Yield: 1½ dozen.

MISS EMMA GAILLARD WITSELL

Bran Muffins

1 cup bran	2 tablespoons sugar
2 cups plain flour	3 tablespoons baking powder
1 cup buttermilk	½ teaspoon salt
3 tablespoons shortening	1 cup seedless raisins

2 eggs

Sift and mix all dry ingredients; then add buttermilk and eggs, then shortening. Bake in hot oven 350°F. for about 20 to 30 minutes. Grease tins well. Makes about 20 small muffins.

MRS. R. C. MULLIN (Hasell Townsend)

Hominy or Rice Muffins

1 cup cold hominy or rice	4 teaspoons baking powder
1 cup milk	2 eggs
1 cup flour	½ teaspoon salt

Soften cereal by adding milk gradually. Add flour, baking powder, and salt sifted together. Add eggs, well beaten. Pour into greased muffin pans. Bake in quick oven ½ hour.

MRS. ALEX MIKELL (Minnie Robertson)

Huckleberry Muffins

2 cups flour	1 cup huckleberries or
¼ cup shortening	blueberries
½ cup sugar	½ teaspoon salt
1 cup milk	4 teaspoons baking powder

1 egg, separated

Sprinkle berries with a little of the flour. Sift remaining flour with other dry ingredients. Melt shortening and combine with milk and beaten egg yolk. Mix dry and liquid mixtures quickly, and fold in stiffly beaten egg white. Bake ½ hour in 400° oven.

MRS. LEGARE WALKER, JR. (Suzannah Dwight)

Plantation Muffins

2 cups flour	1 cup cold cooked rice
4 teaspoons baking powder	2 eggs, well beaten
½ teaspoon salt	1 cup milk

3 tablespoons melted butter

Mix and sift dry ingredients. Add the rice, stirring well, and then combine with the milk and eggs which have been mixed together. Lastly, stir in the melted butter. Turn into well-greased muffin tins and bake in a quick oven (425°) for 25 minutes. This receipt makes 12 muffins.

MR:. S. EDWARD IZARD, JR. (Anne Kirk)

Pancakes

"My Fathers Receipt for Buckwheat Cakes"

2 cups lukewarm water	1 teaspoon sugar
2 cups buckwheat flour	1 yeast cake
(approx.)	1 tablespoon molasses
1 tablespoon melted butter	¼ teaspoon soda
1 teaspoon salt	1 egg

To 1½ cups of lukewarm water, add enough sifted buckwheat flour to make mixture stiff enough to stir easily. To this, add melted butter, salt and sugar, and yeast cake which has been dissolved in ½ cup of lukewarm water. When this has been added, the batter should be a little softer than muffin batter (it must pour from the spoon easily). If too thick, add a little more lukewarm water; if too thin, add a little more buckwheat flour. Set aside in warm place to rise overnight. In morning, add molasses, soda, and egg. Beat thoroughly. Pour by tablespoonful onto hot griddle, turning once. Serves 6 to 8.

MRS. ALSTON RAMSEY (Hazel Hunter)

Mrs. Fishburne's Corn Pancakes

1 cup yellow corn meal	1¾ cups milk
1 cup boiling water	½ cup flour
2 tablespoons bacon grease	1 teaspoon salt
1 tablespoon sugar	1 teaspoon baking powder

1 egg

Scald corn meal in boiling water. Add bacon grease and sugar. Sift in flour, salt and baking powder alternating this with milk. Add the egg. Drop by dessertspoonful on the griddle. Make pancakes small. These with honey are something special. Serves 4-6.

MRS. BEN SCOTT WHALEY (Emily Fishburne)

Corn Meal Griddle Cakes

1 cup corn meal

Boiling water

4 level tablespoons flour

⅔ teaspoon salt

1 egg

1 cup milk

3 level teaspoons baking powder

Scald meal with enough boiling water to cover it. Let stand 5 minutes, then add flour and salt. Thin to a batter with beaten egg and milk, add baking powder last, beating it in well. Cook at once on hot, well-greased griddle. Serves 4-6.

MRS. T. LADSON WEBB (Anne Moore)

Corn Meal Cakes

"Fried fish, corn meal cakes, and hot coffee, are coastal tradition."

1 cup corn meal

½ cup flour

1 teaspoon sugar

Sweet milk

½ teaspoon salt

1 egg

2 teaspoons baking powder

3 tablespoons shortening

Red pepper to taste

Sift dry ingredients. Add egg and stir in well. Melt shortening and add. Use enough sweet milk to make a soft batter. Pour off most of the fat in which the fish was fried, then fry cakes in same pan. Serve with plenty of butter. Serves 4.

MRS. J. ROSS HANAHAN, JR. (Muriel Viglini)

Hush Puppies

"This name originated around the campfire when they were tossed to the hounds to keep them quiet."

2 cups corn meal	2 tablespoons flour
1 teaspoon soda	1 tablespoon baking powder
1 teaspoon salt	1 egg
6 tablespoons chopped onion	2 cups buttermilk
	Red pepper, to taste

Mix all dry ingredients, add chopped onion; then milk and egg, beaten together. Drop by small spoonfuls into boiling deep fat. They will float when done. Drain on brown paper. Serves 8.

MRS. TAFT WALKER (Mary Taft)

Pop-Overs

1½ cups flour	2 whole eggs
½ teaspoon salt	2 teaspoons melted butter
1½ cups milk	or lard

Put flour and salt in bowl. Add milk and eggs. Beat with a rotary beater for 3 minutes. Add melted butter and stir. Put in well-greased muffin tins. Have tins hot. Bake in hot oven 350° for 40 minutes . Make 12 muffins.

CHEESE-POPS

Mix ½ cup grated sharp cheese with ⅛ teaspoon salt, few grains cayenne. Put small amount of batter in each pan, cover with cheese, then with batter.

MRS. WILLIAM ELLISON (Ruth Welton)

Plantation Puffs

2 cups flour
1 tablespoon sugar
2 rounded teaspoons
   baking powder

Milk
1 teaspoon salt
1 tablespoon melted butter
1 egg

Sift dry ingredients together, add egg and enough milk to make a thick batter. Add melted butter, and drop by spoonfuls into boiling hot shortening. Cook until brown and done in center. Serve hot, sprinkled with powdered sugar. Serves 6—maybe! Delicious for Sunday breakfast.

MRS. LIONEL K. LEGGE (Dorothy H. Porcher)

Light Flour Puffs for Breakfast

1 cup sifted flour
1 cup milk
2 eggs

1 teaspoon baking powder
Small amount of salt
1 teaspoon melted butter
   or lard

Put baking powder and salt in flour before sifting. Beat eggs separately, mix all together, add shortening just before baking in small fancy hot greased pans. Bake as quickly as possible in a hot oven, 450°. Serves 4.

MRS. FRANK CAIN, SR. (Parham Atkins)

Puffit

1 egg (separated)
1 tablespoon white sugar
1 tablespoon melted butter

1 cup sweet milk
2 heaping teaspoons
   baking powder

1 pint sifted flour

Beat egg yolks, add sugar, melted butter. Add flour and baking powder alternately with milk, then egg white beaten stiff. Put in greased pan; bake at 450°F. for 20 minutes. Serves 6.

MISS FRANCES CANNON

Rolls

1 yeast cake	1 egg
1¼ cups milk	1 teaspoon salt
4 cups flour, sifted	1 tablespoon sugar

4 level teaspoons of shortening

Soak yeast cake in lukewarm milk for 10 minutes, add all other ingredients, stirring mixture into soft dough. (Add more milk if needed). Let rise until mixture has doubled in bulk (about 2 hours). Knead or stir well, shape into rolls and place in well-greased pan. Let rise until rolls have doubled in bulk. (About one hour). Bake in moderate oven for 20-25 minutes. Yield: 24 rolls.

MRS. HAMPTON LOGAN, JR. (Virginia W. Watson)

Refrigerator Rolls

2 yeast cakes or packages	3 teaspoons salt
1 cup lukewarm water	2 cups mashed potatoes
1⅓ cups shortening	2 cups potato water
1½ cups sugar	3 eggs

Flour

Dissolve yeast in lukewarm water. Add the shortening, sugar, salt, and mashed potatoes to hot potato water. When cold add yeast and eggs, beaten with a fork. Sift in enough flour to make a stiff dough. Turn out on slightly floured board and knead well. Put into greased bowl, grease lightly the top of the dough and cover tightly. Place in refrigerator until ready to use. When needed, form in desired shape, place in greased pan or muffin tin, and put in warm place until double in bulk—about one hour. Brush with melted shortening and bake in 375-400 degree oven about 20 minutes. This dough will keep in the refrigerator a week or more. Yield: 30 rolls.

MRS. T. LADSON WEBB, JR. (Anne Moore)

Magic Butter Rolls

3 cups bread flour	1 tablespoon sugar
1 teaspoon salt	3 eggs
½ cup butter or oleo	1 teaspoon vanilla
¼ cup evaporated milk	1 cup chopped nuts and
¼ cup hot water	½ cup sugar

2 cakes yeast (or packages)

To 1½ cups sifted flour add salt and butter, combining as for pastry. Combine milk and hot water. When lukewarm put in yeast and 1 tablespoon sugar. Soak until yeast dissolves, then blend and stir into first mixture. Beat smooth. Cover and let stand 20 minutes. Add eggs, beating vigorously. Beat in vanilla and remaining 1½ cups flour. Tie the dough into a square of cheesecloth, loosely, and drop it into a pail of cool water (70° to 80° F.).

In about an hour, the dough will rise to the top of the water. When it does, remove it from the pail and turn out onto a platter. Cut off pieces the size of an egg, using a tablespoon, and roll each one in the ½ cup sugar mixed with the nuts. Twist each piece into a figure 8 and place on a greased cookie sheet. Let stand 5 minutes; then bake at 425° oven 10 to 15 minutes.

MRS. M. L. McCRAE (Ena Mae Black)

Miss Adkins' Crisp Buttermilk Waffles

¾ cup flour	2 teaspoons baking powder
¼ teaspoon soda	2 eggs, well beaten
¼ teaspoon salt	¾ cup (approx.) buttermilk

5 tablespoons cooking oil

Sift together the flour, soda, salt and baking powder. To the beaten eggs add a portion of the above dry mixture, then a small amount of buttermilk, mixing well. Continue to alternate three times, using all flour mixture and enough buttermilk to make a thin batter. Add cooking oil and stir well, just blending. Cook immediately. Yield: 4 waffles.

MISS L. A. PASSAILAGUE

Crisp Waffles

These crisp waffles of the days before the War delighted the people of "Look Back to Glory."

½ cup cooked hominy
1 heaping teaspoon
   shortening
½ cup milk
½ cup water, or more

1½ cups sifted flour
1 heaping teaspoon baking
   powder
½ level teaspoon salt
1 level teaspoon sugar

Stir shortening into hot hominy, add liquids. Then add flour, baking powder, salt and sugar. The batter should be the consistency of thin cream. Grease iron only the first time. Waffles should be wafer thin. Yield: 5 waffles.

MRS. HERBERT RAVENEL SASS (Marion Hutson)

Eggless Waffles

2 level cups sifted plain
   flour
4 teaspoons baking powder
1 teaspoon salt

1 tablespoon sugar
2 rounded tablespoons
   shortening
Milk

Cut shortening into flour and other ingredients well. Add enough milk to make a thin batter. Serves 4-6.

Waffles

3 cups flour, sifted
4 teaspoons baking powder
2 teaspoons salt
¾ tablespoons sugar

2 heaping tablespoons
   butter, melted
1 egg (separated)
Milk

2 heaping tablespoons shortening (melted)

Sift flour, baking powder, sugar and salt together. Add butter, shortening and egg yolk, then add enough milk to make a thin batter and beat for 5 minutes. Add beaten egg white last. Serves 6-8.

MRS. CHARLES S. DWIGHT (Lucille Lebby)

SALADS

Salad? Da' w'en dey teck grass an' ting an' put fancy dress on um lukkuh gal gwine tuh chu'ch.

Defiant men, who stubbornly refuse to eat your salad,
Reflect! The lack of vitamins will make you thin and pallid!
The Charleston Navy Yard is full of lusty sailor-men
Who demonstrate their bursting health and make you think again
Of how Popeye, the Sailor-man, achieved his vim and vigor.
Twas salad greens that amplified his muscles and his figger!

Fiddler's Green Stuffed Avocados

(Good as First Course)

Cut avocados lengthwise, leaving skin on. Remove seed, fill with small creek shrimp or crab meat mixed with sauce made of:

⅓ chili sauce   Dash of lemon juice
⅔ mayonnaise   Capers (if desired)

MRS. JOHN P. FROST (Laura Green)

"Crowded House" Cucumber Salad

"This receipt was brought home to Charleston from Hollywood, where it is a favorite with the movie colony."

2 tender cucumbers, peeled   2 tablespoons lemon juice
    and cut in paper-   ½ teaspoon salt
    thin slices   ½ teaspoon sugar
½ cup sour cream   Dash of cayenne pepper
Combine and chill well. Serves 4-6.

MRS. CLEMENTS RIPLEY (Katharine Ball)

Aunt Julia's Molded Salad

1 package lemon gelatine   ½ cup chopped nuts
1 tablespoon vinegar   1 cup chopped cucumber
1 cup hot water   1 cup celery (diced fine)
Dissolve gelatine in hot water. Add vinegar. Allow to cool and then add nuts, cucumber and celery. Mold. Serves 8.

MRS. CHARLES LYON (Leila Storm Jones)

John Dent's Cole Slaw

"John Dent was Mr. Augustine Smythe's body servant during the War"

For a small head of cabbage:

1 tablespoon butter (full)	1 or 2 eggs
3 tablespoons vinegar	1 teaspoon dry mustard
1 teaspoon salt	Black and red pepper,
1 teaspoon celery seed	to taste

Put butter, vinegar, and seasoning in same pan on fire. Beat up eggs until light. Add boiling vinegar. Stir until thick. Add celery seed when off fire. Serves 6.

Mrs. JOHN BENNETT (Susan Smythe)

Tossed Green Salad

2 heads of lettuce	3 tomatoes, diced
½ pound spinach	1 alligator pear
1 jar artichoke hearts	French dressing

Be sure to dry lettuce and spinach thoroughly. Add other ingredients and toss with French dressing. Serves 6.

Mrs. I. MAYO READ (Posey Myers)

Crab Meat Salad

1 pound crab meat	2 hard-cooked eggs,
1 cup celery, diced	diced
⅛ teaspoon pepper	½ cup mayonnaise or
Lettuce	salad dressing
1 green pepper, chopped	½ teaspoon salt

Remove any shell from the crab meat. Combine all the ingredients and serve on lettuce. Shrimp may be used instead of crab meat. Serves 6.

Miss ELIZABETH R. WILLIAMS

Caesar Salad

(Charleston's Adaptation)

1 head of lettuce, pulled
1 head of romaine—
    cut in 2" pieces
2 eggs, raw

Tin anchovy fillets, cut in
    small pieces
½ cup of Parmesan
    cheese, more if desired

CROUTONS

Previously made—from three slices of bread (preferably French) cut in cubes and fried in olive or vegetable oil with 2 cloves of garlic, split. Drain on brown paper until crisp.

Juice of ½ lemon
Cracked fresh black pepper
    (lots and lots)
Salt to taste
    (remember, anchovies
    are salty)

Tarragon vinegar and olive
    oil (enough to coat
    leaves well but leave
    no excess in bottom
    of bowl)

In a salad bowl rubbed with garlic, toss the above. I sprinkle the cheese, salt and pepper through the salad as I toss, so that it doesn't concentrate on a few leaves. This salad should be made to the maker's taste, but it should be very rich and highly seasoned. I personally like more cheese. Add croutons just before serving. Serves 6-8.

MRS. JOHN McGOWAN (Elizabeth Calvin)

Cream Cheese Aspic

1 can tomato soup
½ can water
1 (3 oz.) pkg. cream cheese
½ small onion, grated
    Dash of Worcestershire

1 package gelatine
⅓ cup each celery, green
    pepper, and nuts
Salt and pepper to taste

Boil soup and water. Soak gelatine in cold water. When soup boils, stir in cream cheese until all is melted. Add gelatine and stir until melted. Pour into salad mold. When cool, add vegetables. Serves 4.

MRS. THEODORE J. SIMONS (Laura Douglas)

211

Cheese Aspic with Curry Dressing

2 (3 oz.) pkgs. cream cheese
¼ cup cream or milk
¾ tablespoon gelatine
    soaked in 1 tablespoon
    cold water

½ cup sharp cheese
    (grated)
1 cup whipped cream
Salt and paprika

Rub the cream cheese smooth, moistening with the cream or milk, in which the gelatine has been dissolved. Add the cheese and whipped cream. Season with salt and paprika. (Dressing listed at end of chapter.) Serves 6.

Mrs. R. S. Cathcart (Katherine Morrow)

Grapefruit Salad

1 (No. 2) can grapefruit
    (2½ c.)
1 (No. 2) can white cherries
    (seeded) (2½ c.)
1 (No. 2) can sliced pine-
    apple (2½ c.)
1 lemon (juice)

1 cup almonds
    (blanched and chopped
    coarsely)
2 envelopes gelatine
    dissolved in ½ cup
    of cold water
Salt

Drain off all juices and let them come to boil. Add gelatine and juice of one lemon, add fruit and almonds. Salt to taste. Pour into molds and let harden. Serve on lettuce with mayonnaise. Serves 6.

Mrs. Elizabeth Hanahan (Elizabeth B. Lucas)

Cucumber Jelly

4 large cucumbers
4 tablespoons of vinegar
¼ teaspoon salt
4 tablespoons gelatine

½ cup water
Dash cayenne pepper
1 teaspoon grated onion
2 cups boiling water

2 tablespoons lemon juice

Peel, remove seeds and grate cucumbers. Soak gelatine in small amount of water; when soft, add boiling water; then vinegar and lemon juice; then the cucumbers and seasoning. Put in ice box to jell. Serves 8.

Mrs. A. T. S. Stoney (Loulie Jenkins)

Jellied Cucumber Salad

3 or 4 cucumbers	3 (3 ounce) packages
½ cup vinegar	cream cheese
Sugar to taste	2 tablespoons gelatine
¾ teaspoon salt	¼ cup cold water
1 envelope gelatine	1 can pimento, chopped
1 cup cold water	1 cup chopped nuts
1 cup boiling water	Green vegetable coloring
Cream to soften cheese	Salt and pepper to taste

Peel and grate cucumbers. Strain and add vinegar and sugar to taste. Add salt, then gelatine dissolved in 1 cup cold water and 1 cup boiling water (or 1 pint liquid). Color with green coloring and pour in mold. Let partly jell for ½ hour. Mix cream cheese, cream, 2 tablespoons gelatine dissolved in ¼ cup cold water (dissolved over hot water), pimentos, chopped nuts and salt and pepper to taste. After cucumber part has jellied put this mixture in top and let stand overnight to mold. Serve with mayonnaise and lettuce. This serves 12. The first half may also be made with lime gelatine, vinegar added. Given me by Kitty Cathcart Hamm.

MRS. LIONEL K. LEGGE (Dorothy H. Porcher)

Tomato Aspic

2 envelopes gelatine	4 cups tomato juice
Few bay leaves	(small size—2¼ cups @ can)
6 whole pepper corns	2 or 3 ribs celery
1 large onion, sliced	2 teaspoons tarragon vinegar
Salt to taste	

Soak gelatine in ½ cup cold water. Put other ingredients in saucepan to boil and simmer slowly for fifteen minutes, which will reduce the juice to a pint. Add gelatine and vinegar. Strain, put in tin or glass mold. I always wipe out any mold with salad oil, makes it much easier to turn out. Serves 4.

MRS. FRANCES B. STEWART (Katherine Felder)

Asparagus Mousseline

1 can asparagus tips	2 sprigs parsley
½ rib celery	2 small onions
1 cup consommé	4 slices carrot
1 teaspoon salt	1 tablespoon gelatine
½ teaspoon paprika	¼ cup cold water

1 cup cream (whipped stiff)

Line small molds with top half of tips. Cook together for 15 minutes remainder of asparagus, celery, consommé, parsley, onion and carrot. Put all through sieve, making 1 cup liquid. Add salt, paprika and gelatine which has been soaked in cold water and dissolved over heat. Put mixture on ice to cool. When it begins to set, gently but thoroughly, stir in whipped cream. Pour into molds over tips. Set to congeal. Unmold and serve on lettuce with mayonnaise. Serves 6.

MRS. JAMES HAGOOD (Antoinette Camp)

Vegetable Salad

6 potatoes	2 slices cooked ham or
6 beets	1 can deviled ham
5 carrots	1 teaspoon mustard (p. 332)
1 large onion	½ pint mayonnaise

Cut up boiled potatoes and beets. Grind raw carrots and onion through fine meat chopper. Grind ham (if slices are used). Mix prepared mustard with mayonnaise and thoroughly mix through salad. Add all together, and pour into mold. Serve ice cold. Serves 8-10.

MRS. SIMONS VANDER HORST WARING (Louisa Johnson)

Ginger Ale Fruit Salad

1 package lemon gelatine	1½ cups ginger ale
½ cup hot water	½ cup chopper pecans

1 (No. 2) can fruit cocktail (2½ c.)

Dissolve gelatine in hot water. Add fruit cocktail (without juice), ginger ale, pecans to gelatine. Pour into mold. A dash of ginger adds to the flavor. Serves 5.

MRS. HENRY J. MANN (Florence Hossley)

Bing Cherry Mold

One No. 2 can bing cherries (2½ c.)
1 package cherry gelatine
1 cup port wine
1 envelope gelatine
1 (3 oz.) pkg. cream cheese

Cream

Heat one cup cherry juice and the port. Pour remaining cherry juice over plain gelatine. Put both gelatines together and dissolve in the hot cherry juice and port. Stir and mix together. Add cherries that have been cut in half and pitted. Put in ring mold. Serve with cream cheese that has been softened with cream. Serves 6.

MRS. CHARLES PAUL III (Selby Fechtig)

Fruit Salad

Ingredients: 2 (No. 2) (5 c.) cans orange and grapefruit sections, (No. 2) (1 c.) can pineapple chunks, 1 box plain gelatine, juice of 1 lemon. Add ¾ cup of the liquid from the cans to the 4 envelopes of gelatine. Heat ¾ cup of the liquid from the cans. Dissolve the gelatine mixture in the hot liquid and add to the fruit and lemon juice. Pour into greased molds. Serves 8-10.

MRS. KINLOCH McDOWELL (Annie Bissell)

Frozen Heavenly Hash

1 can shredded pineapple
½ pound marshmallows, cut into quarters
½ pound almonds that have been blanched and cut with scissors into long slender slips.

This mixture is allowed to stand in refrigerator ovenight.

Next morning a dressing is made with the yolks of 4 eggs, 4 tablespoons of sugar and 2 tablespoons of vinegar mixed together in a double boiler and cooked until the mixture is thick and smooth. This dressing is added to the above salad mixture and ½ pint of heavy sweet cream is whipped and folded in. The final mixture is turned into a mold and frozen 4 hours. Serves 6.

MISS EVA BLACKMER

Mayonnaise

"A French receipt which came into our family in the Eighteen Seventies."

1 egg yolk-raw	1 tablespoon lemon juice
1 egg yolk—hard-boiled and chilled	½ teaspoon salt
1 cup olive oil	1 egg white—hard-boiled and chopped fine

Combine yolk of raw egg and yolk of hard-boiled egg. Add salt and lemon juice. Whip with a fork. Add olive oil, a teaspoon at a time, whipping meantime and being careful not to curdle mixture. Add chopped white of egg. Yield: 1 pint.

Mrs. Clements Ripley (Katherine Ball)

Bahamian Salad Dressing

¼ tablespoon salt	½ tablespoon mustard
¾ tablespoon sugar	(page 332)
2½ tablespoons melted butter	1 egg, slightly beaten
	¾ cup cream

Mix the ingredients in the order given (reading across). Cook over boiling water stirring all the time until it thickens. Then strain, if necessary, and cool before mixing it on salad or cole slaw. This is very good served with hearts of artichoke salad.

Mrs. Francis J. Pelzer (Mary Randolph)

Curry Dressing

¾ teaspoon salt	¼ teaspoon pepper
¼ teaspoon curry powder	5 tablespoons olive oil
3 tablespoons vinegar	

Mix ingredients in order given and beat until well blended.

Mrs. R. S. Cathcart (Katherine Morrow)

Dressing for Grapefruit Salad

1 cup catsup
1 cup onions, (small
    pickled pearl onions
    are best)

1 cup pecans
1 cup salad oil
½ cup parsley
1 cup hard-boiled egg

Salt and pepper

Cut onions fine and chop parsley with hard-boiled egg and pecans. Mix with other ingredients, season with salt and pepper and serve on grapefruit sections with lettuce.

MRS. M. BISHOP ALEXANDER (Ferdinand Williams)

Minute Egg Dressing

1½ slices bread
1 egg
½ cup olive or salad
    oil
¼ teaspoon red pepper—
    to taste

¼ teaspoon salt—to taste
½ tablespoon butter or
    margarine
1 clove garlic
¾ cup grated Italian
    cheese,—Parmesan

1 tablespoon vinegar (approx.)

Cut bread into tiny cubes. Place butter in iron frying pan over lowest heat. Add bread and cook until crisp, stirring occasionally to prevent burning. Put egg into bowl, mince garlic and add. Beat well with rotary beater. Add oil, a little at a time, and continue beating until mixture begins to thicken. (In order to get the mixture to thicken, it may be necessary to use a little less or a little more than ½ cup oil). Add cheese, red pepper and salt. Beat well. Add vinegar. Beat well. Just before serving, add bread cubes. Pour over lettuce and toss well. Serves 4. The lettuce may be romaine or iceberg and should be coarsely cut or torn into pieces.

MRS. ALSTON RAMSAY (Hazel Hunter)

Sour Cream Dressing

1 cup sour cream
¼ teaspoon salt

1½ tablespoons lemon juice
¼ cup honey

Combine and beat stiff.

French Dressing

2 round teaspoons salt
1 round teaspoon sugar
½ teaspoon mustard
½ teaspoon black pepper
½ teaspoon celery salt

1 teaspoon Worcestershire
    sauce
1 clove garlic
1 cup olive oil
¼ cup vinegar

Put in quart jar and shake well before using. Half malt and half tarragon vinegar is good.

Roquefort Cheese Dressing

1 (3 oz.) pkg. cream cheese
¼ pound Roquefort cheese

1 cup French dressing
½ cup mayonnaise

½ pint whipped cream

Mix together and serve at once.

MRS. T. LADSON WEBB, JR. (Anne Moore)

French Dressing

5 tablespoons olive oil
3 tablespoons tarragon
    vinegar

2 tablespoons sweet wine
Salt

Mix thoroughly. Other seasoning may be added according to taste.

MRS. AUGUSTINE T. S. STONEY (Loulie Jenkins)

Anchovy Salad Dressing

1 can anchovies (2 oz.)	2 green onions
1 clove garlic (medium size)	1 cup parsley
Anchovy paste (2 oz.)	1 cup stiff mayonnaise

Tarragon or wine vinegar

In a chopping bowl, chop anchovies, onions, garlic and parsley until they are almost a paste. Add two or three tablespoons anchovy paste. Add this mixture to the mayonnaise. Put into the refrigerator at least ovenight. When ready to use, season and thin with tarragon or wine vinegar. Consistency should be that of thin mayonnaise. Keep in refrigerator until ready to serve. This is best used over a bowl of mixed salad greens. The more kinds the better. Toss lightly, as dressing must stay on greens, and salad must be served immediately.

Mrs. Lawrence A. Walker, Jr. (Phyllis Corson)

Aunt Em's Salad Dressing

1 can tomato sauce	Red pepper
1 grated onion	½ cup sugar
1 tablespoon celery seed	¾ cup vinegar
⅓ cup catsup	Dash Worcestershire sauce
1 teaspoon salt	2 cups oil

Dry mustard

Mix well and serve.

Mrs. Laurence O. Stoney (Jane H. Saunders)

Cream Salad Dressing

2 eggs (yolks only)	½ teaspoon mustard
1 tablespoon sugar	Salt and pepper
3 tablespoons vinegar	½ cup cream (well
1 teaspoon butter	whipped)

Beat eggs well, add sugar and seasonings, then vinegar. Cook in double boiler, stirring all the time until about the thickness of rich cream. Take from the fire and beat in cream.

Mrs. Louis T. Parker (Josephine Walker)

French Dressing

(For Fruit Salad only)

⅓ cup sugar
1 teaspoon celery seed
1 cup cold oil
4 tablespoons vinegar

1 teaspoon salt
1 teaspoon paprika
½ teaspoon onion juice
1 teaspoon dry mustard

Mix dry ingredients. Add onion juice and ½ of vinegar. Add oil and beat with rotary or electric beater. Add remaining vinegar and beat. Let stand several hours in refrigerator before using. This should be very thick and is delicious for all types of fruit salad.

MRS. CARLTON G. DAVIES (Harriet Goodacre)

Victor Hugo Salad Dressing

1 tablespoon grated onion
Dash of cayenne pepper
½ cup oil (olive and
    salad)

⅓ cup catsup
1 teaspoon salt
¼ cup sugar
¼ cup vinegar

Juice of one lemon

Combine and beat well with rotary beater.

MRS. HAROLD PETTIT (Corinne Neely)

Sauce à la Russe

½ cup catsup
2 tablespoons lemon juice
3 good dashes hot sauce
½ teaspoon salt
1¼ cups mayonnaise

1 tablespoon vinegar
2 tablespoons horseradish
1 tablespoon Worcestershire
    sauce
1 tablespoon grated onion

Mix together. Chill overnight and do not stir when you empty sauce into serving bowl. Dot the top with about five teaspoons of red or black caviar. Serve with quarters of crisp lettuce.

MRS. W. W. HUMPHREYS (Martha Lynch)

St. Philip's Church 1835

DESSERTS

".... w'en de preachuh eat to de 'ooman house, him fuh nyam de bes'! Nuttin' but de bes' fuh suit."

> Now some receipts say "Stir",—some "Whisk"
> With rapid motion, light and brisk.
> But whether whisk or whether stir,
> Result is soft as kitten's fur.
> No man can stay depressed or wroth
> While eating Syllabub's fragrant froth!

Eve's Pudding and the Christmas Plum Pudding

"Eve's Pudding and the Christmas Plum Pudding we have always been told were brought to America in 1799 by Mrs. de Berniere, wife of Col. John Anthony de Berniere, retired officer of the British Army. It has been used by the descendants—the de Berniere's in America ever since through at least six generations. How long it was in use in the family before their coming to America I do not know."

MISS MARY DE BERNIERE BARNWELL

Eve's Pudding

If you want a good pudding mind what you're taught,
Take of eggs six in number when bought for a groat,
Of the fruit with which Eve her husband did cozen
Well pared and well chopped at least half a dozen.
Six ounces of bread, let Moll eat the crust,
And crumble the other as fine as the dust.
Six ounces of currants from the stones you must sort
Lest you break out your teeth and spoil all the sport.
Six ounces of sugar won't make it too sweet,
Some salt and some nutmeg will make it complete.
Three hours let it boil without haste or flutter
But Adam won't eat it without wine and butter.

MRS. EDWARD K. PRITCHARD (Julia Myers)

223

Eve's Pudding

6 large apples (pared
    and chopped fine)
6 eggs
6 ounces finely
    crumbled bread

6 ounces currants
6 ounces sugar
Salt and nutmeg
    to taste

Boil three hours in a floured cloth tied very tight. Serve with hard sauce flavored with wine. Serves 6.

MRS. ALEX MIKELL (Minnie Robertson)

Great Aunt Janie's
Christmas Plum Pudding

1 lb. chopped raisins
1 lb. chopped suet
1 lb. grated stale bread
    or half bread and
    flour
1 lb. currants
1 lb. sugar

8 eggs (slightly beaten)
1 cup brandy
1 cup wine
1 pint milk
2 grated nutmegs
1 tablespoon mixed spices
1 saltspoon of salt

Mix the above thoroughly. Boil 6 hours in a floured cloth tied tight. It should be served with burning brandy or plum pudding sauce. Serves 12.

MISS MARY DE BERNIERE BARNWELL

Brandy Pudding

1 cup granulated sugar
4 eggs, separated

1 cup brandy
1 pint cream, whipped

12 lady fingers

Cream egg yolks and sugar. Add brandy slowly. Cook in top of double boiler stirring constantly. Remove from fire and fold in the stiffly beaten egg whites. When the mixture cools, fold in the whipped cream and pour into a mold which has been lined with lady fingers. Let stand several hours in ice box before serving. Serves 6.

MRS. HENRY F. CHURCH (Rea Bryant)

Plantation Plum Pudding

1 pint bread crumbs
1 pint brown sugar
1 pint finely chopped suet
2 lbs. seeded raisins
1 lb. currants
¼ lb. finely cut citron
5 eggs

2 wine glasses sherry or
    brandy
1 teaspoon powdered cloves
1 teaspoon nutmeg
1 teaspoon cinnamon
1 teaspoon soda
½ pint flour

¼ lb. coarsely chopped almonds

Sift flour on fruit, mix eggs and brown sugar and add other ingredients. Put in four one-pound coffee cans, tie covers on with string and steam on a rack with the water-level just below the rack in a large pot for about three hours. Serve with vanilla ice cream and sherry sauce. Serves 10-12.

MRS. M. B. ALEXANDER (Ferdinand Willams)

Plum Pudding (without suet)

1 pound seeded raisins
1 pound currants
½ pound citron, chopped
¼ pound flour
½ pound butter
½ teaspoon salt
½ pound brown sugar

6 eggs (well beaten)
½ pound bread crumbs
½ pint milk
1 whole nutmeg, grated
4 tablespoons sherry or
    brandy
Rum

Dredge fruit in most of the flour. Cream butter and sugar, add eggs, any remaining flour and bread crumbs scalded in milk. Add fruit, nutmeg, spirits and mix well. Pour into well greased tins covered tightly and steam for 6 hours. Serve with hard sauce. If the pudding is not used immediately, it should be steamed for 1 hour again before serving. Fills two 1-pound coffee tins or 1 large melon mold. Rum may be poured around the pudding and ignited before serving. Serves 8-10.

MRS. J. ADDISON INGLE (Helen Jervey)

Sweet Potato Pone

4 cups grated raw yams
2 cups molasses or dark
　　corn syrup
1 cup brown sugar
1 teaspoon cinnamon
¼ cup seeded raisins

1 cup warm water
1 cup chopped citron
Grated rind of 1 orange
Grated rind of 1 lemon
1 teaspoon chopped or
　　powdered ginger

2 tablespoons coconut
(optional)

Mix ingredients; pour into greased baking dish. Bake in moderate oven until nice crust forms on top (about 45 minutes). Serve hot with unsweetened cream, plain or whipped. Serves 6.

MISS SALLIE CARRINGTON

Sweet Potato Pudding

1 pint grated sweet potato
½ cup sugar
½ cup syrup
½ cup butter or margarine,
　　melted

3 eggs, separated and
　　beaten
1 pint milk, ½ pint water
½ cup each citron, raisins,
　　currants, dredged with
　　flour

Cinnamon, cloves, nutmeg

Season to taste with cinnamon, cloves and nutmeg. Mix in order given, except the stiffly beaten whites, which go in last. Bake thoroughly in moderate oven, at least 1½ hours. Serve with hard sauce, made of 1 large spoonful butter or margarine rubbed up with granulated sugar and seasoned with brandy or sherry wine. Serves 6-8.

MISS MARY A. SPARKMAN

Hampton Polonaise

"A bride of 1865 brought this receipt from Columbia to Charleston. It is still to be met on gala occasions in the homes of her children."

1 medium size oblong cake (preferably cup or pound)
3 gills (1½ cups) milk
3 eggs

1½ tablespoons cornstarch
1 pound almonds
¾ pound citron
2 ounces chocolate
Rose water

4 large tablespoons sugar

Slice cake as thin as possible across, making 8 layers. Grind citron and almonds together with a few drops of rose water. Leave some whole almonds and sliced citron for decoration. Make a custard with milk, eggs, sugar and cornstarch. Divide into two parts. To one half add grated chocolate, dissolving it in the hot custard. To the other add the citron and almond paste. Put this filling alternately between layers of cake, first chocolate then almond. Cover entire cake with white icing using a lemon flavoring. (See Icings in Cake chapter.) Decorate top and sides with strips of citron and almonds stood on end. Serves 10 to 12.

MRS. A .T. SMYTHE (Harriott R. Buist)

Coconut Pudding

2 cups sugar
6 eggs

1 cup milk
½ cup butter

1 fresh coconut, grated

Cream sugar and butter; add beaten eggs, then milk and coconut. Bake in 375° oven. Watch closely and as soon as it begins to brown, stir thoroughly. Repeat this about four or five times until pudding is thoroughly brown. This is very rich but delicious. Should be eaten sparingly. Serves 6.

MRS. WILLIAM POPHAM (Louisa Stoney)

Date Pudding

1 cup dates	3 tablespoons flour
1 cup pecans	3 tablespoons sweet milk
1 cup sugar	1 teaspoon baking powder
1 egg	½ pint whipping cream

Cut dates fine with knife. Chop nuts not so fine. Mix dates and nuts with flour and baking powder. Beat egg and sugar well and stir in milk. Combine with first mixture. Grease shallow pudding pan and set in water to steam for 45 minutes in 325° oven. Cool and serve with whipped cream. Serves 8.

MRS. A. W. ALLISON (Moneta Slaton)

Rum Regale

1 quart milk	8 tablespoons cornstarch
1 cup sugar	4 eggs
¼ teaspoon salt	¼ stick butter
2 teaspoons vanilla	

Heat milk in top of double boiler. Mix sugar, salt, and cornstarch in large bowl and slowly add scalded milk. Pour this mixture slowly into beaten eggs, return to double boiler and cook until very thick, stirring constantly. Add butter, vanilla and beat until smooth. Cool.

2 nine-inch sponge layers	1 pint whipping cream
½ cup light rum	1 teaspoon vanilla

Split sponge layers in half. Pour ¼ of the rum in dinner plate and place one layer on plate to absorb rum. Repeat for remaining layers. Put cake together with custard filling and chill for 24 hours. Ice with sweetened whipped cream . Serves 10-12.

MRS. CORNELIUS HUGUENIN (Evelyn Anderson)

Syllabub

From "The Carolina Housewife" by a Lady of Charleston (Miss Sara Rutledge, daughter of Edward Rutledge, signer of the Declaration of Independence).

To 1 quart of cream put ½ pint of sweet wine and ½ pint of Madeira, the juice of 2 lemons, a little finely powdered spice, and sugar to taste. The peel of the lemon must be steeped in the wine until the flavor is extracted. Whisk all these ingredients together, and as the froth rises, take it off with a spoon, lay it upon a fine sieve. What drains from it put into your pan and whisk again. Put the froth into glasses. Serves 12.

MISS JENNIE ROSE PORCHER

Country Syllabub

From "Directions for Cookery in its Various Branches" by Miss Leslie, Seventh Edition 1839.

Mix half a pound of white sugar with a pint of fine cider, or of white wine, and grate in a nutmeg. Prepare them in a large bowl, just before milking time. Then let it be taken to the cow, and have about three pints milked into it, stirring it occasionally with a spoon. Let it be eaten before the froth subsides. If you use cider, a little brandy will improve it.

MISS MARY DEAS RAVENEL

Lemon Pudding

1 cup sugar	2 eggs, separated
3 tablespoons flour	1 lemon
1 cup milk	¼ teaspoon salt

Combine sugar and flour. Add milk, well-beaten egg yolks, salt, lemon juice and grated rind. Carefully fold in stiffly beaten egg whites. Pour into buttered baking dish. Set in pan of warm water. Bake in slow oven 350° about 35 minutes, or until a knife blade inserted comes out clean. When done, this pudding forms a light fluffy cake on top and a rich sauce on bottom. Serve warm. Serves 4.

MRS. JAMES PERRY (Llewellyn La Bruce)

Charleston Mud Hens

1 cup sugar	Pinch of salt
¼ pound butter	1 teaspoon vanilla
3 large eggs	1 pound brown sugar
1½ cups plain flour	1 teaspoon lemon juice
1 level teaspoon baking powder	1 cup nuts, broken

Cream sugar and butter, add 3 yolks and 1 white of egg, add flour which has been sifted with baking powder and salt. Add vanilla. Pat evenly with floured hand on 17½" x 11½" greased, floured cookie sheet. Cream brown sugar, lemon juice and 2 egg whites, then spread evenly on top of first mixture. Sprinkle nuts on top. Bake in 375° oven about 20 minutes. Cut in 35 squares or break in small pieces (serving 24) and top with whipped cream (1 pint).

MRS. MARY H. BAILEY (Mary Huguenin)

Berry Dumpling

1½ cups flour	1 egg
1 teaspoon baking powder	¼ cup milk
½ teaspoon salt	1 teaspoon vanilla
2 tablespoons shortening	¼ cup sugar
1 quart berries (blackberries or huckleberries)	

Mix and sift dry ingredients; cut in shortening; add beaten egg and milk. Mash berries thoroughly, mix well with sugar and vanilla. Combine the two mixtures until completely blended. Pour into a floured cloth, tie securely, and place in large pot of boiling water; boil for about two hours. Serve with generous portion of hard sauce flavored with rum or whiskey. (A 30-inch square of unbleached muslin makes a good dumpling cloth). The dumpling will be semi-soft, not stiff. Serves 6.

MRS. HARRY M. RUBIN (Ruth Ensel)

Angel Food Charlotte Russe Cake

1¼ cups egg whites	1¼ teaspoons cream of
1 cup sifted cake flour	tartar
1½ cups sugar	1 teaspoon vanilla extract
¼ teaspoon salt	¼ teaspoon almond extract

Sift flour before measuring, then sift four times with ½ cup of the sugar. Sift remaining cup of sugar. Add salt to egg whites and beat until foamy. Add cream of tartar, beat until they hold in peaks. Add sifted sugar a few tablespoons at a time, beating after each addition. Fold in vanilla and almond extracts. Fold in flour and sugar mixture ½ cup at a time. Pour into angel food cake pan and bake in moderate oven of 375° for 35 minutes. Turn pan upside down and let cake cool for an hour before removing.

FILLING

¼ cup cool water	¾ cup sherry
1 envelope gelatine	1 cup whipping cream

½ cup sugar

Dissolve gelatine in water. Heat sherry to boiling point, stir into gelatine mixture. Let cool. Whip cream, add sugar and fold into cooled gelatine mixture. Let congeal in refrigerator. Cut cake into two layers and place filling between layers and in hole. Ice with the following icing:

ICING

4 egg whites	1 tablespoon corn syrup
1 cup sugar	(white)

⅛ teaspoon cream of tartar

Place all ingredients in top of double-boiler and heat, stirring occasionally, until very hot. Pour into small bowl of electric mixer and beat at high speed ten minutes or until it holds in peaks. Let cake stand overnight in refrigerator before serving. Serves 8-10. This cake can be frozen very successfully if wrapped in heavy paper. Remove paper before starting to thaw cake to keep icing intact.

MRS. RUDOLPH SIEGLING (Elizabeth Carter)

Charlotte Russe

1 pint whipping cream	¼ cup cold milk
1 teaspoon vanilla	¼ cup warm milk
5 egg whites	½ cup sugar
Sherry	½ tablespoon gelatine

Lady fingers, split

Whip cream until stiff, add vanilla and sugar, also sherry to taste. Soften gelatine in cold milk, then dissolve in warm milk. When cool add to above mixture, beating the cream all of the time. Add beaten egg whites. Pour in bowl or dessert glasses lined with lady fingers. Serves 6.

MRS. J. STANYARNE STEVENS (Caroline Simonds)

Mrs. Edmund Felder's Caramel Charlotte Russe

½ envelope gelatine	1 pint cream, whipped
1 cup white sugar	¼ cup sugar
½ cup boiling water	1 teaspoon vanilla
¼ cup cold water	6 or 8 lady fingers, split

1 cup blanched almonds, chopped

Soak gelatine in ¼ cup cold water. Caramel 1 cup white sugar well by browning in frying pan. Add boiling water to sugar and stir. Pour this into bowl and add gelatine and almonds. Cool, then add cream whipped with sugar and vanilla. Pour into bowl lined with lady fingers. Chill and serve, with or without whipped cream on top. Serves 6.

MRS. LIONEL LEGGE (Dorothy H. Porcher)

232

Angel Ice Box Cake

1 angel cake	½ cup nuts
1½ pints cream, whipped	Sherry wine
3 slices crystallized pineapple	Sugar to taste
½ cup crystallized cherries	

Cut top off cake to depth of ½ inch and scoop out the inside of the cake leaving a shell, but saving the inside. Cut up fruit and nuts and soak overnight or for several hours in sherry, saving a few cherries for a garnish. Drain well, add whipped cream, flavored with sherry and sugar, reserving enough cream to "ice" outside of cake; mix in crumbled inside of cake and stuff mixture into the shell; top with piece cut off top then cover the whole cake with rest of whipped cream and decorate with cut-up cherries. Serves 12 or more.

MRS. JOSEPH HENRY MOORE (Sally Horton)

Meringue Dessert with Lemon Filling

MERINGUE

8 egg whites	1 teaspoon vanilla
1 teaspoon cream of tartar	2 cups of sugar
1 teaspoon vinegar	

Beat egg whites, add sugar and cream of tartar, then vinegar, and vanilla. Put in an ungreased spring-form pan and bake in 275° oven for about 2 hours. Top with lemon filling.

FILLING

5 egg yolks	1 cup sugar
Juice of 3 lemons	2 tablespoons flour or
1 tablespoon butter	cornstarch

Mix all ingredients together and cook in double-boiler until thick, cool a little and top the meringue with this filling. Ice the whole dessert with whipped cream (1 pint). Serves 10-12.

MRS. HAROLD G. DOTTERER (Harriet Lipscomb)

233

TORTES
Almond

½ pound powdered sugar
½ pound almonds, blanched
  and ground
1 pint heavy cream

½ pound dates
5 eggs, separated
2 teaspoons baking powder
Sliced almonds

Beat egg yolks; add date pulp, sugar and almonds. Sprinkle baking powder over egg whites, beaten stiff, and fold in. Fold stiff whites into yolk mixture. Bake in 350° oven for 45 minutes in detachable-rim pie plate. When cool, split in 2 layers and put whipped cream and sliced almonds between and on top. Serves 6.

Black Walnut

1 cup zweibach crumbs
1½ cups chopped nuts
6 eggs

1 cup powdered sugar
1 teaspoon vanilla
Pinch of salt

Roll zweibach to make 1 full cup crumbs. Add chopped nuts, beaten egg yolks, and fold in beaten egg whites last, after sugar, vanilla and salt. Butter pans, do not flour. Bake in 2 layer cake pans 12 to 15 minutes in a 350° oven. Let stand 24 hours. Top with sweetened whipped cream, sprinkle with nuts. Serves 6.

Macaroon Filling for Torten Crust

7 egg whites
¾ pound almonds

Juice and grated rind
  of 1 lemon
½ pound powdered sugar

Steam sugar (sifted) and egg whites in double-boiler 5 minutes, stirring constantly. Cool. Blanch and grind almonds, add sugar, eggs and lemon. Bake 45 minutes in 350° oven. Serves 6.

(See Torten Crust, p. 264)

MISS SYDNEY DENT

Huguenot Torte

4 eggs	2 cups chopped tart
3 cups sugar	cooking apples
8 tablespoons flour	2 cups chopped pecans
5 teaspoons baking powder	or walnuts
½ teaspoon salt	2 teaspoons vanilla

Beat whole eggs in electric mixer or with rotary beater until very frothy and lemon-colored. Add other ingredients in above order. Pour into two *well-buttered* baking pans about 8 by 12 inches. Bake in 325° oven about 45 minutes or until crusty and brown. To serve, scoop up with pancake turner (keeping crusty part on top), pile on large plate and cover with whipped cream and a sprinkling of the chopped nuts, or make 16 individual servings.

MRS. CORNELIUS HUGUENIN (Evelyn Anderson)

Apple Torte

1 egg	1 cup finely chopped
¾ cup sugar	tart apples
½ cup flour	½ cup chopped California
½ teaspoon salt	walnuts
1 teaspoon baking powder	1 teaspoon almond extract

Beat egg until light and fluffy. Add sugar gradually and beat until it is dissolved. Sift dry ingredients together and fold into egg and sugar mixture. Stir in apple, nuts and almond extract. Lightly grease the bottom of an 8" x 8" pan. Pour in mixture and bake 35 to 40 minutes in 350° oven. Serve warm with whipped cream. Serves 6.

MRS. M. L. McCRAE (Ena Mae Black)

Apple Meringue

6 large apples
4 egg whites
Currant jelly

1½ cups confectioners
sugar
1 teaspoon vanilla

Boil the apples after having peeled and cored them. Make a meringue of the whites, sugar, and vanilla. Stuff the holes of the apples with currant jelly, then cover the apples with the meringue. Brown in a moderate oven for three minutes. Serves 6.

MRS. THOMAS R. WARING (Laura Witte)

Snow Peaks

½ cup milk
2 squares chocolate
3 tablespoons shortening
½ cup sugar

1 egg
½ cup flour
½ teaspoon salt
1 teaspoon baking powder

½ teaspoon vanilla

Heat milk over hot water. Add coarsely grated chocolate and cook until thick. Stir to keep smooth. Blend shortening, sugar and egg until light. Add chocolate mixture, then the sifted dry ingredients and vanilla. Pour into 6 greased custard cups. Bake in 350° oven about 20 minutes. Serve warm with Mallow Mint Sauce. Serves 6.

MALLOW MINT SAUCE

½ cup sugar
⅓ cup water
⅛ teaspoon cream of tartar

8 marshmallows
Few drops peppermint or
crushed mint candy

Boil sugar and water 3 minutes. Add cream of tartar. Put in the marshmallows which have been cut into pieces. Stir till smooth. Flavor with peppermint.

MRS. M. L. McCRAE (Ena Mae Black)

Mocha Sponge

6 squares unsweetened
   chocolate
6 eggs
1 envelope gelatine
½ cup cold water

1 teaspoon vanilla
Pinch salt
1½ cups granulated sugar
1 pint whipped cream
Heavy rum, to taste

1 cup very strong hot coffee

Melt chocolate in double-boiler. Separate eggs. Beat yolks until lemon-colored, add sugar slowly, beat some more, adding chocolate slowly. Dissolve gelatine in water, then pour into hot coffee, stir and strain into mixture, beat well, add vanilla and salt. Fold in whites of eggs beaten until stiff. Beat mixture thoroughly, put into oiled ring mold. Chill. Serve with whipped cream flavored with heavy rum. Serves 8 to 10.

MRS. FRANCIS B. STEWART (Katherine Felder)

Coeur à la Crème

6 (3 oz.) packages
   cream cheese
1 pint heavy cream
1 cup coffee cream
1 envelope of gelatine

½ cup cold water
1¼ cups sugar
½ cup sweet or cream
   sherry
Strawberries or raspberries

Soften cheese, one package at a time, with heavy cream, stirring until smooth. Add sugar and sherry. Dissolve gelatine in cold water, heat the coffee cream (do not boil), pour on gelatine, strain into mixture, and stir thoroughly. Pour into an oiled mold. Chill. Serve with strawberries or raspberries. Serves 6.

MRS. FRANCIS B. STEWART (Katherine Felder)

Baba au Rhum

1 package yeast	½ teaspoon salt
¼ cup lukewarm water	1 cup sifted flour
¼ cup milk, scalded	3 eggs
½ cup butter	1 tablespoon rum
2 tablespoons sugar	½ cup citron, chopped

½ cup flour

Dissolve yeast in water. Heat milk and butter, pour into large bowl, stir in salt and sugar, add yeast, and stir in one cup flour. Add eggs, beating in one by one, add rum and citron, and ½ cup flour. Cover and let rise in warm place until double in bulk. Put in greased muffin pans and let rise until double. Bake in preheated oven at 400° for 10 minutes. Remove and pour over them the following sauce. Yield: 1 dozen.

SAUCE

1 cup brown sugar	½ cup water
1 cup white corn syrup	1 tablespoon butter

½ cup rum

Place first four ingredients in saucepan and heat to boiling point, stirring occasionally. Add rum. Babas can be frozen. Pack lightly in jars. To thaw—place in top of double-boiler and heat. Serve hot with whipped cream or with a spoonful of whipped-up ice cream on top.

MRS. RUDOLPH SIEGLING (Elizabeth Carter)

Never-Fail Baked Custard

5 eggs	5 heaping tablespoons
1 quart milk	sugar

1 teaspoon vanilla

Heat milk; cream yolks and sugar thoroughly. Add milk slowly. Beat egg whites until foamy (not too stiff), fold into mixture. Add vanilla. Pour in casserole; set in pan of hot water. Bake slowly in 325° oven. When done inserted knife comes out clean. Serves 6.

MRS. MARY H. BAILEY (Mary Huguenin)

Rum - Bumble

1½ tablespoons gelatine	⅓ cup rum
2 tablespoons cold water	4 tablespoons rye whiskey
6 tablespoons boiling water	2 egg whites
1 cup sugar	1 pint cream

½ cup almonds

Soften gelatine in cold water. After 5 minutes dissolve in boiling water. Add sugar, rum and whiskey, stirring until sugar melts. Strain; when it begins to thicken, beat till frothy. Add well beaten egg whites, then cream, beaten, and gradually put in all of it. Beat very light. Put in mold and chill. Serve with whipped cream and sprinkled with ½ cup chopped toasted almonds. Serves 6.

Mrs. John Bennett (Susan Smythe)

Chocolate Pots de Crème

1 pound triple	2 cups milk
vanilla sweet chocolate	6 egg yolks

1 tablespoon sugar

Melt chocolate and milk in double boiler. Beat eggs and sugar until thick. When chocolate is melted and thickened, pour over beaten egg yolks, stirring constantly. Pour into individual pots de crème dishes and put in shallow pan of water. Cook in 350° oven until custards are firm. Cool and place in refrigerator and serve with Mocha Sauce. Serves 10.

MOCHA SAUCE

1½ tablespoons instant coffee	2 egg yolks
	¼ cup sugar
½ cup hot water	Pinch salt

½ pint cream (whipped)

Dissolve instant coffee in hot water. Beat egg yolks with sugar and salt. Add coffee and cook in double-boiler, stirring constantly until custard is very thick. Cool. Chill in refrigerator and fold in whipped cream just before serving.

Mrs. Henry P. Staats (Juliette Wiles)

Strawberry Short Cake

2 cups flour (measured
   before sifting)
3 teaspoons baking powder
¼ teaspoon salt
2 tablespoons sugar

4 tablespoons butter
1 cup milk
1 quart strawberries with
   ¾ cup sugar
Butter to spread

Pulverized sugar

Mix dry ingredients and sift; rub in the butter and add milk. Grease 2 pans and spread with the mixture. Bake 20 minutes in a quick oven. Reserve a few large berries and mash the others with sugar. Take cakes from oven and spread with butter, then fill with berries (after draining them). Put some of the whole berries on top of the cake and sprinkle with pulverized sugar. Serve (hot or cold) with the juice as a sauce, or with whipped cream, or both. Serves 6-8.

Mrs. Louis T. Parker (Josephine Walker)

Coffee Jelly with Macaroon Cream

4 teaspoons of granulated
   gelatine
½ cup cold water
1 cup boiling water

1½ tablespoons of sugar
2 cups strong coffee
½ teaspoon of vanilla
   extract

Dissolve gelatine in cold water. Add boiling water and sugar. Stir well. Let cool for thirty minutes, then add the coffee, and vanilla, stir again and put in a nine (9) inch ring mold. Chill for 5 hours. Turn jellied coffee onto chilled plate and fill the center with macaroon cream.

MACAROON CREAM

1½ cups whipping cream
3 tablespoons sugar

1 jigger good rum
1 cup crumbled macaroons

Whip cream, add sugar, rum and macaroons. Serves 6.

Mrs. Walter Metts (Jane Stauffer)

Macaroon Soufflé

1 dozen macaroons,
    crumbled
1 cup milk
3 egg yolks

3 egg whites
½ cup chopped fresh
    fruits

½ pint whipping cream

Scald macaroons in milk, pour gradually over beaten egg yolks and cook over hot water until slightly thickened. Fold into the mixture the stiffly beaten egg whites and bake in a buttered mold set in a pan of water. Bake at 375° about 20 minutes. Turn out and sprinkle with chopped fresh fruits and surround with whipped cream. Serves 6.

MISS EUGENIA FROST

Wine Soufflé

This dessert is particularly good after Christmas, or any other heavy dinner.

7 egg whites
Pinch of baking powder
½ cup of broken English
    walnuts

7 tablespoons sugar
½ cup of raisins
Sherry wine

Soak walnuts and raisins in sherry wine the night before using. Beat egg whites stiff and add sugar gradually, then baking powder and lastly nuts and raisins which have been removed from the wine. The nuts and raisins should be folded in lightly and the entire mixture put in a greased baking dish. This must be placed in a pan of hot water and cooked in a 375° oven for 15 or 20 minutes. Serve immediately. Serves 6.

MRS. JOHN SIMONDS (Frances Rees)

Chocolate Soufflé

2 tablespoons butter
2 tablespoons flour
¾ cup milk
1½ squares bitter
    chocolate

2 tablespoons hot water
⅓ cup sugar
3 egg yolks
3 egg whites
1 teaspoon vanilla

Melt butter, blend in flour. Gradually add milk, stirring until it reaches the boiling point. Melt chocolate, add sugar, and hot water. Combine with milk mixture. Add egg yolks (well beaten). Cool, then add vanilla and lastly fold in the stiffly beaten egg whites. Put in buttered ramekins or baking dishes. Bake 25 minutes in 350 degree oven. Serves 4-6.

MRS. MARY H. BAILEY (Mary Huguenin)

Orange Cake with Whipped Cream

1 cup sugar
½ cup butter
2 eggs
2 cups flour
½ teaspoon baking powder
1 cup sour milk

1 teaspoon soda
1 cup raisins
Rind of 1 large orange
1 pint whipping cream
½ cup orange juice with
    ½ cup sugar

Salt

Cream butter and sugar. Beat eggs and add to mixture. Sift soda and a pinch of salt and baking powder with flour. Add to mixture, alternating with sour milk. Put orange rind and raisins through food chopper and add. Bake 40 minutes in moderate oven (350°) in flat glass baking dish (greased with shortening). When cool pour over cake ¼ cup orange juice mixed with ½ cup sugar. Cut in squares and serve with whipped cream. Serves 10 or more.

MRS. ARTHUR HOPKINS (Martha Carrington)

Wine Jelly

2 cups sugar
4⅔ cups cold water
2 lemons (rind cut in pieces)

2 cups sherry
1 cup rum
Juice of 3 lemons

3 envelopes gelatine

Bring sugar, 2 cups cold water and rind of lemons to a boil and boil for 15 minutes. While this is cooking, soak gelatine in ⅔ cup cold water. Pour hot mixture on gelatine and stir until dissolved. Add 2 cups cold water, strain to remove lemon peel. Add sherry, rum and lemon juice. This makes one-half gallon.

MRS. FRANCIS J. PELZER (Mary Randolph)

Wine Jelly

2 envelopes gelatine
½ cup cold water
1 cup boiling water
2 cups sweet sherry wine
Pinch of salt

¼ cup lemon juice, strained
¼ cup orange juice, strained
⅔ cup sugar

Soak gelatine in cold water about 10 minutes. Add boiling water; stir well; cool partially. Then add sugar, salt, lemon juice, orange juice and wine. Place in mold to congeal. Serves 6.

MRS. THADDEUS STREET (Mary Leize Simons)

Tropical Gingerbread

½ cup butter
½ cup sugar
½ cup molasses
1 teaspoon soda
2 eggs
1½ cups flour

1 teaspoon cinnamon
1 tablespoon ginger
¼ teaspoon each:
  allspice, cloves and
  nutmeg
½ cup cold water

1 can moist coconut

Cream butter and sugar, add all other ingredients in above order. Bake in a greased shallow pan in 350° oven for 30 to 40 minutes. Cut in squares and serve with cream (whipped). Serves 6-8.

MRS. A. KINLOCH MCDOWELL (Annie Bissell)

Bossis Plantation Molasses Cake in Casserole

½ cup butter
½ cup molasses
½ cup brown sugar
1 egg
½ teaspoon soda

½ cup hot water
2 cups flour (sifted)
1 teaspoon baking powder
1 teaspoon each: cinnamon,
    cloves, ginger (mixed)
Raisins, (optional)

Cream butter and sugar. Add sifted flour, baking powder, spices. Then add egg and molasses. When ready to bake, add soda, water and raisins. Cook in 350° oven for 30 minutes. Serve with hot melted butter or lemon sauce. Serves 6. (See p. 247 for lemon sauce.)

(See p. 247 for lemon sauce.)

MRS. THOMAS PORCHER WHITE (Gulie Simmons)

Southern Spicy Gingerbread

2 eggs
¾ cup brown sugar
¾ cup dark molasses
¾ cup shortening
    (½ butter)
2½ cups flour

1 cup boiling water
2 teaspoons soda
2 teaspoons ginger
1½ teaspoons cinnamon
½ teaspoon cloves
½ teaspoon nutmeg

½ teaspoon baking powder

Add beaten eggs to sugar, molasses and melted shortening and beat well. Add dry ingredients which have been mixed and sifted, then the boiling water. Bake in small individual pans or shallow pan, greased, in moderate oven 350° for 30 or 40 minutes. Serve with lemon sauce. Serves 8. (See p. 247 for lemon sauce.)

(See p. 247 for lemon sauce.)

MRS. RICHARDS LEWIS (Gabriella Parker)

Mrs. Dill's Bucket Dumpling

1 pint of flour
2 eggs
2 level teaspoons baking
    powder

1 large tablespoon butter
1 large tablespoon shortening
⅔ cup milk
1 qt. sweetened blackberries

Mix butter, lard, flour and baking powder. Add eggs, slightly beaten, then milk. Put in a lard can or mold and smear around sides. Place one quart of berries in center. Cover mold and steam in boiling water for three hours. Serve with hard sauce. This dumpling is more delicious than when made with biscuit dough. If berries are sour, you may add a little sugar. Any other fruit in season, such as apples, peaches or huckleberries may be substituted for blackberries. Serves 6-8.

MRS. W. DAVIS ROGERS (Julia Dill)

Peach Upside-Down Cake

⅓ cup shortening
⅔ cup sugar
⅔ cup milk
1 teaspoon vanilla

2 eggs
2 teaspoons baking powder
1⅔ cups flour
⅛ teaspoon salt

¼ teaspoon almond flavoring

Cream shortening and sugar. Add remaining ingredients and beat well. Pour over peach mixture. Serves 6.

PEACH MIXTURE

⅓ cup butter

1 cup light brown sugar

1½ cups sliced peaches

Place butter and sugar in a sheet cake pan and heat slowly, stirring constantly until well browned. Add peaches. Cover with cake batter; bake ¾ hour at 350°. Turn out peach side up. Serve hot or cold with whipped cream . Other fruits may be substituted for the peaches.

MRS. S. EDWARD IZARD, JR. (Anne Kirk)

245

Pineapple Fritters

*These fritters are a specialty at the old Ceasar's Head Hotel,
Ceasar's Head, South Carolina, where many Charlestonians summer.*

1 egg
1 cup milk (scant)
3 tablespoons sugar
2½ teaspoons baking
    powder

1 cup crushed and drained
    pineapple
2 tablespoons butter, melted
2½ cups flour to make
    stiff batter

Combine in order given. Add pineapple to batter last. Drop
a tablespoonful at a time in hot, deep fat. Serves 6-8.

SAUCE FOR PINEAPPLE FRITTERS

1 cup brown sugar
    (light)
2 tablespoons flour
½ lemon (juice)

1 cup water
1 cup pineapple juice
2 tablespoons butter

Combine and cook until clear.

Mrs. Eugene Geer (Winifred Williams)

Plum Pudding Sauce

1 cup sugar
¼ stick butter

1 egg
Rum, whiskey or sherry
    to taste

Add just enough water to wet sugar and cook until it begins to
thicken. Take off heat, add butter then pour slowly over beaten
whole egg and bring to a boil. Then add rum, whiskey or sherry to
taste.

Mrs. Walker Coleman (Felicia Chisolm)

Mrs. W. Lucas Simons' Orange and Lemon Sauce

Grated rind of 2 oranges	Juice of 2 lemons
Juice of 4 oranges	1 cup sugar
Enough water to make	4 egg yolks
1 pint liquid	2 tablespoons corn starch

Boil together for five minutes all ingredients except egg yolks and starch, then pour over egg yolks into which paste made with corn starch and a little water has been beaten Boil again for 5 minutes or until thick and clear.

LEMON SAUCE

¾ cup lemon juice instead of orange and lemon.

MRS. ARTHUR J. STONEY (Anne Montague)

Wine Sauce

2 tablespoons butter	1 egg white
½ cup powdered sugar	3 tablespoons of sherry

Cream butter and sugar. Add white of egg well beaten and beat for a minute. Add wine, a little at a time. Place bowl containing mixture in a pan of boiling water and stir for 3 minutes.

MRS. J. ADDISON INGLE (Nell Jervey)

Hard Sauce

1 stick butter (real)	1 egg white
1 cup white sugar	¼ cup rum or whiskey

Cream butter and sugar until very light, add beaten egg white, continue beating and add flavoring a little at a time until sauce is very fluffy. Sprinkle grated nutmeg on top of sauce.

MRS. A. KINLOCH MCDOWELL (Annie Bissell)

FIGS

ICE CREAMS

Miss Sally, ef uh chu'n um fuh yuh, kin uh lick de dashuh?

The summertime in Charleston
Can be a pleasant season.
No need to let the temperature
Deprive you of your reason!
Dress coolly then, and bow the blinds
Against the heat and gleam;
And leisurely consume a dish
Of frosty fig ice cream.

Fig Ice Cream

2 eggs	¾ cup sugar
½ pint milk	3 quarts figs
1 quart whipping cream	1 tablespoon lemon juice

1 teaspoon vanilla

Make custard of milk and eggs. (See Custard Ice Cream, p. 254.) Whip cream until frothy on top. Add custard when cold, figs which have been peeled and mashed through a potato ricer or sieve, and sprinkled with the lemon juice, sugar, and vanilla. Freeze in churn. (If no churn is available this may be frozen in a refrigerator provided it is taken out and beaten with an egg beater when it is partly frozen and returned to freezing tray.) This ice cream can be made with any fruit. Serves 16.

MRS. J. STANYARNE STEVENS (Caroline Simonds)

Frozen Eggnog

5 eggs	1 pint whipping cream
⅓ cup sugar	4 jiggers of rum

2 jiggers of rye

Separate egg yolks and whites. Beat yolks well. Add about ½ the sugar, then rum, and rye. Let this stand, stirring occasionally, while beating the whites very stiff and gradually adding rest of sugar. Whip cream and add all together. Put in freezing tray in refrigerator. This will never freeze very stiff. Serves 8.

MRS. WALKER COLEMAN (Felicia Chisolm)

Cherry Bisque Ice Cream

1 pint milk (scalded)
2 eggs (well beaten)
1 cup sugar (or more)
Pinch of salt
1 heaping tablespoon flour
1 teaspoon vanilla
1 quart single cream

6 or 8 tablespoons rum
  or whiskey
1 dozen macaroons
  (crumbled)
¼ pound crystallized
  cherries (cut in
  small pieces)

Beat egg; add sugar, flour and salt. Stir in milk while hot. Return to stove and let thicken, stirring all the time to keep from lumping. Set aside to cool. (If any lumps, strain custard.) Whip cream (not stiff) and stir into custard; add vanilla and rum or whiskey and freeze. When almost frozen open freezer and mix in macaroons and cherries. Freeze again until hard. Yield: 1½ qts. Serves 10-12.

MRS. ANDREW SIMONS (Katherine Hunt)

Coconut Ice Cream

1 tablespoon flour
2 tablespoons milk
1 cup milk
⅓ cup light corn syrup
Extra coconut for toasting

1 egg
½ cup top milk (half and
  half)
1 teaspoon vanilla
½ cup shredded coconut

Blend flour with 2 tablespoons milk. Add 1 cup milk and syrup. Beat egg whole, add. Cook over hot water, stirring until thick. Cool. Add top milk, vanilla and coconut. Freeze to mush, using 8 parts crushed ice to 1 part ice cream salt. Remove dasher. Cover. Pack in 4 parts ice to 1 part salt for three hours. When serving, sprinkle toasted coconut over top. Makes 1 quart. May be frozen in electric refrigerator, stirring once after mush has formed. Serves 8.

MRS. ARTHUR J. STONEY (Anne Montague)

Peppermint-Stick Ice Cream

1 cup milk
1 pint heavy cream

½ pound peppermint
stick candy, crushed

Heat milk in top of double-boiler; add candy and stir constantly until dissolved. Pour into tray of refrigerator and chill. Whip cream until thickened, but not stiff, and fold into chilled candy mixture. Pour back into tray and freeze with control set at coldest point, until firm. Stir once or twice during freezing. Serve with hot fudge sauce. Serves 6 to 8.

MRS. JOHN LAURENS (May Rose)

Chilled Pineapple Ice Cream

1 pint cream, whipped
1 fresh pineapple, diced
(about 2 cups)

Sugar to taste
Flavor with rum

Mix. Put in refrigerator tray 12 hours before using. Serves 6-8.

MRS. JOHN BENNETT (Susan Smythe)

My Mother's Lemon Ice Cream

2 lemons
2 cups cream

2 cups milk
1 cup sugar

1 egg white

Squeeze juice of one lemon, cut other lemon into very thin slices; add juice and sliced lemon to cup of sugar and let stand for one hour, stirring until sugar is dissolved.

Whip cream, add milk and chill, then add lemon and sugar mixture and stiffly beaten egg white.

If made in refrigerator, ice cream should be beaten thoroughly when it is of mushy consistency. If made in dasher-type ice cream freezer, it is not necessary to whip cream. Serves 6.

MISS MARGARET WATSON

Custard Ice Cream

1 cup milk
1 cup light cream
6 egg yolks
2 cups heavy cream
¾ cup sugar
¼ teaspoon salt
1½ teaspoons vanilla

Scald 1 cup milk and 1 cup light cream. Add gradually to the slightly beaten egg yolks, mixed with the sugar and salt. Cook in double-boiler, stirring constantly, until the custard thickens and coats a spoon. Pour into a bowl and flavor with the vanilla. Cool. Beat the heavy cream until thick but not stiff. Fold into the custard. Pour into freezing tray, set the refrigerator to coldest point, and freeze until firm. Remove from refrigerator, beat and mash mixture in tray until smooth. Freeze again until firm. Remove and beat and mash again. Freeze until firm. Set control back to normal position. Serve with hot fudge sauce or fruit sauce. Serves 8 to 10.

MRS. JOHN LAURENS (May Rose)

Vanilla Ice Cream

1 pint heavy cream
½ cup sugar
½ cup milk
½ teaspoon vanilla
Pinch of salt
1 egg

Beat cream until thick, then add rest of the ingredients. Freeze one hour or until hard. Then remove mixture to bowl and beat it again. Re-freeze. Serves 4-6.

MRS. J. K. DONAHUE (Esther Laushe)

Buttermilk Ice Cream

1 quart buttermilk
1 pint cream
1½ cups sugar
Flavor with vanilla
or wine

Blend these ingredients and put in freezing unit of refrigerator. Stir well after it begins to freeze and return to refrigerator. Serves 8.

MRS. CHARLES DWIGHT (Lucille Lebby)

Macaroon Ice Cream

1 pound macaroons
½ cup sherry
1 pint whipping cream
Sugar to taste

Crumble macaroons and soak them in sherry. Add cream, beaten stiff. Sweeten to taste. Put in pan and let stay in freezer for half an hour. Take out and beat mixture with a fork. Put back in freezer for another half hour. Cover with wax paper and leave in box until ready to serve. The sherry wine in the cream takes longer to freeze; about three hours. Serves 6.

MISS I. L. DAWSON

Macaroon-Apricot Ice Cream

1 pint whipping cream
1 pint coffee cream
12 macaroons if large,
    more if small
1 can apricots (about
    2 cups)
Sugar to taste

Lightly whip heavy cream, adding coffee cream, and crumble the macaroons into this. Add the apricots which have been mashed through strainer. Use all the juice and pulp. Sweeten to taste. Freeze. Stir before it begins to freeze hard. Serves 8.

MRS. J. P. FROST (Laura Green)

Biscuit Tortoni

1 cup sugar
3 tablespoons water
1 dozen stale macaroons
3 eggs
1 pint cream
1 teaspoon vanilla
1 tablespoon sweet sherry

Cook sugar and water until it makes a syrup. Beat the egg yolks. Beat egg whites until stiff; then add syrup slowly. Fold in beaten egg yolks and whipped cream. Season with vanilla and sherry. Cut wax paper and line freezing trays. Put layer of macaroons, crumbled, layer of mixture, etc. Top with macaroon crumbs. If serving at night prepare in the morning. Freeze. Serves 7.

MRS. G. SIMMS MCDOWELL (Henrietta Phillips)

Pistachio Ice Cream

4 cups light cream
1 cup sugar
1 tablespoon almond
    extract

¼ teaspoon salt
½ cup pistachio nuts
1 cup almonds
Green coloring

Chop pistachio nuts and almonds fine. Whip cream, then add other ingredients, and nuts. Color with delicate green coloring, freeze. Good served with peach sauce made as follows: Turn 1 can of peaches into a saucepan. Add ⅓ cup of sugar, and cook slowly until syrup is thick. Cool and cut the fruit into small pieces. Serves 4-6.

MRS. LIONEL LEGGE (Dorothy H. Porcher)

Mrs. Alston Pringle's Marshmallow Ice Cream

1 pound marshmallows, cut
    up
1 large can grated pineapple

1 pint cream, whipped
1 cup sherry

Put marshmallows and pineapple together and let stand overnight. When ready to freeze, add whipped cream and sherry. Serves 12-14.

MRS. JOHN SIMONDS (Frances Rees)

Mint Parfait

16 marshmallows
¾ cup milk
½ pint whipping cream
3-ounce bottle crème de menthe cherries

5 drops essence of
    peppermint
Green coloring, if desired

Steam marshmallows and milk together over hot water until mixture is smooth. Add cherries (finely chopped) and juice. Add peppermint essence. Cool, and when slightly stiffened, combine carefully with stiffly beaten cream. Pour into trays and freeze without stirring. Serve in sherbet, or parfait glasses. Serves 6.

MRS. ARTHUR J. STONEY (Anne Montague)

Coffee Mousse

1 quart whipping cream   2 cups strong coffee
1 cup sugar   2 eggs
Tiny pinch of salt

Melt sugar and salt in cold coffee. Beat cream until stiff. Add sugar and coffee mixture slowly. Beat in the raw eggs. Freeze in deep ice tray. Serves 8.

Mrs. ALBERT SIMONS (Harriet Stoney)

Peach Mousse

1 cup sugar   ¼ cup water
1 cup mashed peaches   2 cups heavy cream
½ tablespoon gelatine   2 tablespoons lemon juice

Mash fruit and put through sieve. Soak gelatine 5 minutes in ¼ cup cold water. Dissolve thoroughly by placing it over a pan of boiling water. Add gelatine, lemon juice, and sugar to crushed fruit. Place in refrigerator. When mixture is thoroughly chilled and beginning to congeal, fold in cream, which has been whipped stiff. Pour into refrigerator tray and chill. Serves 6 to 8.

Mrs. W. HAMPTON LOGAN, JR. (Virginia Watson)

Orange Ice and Vanilla Mousse

Juice of 8 large oranges   1 pint cream, whipped
Juice of 2 lemons   1 teaspoon gelatine,
½ cup sugar   dissolved in water
1 egg white, beaten stiff   ½ cup sugar
1 teaspoon vanilla

Mix orange and lemon juice and ½ cup sugar. Place in freezer. When nearly hard remove from freezer and beat in the beaten egg white. Place back in freezer and when hard add mousse. To make mousse, whip the cream, add ½ cup sugar, gelatine and vanilla. Place on top of orange ice and freeze. Serves 6.

Mrs. WILLIAM A. HUTCHINSON (Eva Austin)

Raspberry Mousse

2 eggs	2½ tablespoons gelatine
1 quart cream	1 quart milk
1 pint raspberry jam	½ cup cold water

Beat eggs into cream and jam. Soften gelatine in cold water, then dissolve in hot milk. After that cools, pour in the mixture and put in refrigerator. Serves 8.

Miss Caroline Rutledge

Pineapple Sherbet

2 cups buttermilk	1 egg white, beaten stiff
1 cup sugar	1 teaspoon vanilla
1 nine-ounce can crushed pineapple	½ teaspoon unflavored gelatine
2 teaspoons cold water	

Drain pineapple. Combine buttermilk, sugar, pineapple, and vanilla. Add gelatine, which has been soaked in cold water and dissolved over hot water. Fold in egg white. Freeze firm 3 to 4 hours. Stir once during freezing. Serves 6.

Mrs. J. K. Donahue (Esther Laushe)

Fruit and Milk Sherbet

3 lemons, juice	½ cup white syrup
3 oranges, juice and pulp	½ cup sugar
3 large bananas, mashed fine	1 pint milk

To mashed bananas add fruit pulp, juices, sugar, and syrup. Stir into the milk. Pour into refrigerator tray and freeze until firm. Stir twice during freezing. Serves 6.

Mrs. John Laurens (May Rose)

Pineapple Milk Sherbet

1 cup pineapple juice   ⅔ cup sugar
3 tablespoons lemon juice   2 cups milk

Mix pineapple juice, lemon juice, and sugar. Chill, then add to milk. Freeze one hour, beat thoroughly, then freeze about 3 hours. Serves 4.

MRS. LOUIS T. PARKER (Josephine Walker)

The Ravenel Twins' Delectable

1 cup chopped pecans   1 cup preserved ginger,
1 cup marashino cherries,   chopped
    chopped   Syrup from ginger
                2 quarts orange sherbet

Mix pecans, cherries, ginger and syrup. Place a large table-spoon of the sherbet in a punch cup, top with a teaspoon of the sauce. Serve with a small coffee spoon. Delicious at a reception or tea, with sherbet in punch bowl and sauce in small bowl. Serves about 50.

MISS M. DEAS RAVENEL

Mrs. S. G. Stoney's Watermelon deLuxe

1 good, well-shaped   1 dozen limes
    watermelon   3 pounds sugar
1 bottle claret   3 quarts water

Cut melon in half, length-wise, and chill. (Only half of melon is used). Take out the heart in pieces, removing seeds. Have ready sherbet given below, pile into melon shell with pieces of melon mixed into sherbet.

SHERBET:

Boil sugar and lime skins with water until syrup is pleasantly flavored. Pour in claret, lime juice, and enough water to fill a 6-quart churn. Churn until hard. Serves 12-14.

MRS. W. S. POPHAM (Louisa Stoney)

Watermelon Balls with Raspberry Ice

1 well-shaped watermelon   Sugar
Anisette liqueur   Mint leaves
3 quarts raspberry ice (Sherbet)

Choose well-shaped watermelon, chill well, then cut lengthwise. With ball cutter cut out as many balls as possible. Sprinkle balls with small amount of sugar, a very little of the liqueur and a few fresh mint leaves very finely cut. Using the most uniform half, trim out uneven bits of melon left from the balling process, then pack well with red raspberry ice (three quarts of ice are sufficient for ordinary sized melon). Decorate top with semi-sweet chocolate drops in seed pattern. To serve: Place packed melon half on large silver platter or tray and surround with few small magnolia leaves and mounds of melon balls. Serves 12-14.

MRS. JOHN McGOWAN (Elizabeth Calvin)

Chocolate Sauce

2 ounces bitter chocolate   4 tablespoons butter
1 cup boiling water   1 cup sugar
1 teaspoon vanilla   Pinch of salt

Melt chocolate in top of double-boiler. Add butter and stir. When melted, add cup of boiling water slowly, stirring constantly. Then add sugar. Take off double-boiler and put over fire. Bring to a boil and cook about five minutes. Add pinch of salt and vanilla.

MRS. WALKER COLEMAN (Felicia Chisolm)

Caramel Sauce

1½ cups sugar   ¾ cup cream
1 tablespoon butter

Put 1 cup sugar and the cream in top of double-boiler. When thoroughly heated, add ½ cup of the sugar that has been browned into liquid in skillet. Stir until fully dissolved and add the butter. Serve hot on vanilla ice cream, cake, etc. Yield: ¾ pint.

MRS. THOMAS CARRUTHERS (Ellen D. Everett)

Tutti-Frutti Sauce

1 quart grain alcohol   1 cup fresh fruit
1 cup sugar

Use 1 gallon crock with a tight cover. Begin in March; put alcohol in, then equal sugar to fruit, one cup of each, as the fresh fruits come in the market except peaches, pears, bananas and apples. Start first with pineapple, then use your own ingenuity in procuring a variety of fruits and berries. Always remove seeds or stones. In November add 1 cup seeded raisins and 1 cup broken pecan meats (no sugar for these last two). Heavy rum may be substituted for alcohol. Stir after addition of fruit with wooden spoon. This is ready for Christmas.

MRS. ANDREW J. GEER (Mary Owen)

Sugarless Fudge Sauce

⅓ cup cocoa   ⅛ teaspoon salt
¼ cup cold water   1 tablespoon oleo
1½ cups light corn syrup   1 teaspoon vanilla

Mix cocoa, water, syrup and salt. Cook, stirring often, until mixture becomes a heavy syrup. Stir in margarine and vanilla. Serve hot or cold. If desired sweeter, add honey to taste after sauce has finished cooking. Makes 1⅔ cups.

MRS. R. M. ANDERSON (Dorothy Middleton)

Sherry Sauce

"This sauce is so easily and quickly made and makes something really special of vanilla ice cream."

½ cup milk   1 cup sugar
2 tablespoons sherry   4 tablespoons butter

Boil milk, sugar and butter together for five minutes. Add sherry.

MRS. PRIOLEAU BALL (Teresa Daniel)

PIES

"W'en unnuh fuh mek pie-crus', tek vuh flour en' put een 'nuf fuh tek up de slack."

Your fav'rite man demands an apple pie?
Then scan the best receipts with searching eye,—
Transparent Tarts, Rum Pie, or Bakewell Tart?
What matter if it seems to satisfy?
For often, by ignoring his behest,
You may convince him Wifie knoweth best!

Plain Pastry

DOUBLE CRUST

2¼ cups sifted flour	1 teaspoon salt
¾ cup shortening	¼ cup water

Sift flour and salt into bowl. Reserve ⅓ cup flour. Cut shortening into remaining flour with two knives or with pastry mixer. When lumps are size of small peas, add the ⅓ cup flour blended to paste with the water. Mix thoroughly but lightly until mixture can be formed into a ball. Put wax paper over biscuit board, or any smooth surface. Place half of dough on it, cover with another sheet of wax paper. Roll with short, light strokes to 12 inch round and ⅛ inch thickness. Place lightly in pie plate, easing into angle at base. Trim ½ inch beyond outer edge of plate. After filling and upper crust are in place, crimp this edge as desired.

SINGLE CRUST

1½ cups flour	½ cup shortening
½ teaspoon salt	3 tablespoons water

Proceed as above. Reserve ¼ cup flour. Bake 8-10 minutes at 475°.

MRS. JOHN BOONE (Ellen Gleason)

Torten Crust

¼ cup butter 1 tablespoon sugar
1 cup flour 1 egg yolk
Pinch salt

Cream butter and sugar, add other ingredients, pat ¼ inch thick in pie pan, fill with pie filling and bake. (See filling page 234).

MISS SYDNEY DENT

New Pie Crust

2 cups sifted flour ½ cup vegetable oil
1½ teaspoons salt ¼ cup cold milk

Blend all together thoroughly but lightly with knives or pastry mixer. Divide and roll between sheets of wax paper as plain pastry. This amount makes enough for a 2-crust pie. For one-crust pie shell use ½ the measurements. Place rolled dough in pie plate. Prick thoroughly with fork. Bake 8-10 minutes in very hot oven (475°).

MRS. WALTER PRINGLE III (Adelaide Godfrey)

Lemon Meringue Pie

4 eggs 1 cup sugar
1 tablespoon flour 1 large lemon

Separate eggs. Beat yolks until very light. Add ½ cup sugar and the flour well blended. Add juice and grated rind of lemon. Cook over flame until it thickens. Stir constantly, as it scorches easily. Cool. Beat egg whites very stiff. Add ½ cup sugar slowly, beating all the while. Leave half of whites for meringue. Add other half to yolk mixture folding gently. Fill partly cooked pie crust with mixture. Top with meringue. Bake slowly in medium oven for 20 minutes.

MRS. WALTER A. DAVIS (Genevieve Lockwood)

Chocolate Meringue Pie

¾ cup sugar
3 tablespoons cornstarch
3 tablespoons flour
½ teaspoon salt

2½ cups milk
2 squares chocolate
2 egg yolks
1 teaspoon vanilla

Grate or cut chocolate into 2 cups milk, place over hot water to melt. Combine first four ingredients and blend with ½ cup milk. When chocolate is melted and milk is scalded, add to egg yolks well beaten. Stir constantly. Add flour and sugar mixture. Cook over boiling water stirring constantly until thick, add vanilla. Cool. Place in pastry shell and top with meringue made of:

3 egg whites   6 tablespoons sugar

Beat eggs until stiff, then add sugar gradually. Spread on pie. Bake in oven 300° about 7 minutes.

MRS. LIONEL K. LEGGE (Dorothy Porcher)

Coconut Cream Pie

1 cup sugar and 4
   tablespoons
¼ teaspoon salt
2¾ cups milk
4 eggs (separated)

3 rounded tablespoons
   cornstarch
2 teaspoons vanilla
¼ cup coconut juice
¼ stick real butter
1 large coconut (finely grated)

Scald milk, pour slowly over 1 cup sugar, cornstarch and salt mixed together, then pour this mixture slowly over beaten egg yolks. Return to double-boiler, add coconut juice and cook until thick, stirring constantly. Remove from heat, add butter, vanilla and coconut (reserving ¼ cup). Cool, pour into baked pie shell. Beat egg whites until stiff, add 4 tablespoons sugar and spread meringue over pie, touching crust. Sprinkle coconut on top and bake at 300° until brown. Serves 8.

MRS. CORNELIUS HUGUENIN (Evelyn Anderson)

Peach Meringue Pie

5-6 ripe peaches	2 egg whites
1-2 tablespoons sugar	4 tablespoons confectioners
Few drops lemon juice	or granulated sugar

Prepare a baked pie shell—7 inch. Peel and slice fresh peaches, sprinkling a little sugar over them according to their sweetness, also the lemon juice.

Whip eggs until stiff, then beat in the sugar, ½ teaspoon at a time—this is important. Continue beating until mixture is very heavy and stands in peaks. Place the peaches in the shell, cover with meringue. Bake in slow oven (300°) for 15 minutes or a little longer, until top of meringue is brownish.

MRS. PETER GETHING (Janet Quinn)

Huckleberry Pie

3½ cups berries, fresh or canned	1 tablespoon flour
	Little butter
¾ cup sugar and 2 teaspoons	1 lemon
	Little cream

Wash and drain fresh berries or drain canned ones. Put in pastry-lined 9-inch pie plate. Mix flour with ¾ cup sugar. Pour over berries. Dot with butter. Sprinkle with lemon juice and some of rind cut in small pieces. Cover with top crust, brush with cream, sprinkle with sugar. Bake in hot oven (425°) 15 minutes, decrease heat to moderate (350°) and bake 20-30 minutes longer.

MRS. THOMAS LEGARE, JR. (Laura Hasell)

Apple Crumb Pie

5-6 tart apples	1 cup flour
2 tablespoons sugar	1 cup brown sugar
1 teaspoon nutmeg	½ cup butter
3 tablespoons milk	

Mix sugar and nutmeg. Pour over apples sliced very thin into pie pan lined with pastry. Place brown sugar and flour in a bowl, cut butter into this until crumbly. Pour this over apples, and on top, pour milk. Bake in moderate oven (350°) until done.

MRS. JAMES SNOWDEN, JR. (Anne Hutchins)

Pecan Pie

½ cup pecan meats
1 cup sugar
1 cup dark corn syrup
3 eggs, beaten lightly
1 tablespoon melted butter
1 teaspoon vanilla, scant

Mix sugar, butter, syrup and vanilla. Add to beaten eggs. Then add pecans. Pour into pie pan lined with good rich pastry. Bake in 375° oven for 40 minutes. May be served with whipped cream.

MRS. JAMES HAGOOD (Antoinette Camp)

Pecan Pie

⅔ cup brown sugar
⅓ cup white cane syrup
2 tablespoons milk
1 heaping tablespoon corn
    meal
1 egg
1 pinch salt
1 teaspoon vanilla
1 cup pecan meats
Butter size of an egg

Mix in order listed, pour into pie pan lined with pastry. Bake in 375° oven for 25 minutes.

MRS. RICHARD HANCKEL (Ruth Farmer)

Pumpkin Pie

1 cup stewed pumpkin
1 cup brown sugar
1 teaspoon ground ginger
1 teaspoon ground cinnamon
¼ teaspoon salt
2 cups milk
2 tablespoons melted
    butter

2 eggs

Add sugar and seasonings to the pumpkin and mix well. Add slightly beaten eggs and milk. Lastly, stir in melted butter. Turn into pie plate lined with pastry and bake in hot oven (425°) for 5 minutes. Lower heat to moderate (350°) and bake until filling is set. A knife inserted in center will come out clean when center is done. Serve thoroughly cold.

MRS. S. EDWARD IZARD, JR. (Anne Kirk)

Mrs. Colcock's Mince Meat

1 beef tongue	2 pounds sugar
2 pounds raisins	1 dozen apples
1 pound citron	½ ounce cinnamon
2 pounds beef suet	¼ ounce mace
1 quart wine (sherry)	¼ ounce nutmeg
1 pint whiskey	1 teaspoon salt

Cover tongue with boiling water and *simmer* gently until tender, stand aside to cool. Shred the suet and chop it fine. Pare, core and chop apples, stone raisins, shred citron. When meat is perfectly cold, chop it fine. Mix thoroughly with other prepared ingredients, adding the spices. Pack in stone jar. Pour wine and whiskey over mixture. Cover closely and store in a cool place. It will keep all winter. When ready to use, dip out quantity desired, thin with cider or wine, if necessary. Place in pie pan lined with pastry, cover with top crust, pricking or cutting designs in cover to allow steam to escape. Bake in a hot oven 450° for 30 minutes. For special occasions serve vanilla ice cream on slices of steaming hot mince pie.

MRS. GABRIEL CANNON (Jeannie Heyward)

Chocolate Angel Pie

2 egg whites	1½ teaspoons vanilla
⅛ teaspoon salt	1 cake sweet chocolate
⅛ teaspoon cream of tartar	(¼ pound)
½ cup sugar	3 tablespoons hot water
½ cup chopped nuts	1 cup cream

Beat egg whites until foamy, add salt and cream of tartar. Beat until mixture stands in soft peaks. Add sugar gradually, beat until *very stiff*. Fold in chopped nuts and ½ teaspoon vanilla. Turn into lightly greased 8-inch pie plate. Make a nest-like shell, building up side above edge of plate. Bake in a slow oven (300°) for 35 minutes. Cool.

Melt chocolate in double-boiler, add hot water and blend. Cool. Add 1 teaspoon vanilla. Fold in whipped cream. Turn into meringue shell. Chill. Serves 6.

MRS. JOHN E. BURROWS (Bess Smith)

Mulberry Plantation
Lemon Cream Meringue

4 egg whites (at room temperature)
½ teaspoon cream of tartar
1 cup sugar
4 egg yolks
½ cup sugar
2 teaspoons grated lemon rind
3 tablespoons lemon juice
2 cups cream
1 tablespoon sugar

Beat whites until foamy. Add cream of tartar and beat until they start to stiffen. Add cup of sugar gradually (about 2 tablespoons at a time), and continue beating until meringue is glossy and stiff enough to hold its shape. Spread on a lightly buttered 9 inch pie or cake pan. Make outside rim higher than middle. Bake in a slow oven (300°) 40 minutes. While this is cooling, beat yolks until thick and lemon colored. Beat in ½ cup sugar, lemon juice and rind. Cook in double-boiler about 15 to 20 minutes until thick. Cool. Whip 1 cup cream. Fold it into lemon mixture blending thoroughly. Fill center of meringue with this mixture and chill in refrigerator 8 to 16 hours. When ready to serve, cover top with cup of cream whipped with tablespoon of sugar.

MRS. LAWRENCE A. WALKER, JR. (Phyllis Corson)

Caramel Pie

1½ cups sugar
1 stick butter (½ cup)
3 tablespoons cornstarch
1½ cups water
2 eggs
1 teaspoon vanilla
1 tablespoon sugar

Scorch one half the sugar, pour water in, then add rest of sugar and butter. When butter is melted, add cornstarch, which has been mixed with a little water. Stir constantly and cook until very thick. Take off and cool. Add beaten egg yolks and vanilla. Put caramel filling on baked crust in pie plate. Make meringue of egg whites and extra tablespoon of sugar. Place on top of pie, run in oven (300°) to brown.

MRS. J. STANYARNE STEVENS (Caroline Simonds)

Rum Pie

1 tablespoon gelatine	2 tablespoons rum
¼ cup cold water	1 teaspoon vanilla
2 cups cream	Pinch of salt
2 eggs—separated	1 baked 9″ pie shell or
¼ cup and 6 tablespoons	8-10 baked tart shells
sugar	1 square of chocolate

Soak gelatine in water 5 minutes. Scald cream in top of double-boiler. Beat egg yolks with fork; stir in salt and ¼ cup sugar. Add scalded cream slowly to yolks, stirring constantly. Place over boiling water, continue stirring until smooth and slightly thickened, about 5 minutes. Remove from heat, add gelatine, stir until dissolved. Pour into a bowl and chill until it begins to thicken. Beat egg whites stiff, gradually add 6 tablespoons sugar, continue beating until stiff. Fold whites into custard with rum and vanilla. Pour in baked shell, chill until set. Just before serving, shave a square of chocolate with a sharp straight edged knife, sprinkle shavings on pie.

MRS. JOHN LAURENS (May Rose)

Sweet Potato Pie

3 large sweet potatoes	½ teaspoon nutmeg
2 tablespoons butter	1 egg
½ cup sugar	2 egg whites
½ teaspoon cinnamon	4 teaspoons sugar

Boil potatoes until soft. Peel and mash well with 2 tablespoons butter. Add sugar, cinnamon, nutmeg and egg, well beaten. Fill cooked pastry shell and cover with meringue made of beaten egg whites and 4 teaspoons of sugar. Brown in medium oven. Serves 6.

MRS. THOMAS WARING, JR. (Clelia Mathewes)

Transparent Tarts

½ cup butter	1 pound citron, chopped
2 cups brown sugar	5 eggs (or more)
1 cup cream, whipped	

Melt butter, add sugar and citron. Beat in eggs, one at a time. Cook in double-boiler, stirring until consistency of thick custard. Fills about 12 small tart shells. Serve with unsweetened whipped cream.

Miss Martha Carrington

Bakewell Tart

½ pound short pie crust	2 egg yolks
2 ozs. ground almonds (¼ c.)	1 egg white
2 ounces sugar (¼ c.)	Essence of almonds
2 ounces butter (4 tbsps.)	Raspberry jam

Cream butter and sugar until smooth and thick. Add egg yolks and white of egg, also almonds and essence. Beat well. Line a pie plate with pastry. Place a good layer of jam on bottom and cover with the butter and egg mixture. Bake in a quick oven for 30 minutes. Serve hot or cold.

Miss Julia C. Conner

Sherry Tarts

⅓ cup sugar	½ cup milk
⅓ cup flour	3 tablespoons sherry
⅛ teaspoon salt	1 teaspoon sugar
2 eggs	Grated nutmeg
2 cups cream	8 tart shells, medium size

Mix dry ingredients. Add eggs, slightly beaten. Blend thoroughly. Reserve ½ cup cream. Scald rest of cream and milk then pour it gradually over egg mixture, stirring constantly. Cook about 15 minutes in top of double-boiler, continuing to stir so flour will not lump. Cool, add sherry. Whip reserved cream with teaspoon of sugar until it is thick but not quite stiff. Fill shells with custard, top with cream and grate a dash of nutmeg over each. Rum may be substituted for sherry, using only 2 tablespoons.

Mrs. Arthur J. Stoney (Anne Montague)

MIDDLETON PLACE 1741

CAKES

"No, Ma'am', I ain' fuh measure. I jes' jedge by my own repin-ion. I teck muh flour en' muh brown sugah, en' two-t'ree glub uh muhlassis." "What do you mean by glub?" "You know de soun' muhlassis meck w'en 'e come fum de jug? Glub! Glub!"

Whenever I boil or brew or bake,
How hard I try! What pains I take!
There isn't a step I don't discuss.
My measuring is meticulous.
And what's the result of the fuss and fiddle?
My cake sinks heavily in the middle!
Then old Maria follows me
With a hand that's deft and a smile of glee.
With a touch as light as an angel's kiss,
She stirs in a little of that or this,
With lavish seasoning "to taste"
And calm indifference to waste.
Though her method is all a grave mistake,
The result is always a *super*-cake!

Yummy Cake

½ cup shortening
½ cup sugar
1 egg
2 eggs, separated

1 teaspoon vanilla
1½ cups flour, sifted
1 cup brown sugar
½ cup nut meats

Cream shortening, add sugar and continue creaming. Add separately, 1 egg and 2 yolks. Beat well. Add vanilla, then flour. Pour batter in greased 9" x 13" pan and cover with meringue (Method: beat 2 egg whites stiff; add brown sugar slowly and beat until mixture forms heavy peaks; add nuts). Bake in 350° oven 30 or 40 minutes. Cut in squares. Yield: 15 squares.

MISS MATILDA BELL

My Mother's Nut Cake

1½ sticks butter	1 teaspoon baking powder
2 cups sugar	1 teaspoon nutmeg, grated
6 eggs, beaten	Flour, for nuts
4½ cups flour	1 quart pecans, not chopped

Cream butter and sugar. Add eggs, then sifted dry ingredients. Dredge pecans with flour and fold into mixture. Bake in greased tube pan 1 hour and 15 minutes in 325° oven. When done, turn pan upside down and cool before removing. This cake is not very sweet and keeps indefinitely. Delicious with tea or sherry.

Mrs. Charles Prioleau (Anne Little)

Charleston Devils

Another specialty of the Lady Baltimore Tea Room were these delectable chocolate cakes.

½ stick butter	¾ cup buttermilk
1 cup sugar	2 cups flour
1 egg	1 teaspoon soda
4 squares chocolate	1 teaspoon vanilla
1 cup sweet milk	Pinch of salt

Cook sweet milk, chocolate and butter in top of double-boiler, stirring until thick. Set aside to cool. Cream sugar and egg together; add to cooled chocolate mixture. Sift flour, soda and salt three times; add to mixture alternately with buttermilk. Add vanilla. Cook in 9" x 13" pan lined with wax paper 25 minutes in a slow oven. Cut into squares. Makes 3 dozen cakes.

ICING

1 box confectioners sugar	½ block butter or oleo
4 heaping tablespoons cocoa	1 teaspoon vanilla

Add boiling water enough to mix. Stir until smooth and add vanilla. If icing is runny add more sugar. Spread on cakes.

Mrs. Elizabeth L. Hanahan (Elizabeth Lucas)

Lady Baltimore Cake

½ cup butter

1¼ cups sugar

2 cups sifted cake flour

¾ cup milk

2 teaspoons baking powder

¼ teaspoon salt

1 teaspoon almond extract

3 egg whites

Cream butter, add sugar gradually. Cream until light. Add baking powder and salt to sifted flour; sift three times. Add flour mixture alternately with milk in small amounts, beating after each addition. Add almond extract. Beat whites of eggs until they stand in moist peaks, fold well in flour mixture. Bake in 2 greased 8″ layer pans in 375° oven 20 to 25 minutes. Serves 12. Double quantity makes three 9″ layers and serves 16-20.

ICING AND FILLING

1 cup seeded raisins, chopped

1 cup English walnuts, chopped

½ cup sherry wine

2 cups sugar

½ cup water

¼ teaspoon cream of tartar

2 egg whites

1 tablespoon lemon juice

1 teaspoon almond extract

Soak raisins and nuts in wine overnight. Boil sugar and water until the syrup ropes a heavy thread. Add cream of tartar to egg whites and beat until they stand in moist peaks, slowly pour the hot syrup onto the whites while beating constantly, add flavoring and beat until stiff enough to spread, then add raisins and nuts (well drained) and beat again until glazed looking. Spread between layers, on top and sides. Double quantity for 3 layer 9″ cake.

MRS. JOHN LAURENS (May Rose)

Lady Baltimore Cake

Owen Wister immortalized Charleston's Lady Baltimore Tea Room and its glamorous cake in his book "Lady Baltimore." This is the first time this long sought after and particular receipt for it has been given.

1 cup butter	3½ cups cake flour
3 cups sugar	4 teaspoons baking powder
4 eggs	2 teaspoons vanilla
1 cup milk	2 teaspoons almond extract

½ cup water

Use electric mixer, if possible; cream butter, add 2 cups sugar gradually and beat until the consistency of whipped cream. Add eggs, one at a time, and beat thoroughly. Sift baking powder and flour three times and add alternately with milk, using a wooden spoon for blending. Bake in two 11″ greased cake pans in 350° oven 30 minutes. Make a thick syrup of 1 cup of sugar and ½ cup of water. Flavor with almond and vanilla. Spread this over your layers as soon as you remove them from the pans.

FROSTING

2 cups sugar	2 cups seeded raisins
⅔ cup water	2 cups pecans or walnuts
2 egg whites (beaten stiff)	12 figs
2 teaspoons corn syrup	Almond and vanilla extract

Mix sugar, water and syrup. Cook until it forms a firm ball in cold water. Pour gradually into the stiff egg whites, beating constantly. Now add raisins, pecan nuts, and figs all cut fine. Raisins and figs may be soaked overnight in small amount of sherry or brandy, if desired. Add almond and vanilla extracts to taste. Spread between layers, on top and sides of cake.

MRS. HOWARD READ (Adelaide Higgins)

Mocha Cakes

½ cup butter
1 cup sugar
2 cups sifted flour (scant)
3 eggs
1 teaspoon vanilla

3 level teaspoons baking
    powder
Saltspoon of salt
    (small)
½ cup milk

Lemon peel, grated

Cream butter and sugar very light. Add eggs, one at a time. Beat very light. Sift in flour, baking powder and salt. Add milk and vanilla and a small amount of grated peel. Bake in shallow 8″ x 8″ square pans in moderate oven 30-40 minutes. Cut in small squares; ice. Yield: 6 doz.

MOCHA ICING

¼ pound butter
10 ounces x x x x sugar

1½ tablespoons brandy,
    rum, coffee or whiskey

½ pound shelled almonds

Add sugar to butter gradually and beat to a light cream. Add the spirits or coffee. Blanch and parch almonds, grind rather fine. Spread butter mixture on top and sides, a little thicker on top. Then sprinkle generously with ground almonds which should be light brown, but thoroughly parched. Icing melts in hot weather.

MISS VALERIA CHISOLM

Mrs. Fairfax Montague's Old Time Sponge Cake

8 eggs
2 cups sugar

2 cups flour (sifted)
1½ teaspoons vinegar

1 dessertspoon vanilla

Separate eggs and beat in different bowls, adding 1 cup of sugar to each mixture. Put together and add the vinegar and sifted flour. Add vanilla and bake in slow oven (250°) for 30 minutes and in quicker oven for 30 minutes longer, in an angel food cake pan.

MRS. LIONEL LEGGE (Dorothy H. Porcher)

Old-Fashioned Pound Cake

1 pound granulated sugar	½ teaspoon mace
1 pound butter	½ teaspoon vanilla
10 eggs	1 teaspoon lemon extract
1 pound plain flour	1 teaspoon almond extract

1 teaspoon baking powder

Cream butter, add sugar gradually, and continue beating; then add egg yolks beaten until thick and lemon colored. Sift flour and baking powder together and add gradually to mixture, beating after each addition; then add mace and extracts to taste; lastly fold in egg whites which have been beaten until stiff.

Beat vigorously for five minutes. Then put into a well-buttered tube pan (or plain baking pan which has been lined with two thicknesses of buttered brown paper.)

Bake in slow oven (250°) for about 1½ hours in tube pan, or 2 hours in lined pan. (If cake seems a little too brown during last part of baking period, place a large piece of brown paper lightly on top of pan for a little while).

MISS HELEN O'SHAUGHNESSY

Coconut Cake

¾ cup butter (1½ blocks)	¾ cup milk
2 cups sugar	3 cups flour
4 eggs (separated)	3 teaspoons baking powder

1 teaspoon vanilla

Cream butter and sugar. Add well-beaten egg yolks. Then alternately add milk and flour which has been sifted with the baking powder. Then add stiffly beaten egg whites and vanilla. Bake in two 9" layer pans, greased and lined on bottom with waxed paper, in 375° oven for 25 to 30 minutes.

ICING

3 cups sugar	3 egg whites

1 coconut (grated)

Moisten sugar with cold water and boil until it threads. Then pour over stiffly beaten whites of eggs. Spread on cake and sprinkle generously with coconut.

MRS. N. I. BALL, JR. (Anne Barnwell)

Chocolate Angel Food Cake

1½ cups egg whites
1½ cups sugar
¾ cup flour
¼ cup cocoa

1 teaspoon cream of tartar
¼ teaspoon salt
1 teaspoon vanilla
Few drops lemon extract

Beat egg whites until foamy, add cream of tartar and continue beating until stiff, but not dry. Gradually beat in sugar. Add vanilla and lemon extract and cut and fold in flour and cocoa which have been sifted together five times. Turn into angel food tin and bake in moderate oven about 1 hour and 15 minutes. Set oven at 275° and gradually increase heat until 325° is reached. Cover with seven-minute frosting to which has been added 8-10 marsh-mallows.

MRS. CORNELIUS HUGUENIN (Evelyn Anderson)

Chocolate Cake with Mocha Frosting

2 cups brown sugar
½ cup butter, creamed
2 eggs, beaten together
½ cup sour milk
2 squares chocolate, melted

½ cup warm water with
   1 teaspoon soda
   dissolved in it
2 cups flour, sifted with
   ¼ teaspoon baking
   powder

1 teaspoon vanilla

Cream butter and sugar, add eggs, then add milk, water, and flour, alternating liquids and flour, beating until smooth each time. Add vanilla and chocolate and bake in two 9″ greased tins in 350° oven ½ hour.

FROSTING

3 cups confectioners sugar, creamed with 3 tablespoons butter. Use 5 or 6 tablespoons cold strong coffee to soften while creaming. Add 6 teaspoons dry cocoa and a little vanilla. Cool cake before frosting.

MRS. PARKER JONES (Elizabeth Howard)

Scripture Cake

4½ cups (1st Kings 4–22)   Flour
1 cup (Judges 5–25
    last clause)   Butter
2 cups (Jeremiah 6–20)   Sugar
2 cups (1st Samuel 30–12)   Raisins
2 cups (Nahum 3–12)   Figs
2 cups (Numbers 17–18)   Almonds
2 tablespoon (1st Samuel
    14–13)   Honey
1 pinch (Leviticus 2–13)   Salt
6 (Jeremiah 17–11)   Eggs
½ cup (Judges 4–19)   Milk
    (last clause)
2 tablespoons (Amos 4–5)   Leaven

Season to taste with (2nd Chronicles 9–9) spices. Mix like a fruit cake and bake.

Mrs. Harold G. Dotterer (Harriet Lipscomb)

Black Fruit Cake

1¼ pounds butter
1¼ pounds brown sugar
1¼ pounds flour
3 pounds seeded raisins
3 pounds currants
2 pounds chopped citron
12 eggs
1 cup strong coffee

1 tablespoon powdered mace
3 tablespoons powdered
    cinnamon
1 tablespoon powdered
    cloves
2 wine glasses whiskey
    or brandy
1 wine glass rose water

Soften butter by soaking in tepid water in covered bowl for a few minutes. Drain. Cream butter, rub in sugar slowly. Add eggs, one at a time, beating each before adding. Sift in half of flour. Mix fruit with rest of flour and spices. Stir in floured fruit, add coffee and flavoring. Pre-heat oven to 350°. Turn down after 10 minutes to as low as it will burn. Bake 5 to 6 hours, testing with a straw. This is a fine wedding or Christmas cake. Weighs about 15 pounds when iced.

Mrs. McIver Wilbur (Susan Prioleau)

White Fruit Cake

1½ pounds citron (cut fine)
1½ pounds sultana raisins, washed and dried
1½ pounds blanched ground almonds
1 small grated coconut
1½ pounds crystallized pineapple (cut fine)

1 pound butter
1 pound sugar
1 pound flour
2 tablespoons nutmeg
1 teaspoon almond extract
1 tablespoon vanilla extract
½ pint sherry or coconut milk

6 eggs

Cream butter and sugar and add eggs one by one, beating well after each egg is added. Put half of flour over fruit and other half over butter mixture. Mix all ingredients well.

Line the sides and bottom of the greased cake pan with greased brown paper. Four 9 x 5 x 2¾ inch loaf pans could be used. Place cake in pan of water, cover and steam for 3½ hours in oven at 375°. Remove cover, also pan with water, and bake for ½ hour at 325°. Cake will weigh about 8 pounds.

Mrs. Felix Chisolm (Elizabeth Simonds)

White Fruit Cake

1 pound butter
1 pound sugar
1 pound flour
10 eggs
2 pounds candied pineapple (scrape off sugar)
1½ pounds citron

1½ pounds almonds
1 tablespoonful rose water
1 cup good sherry wine
4 teaspoons baking powder
1 grated fresh coconut (optional)

2 pounds candied cherries

Blanch almonds. Cut up fruit and nuts. Cream butter and sugar. Add eggs, two at a time, beating after each addition. Add flavoring. Sift flour and baking powder over finely cut-up fruit and nuts. Mix in thoroughly. Pour batter over fruit mixture and mix well. (I use hands.) Line two tube pans with well-greased brown paper. (Any good baking utensil may be used as long as it is proper depth.) Steam three hours. Bake in oven ½ hour at 325°.

Mrs. James M. Hagood (Louise Taber)

Old Time Wedding Cake

"Old Time Wedding Cake has been used by members of my family for upwards of seventy years. More often at Christmas season than weddings."

2 pounds raisins	1 pound butter
2½ pounds currants	9 eggs
1 pound citron	1 wine glass whiskey
1½ pounds sugar	1 wine glass sherry
¾ pound flour	1 teaspoon mixed spices

1 teaspoon baking powder

Chop raisins and citron, wash and drain currants. Sift flour with baking powder into fruit and mix thoroughly. Separate eggs. Cream yolks, butter and sugar thoroughly. Add stiffly beaten egg whites and then fruit mixture. Mix and knead with hands. Stir in liquor and spices. Divide into two deep 10-inch cake pans lined with well greased wax paper. Cook in covered steamer four and a half to five hours. If you have no steamer, put in a dish pan of water (cover well, and let boil on top of stove).

MRS. PHILIP G. PORCHER, SR. (Mary Cordes)

"Carolina Housewife"
Wedding Cake of 1850!

20 pounds butter	20 nutmegs
20 pounds sugar	1 ounce mace
20 pounds flour	4 ounces cinnamon
20 pounds raisins	20 glasses wine
40 pounds currants	20 glasses brandy
12 pounds citron	10 eggs to the pound

Add cloves to your taste. If you wish it richer, add 2 pounds of currants, and 1 pound of raisins to each pound of flour.

MISS MARY DEAS RAVENEL

Cheese Cake

¾ package zwieback (or graham crackers)
2 tablespoons butter
Sugar (½ cup plus 2 tablespoons)
2 tablespoons of flour
½ teaspoon salt
5½ packages (3 oz.) cream cheese
1 teaspoon vanilla
4 egg yolks
1 cup heavy cream
4 egg whites

Roll zwiebacks into fine crumbs and blend with butter and 2 tablespoons of sugar. Press mixture into bottom and sides of a 9-inch spring-form mold. Blend together ½ cup sugar, flour, salt and cream cheese, add vanilla and egg yolks. Mix well, add heavy cream and mix again. Fold in stiffly beaten egg whites. Pour into mold on top of crumbs and bake in a moderate oven 325° to 350°, about 1½ hours or until "set" in the middle. Cool before serving.

MRS. JACK KRAWCHECK (Esther Bielsky)

Sour Milk Ginger Cake

¼ cup butter
½ cup sugar
1 egg well beaten
½ cup molasses
1⅔ cups flour
½ teaspoon soda
1 teaspoon baking powder
1 teaspoon ginger
½ teaspoon salt
½ cup sour milk
2 tablespoons sugar
1 teaspoon cinnamon

Cream butter and sugar thoroughly, add egg and molasses, blend. Add next five ingredients, sifted, alternately with milk, beat until smooth. Pour into 9" x 13" buttered pan and sprinkle top with sugar and cinnamon. Bake in moderate oven (350°F.) for 45 minutes. Serves about 15 people.

MRS. R. C. MULLIN (Hasell Townsend)

Almond Cake

3 eggs
1½ sticks butter
Few drops of almond
    extract

¾ cup sugar
3 oz. ground almonds,
    (ground very fine)
1 cup flour (sifted)

Beat butter and sugar to a cream, add eggs, well beaten, then flour, almonds and extract. Put in greased loaf-tin lined with grease-proof paper and cover top with grease-proof paper. Bake 1 hour in moderate oven.

MRS. LOUIS McCRADY (Eleanor Laurens)

Chocolate Waldorf Cake

1 cup sugar
2 cups plain flour
    (unsifted)
4 level tablespoons cocoa
2 level teaspoons baking
    soda

Pinch of salt
1 cup cold water
1 teaspoon vanilla
1 cup mayonnaise
    (commercial brand)
2 heaping tablespoons
    seeded blackberry jam

Sift sugar, flour, cocoa, soda and salt together. Add mayonnaise, water, vanilla, blackberry jam. Stir and beat 1 minute. Bake in two 9" layers in 350° oven for 25 or 30 minutes. **Cover with Seven-Minute Icing.**

MRS. W. E. AMOS (Marie Weatherford)

Eggless-Butterless Cake

2 cups flour
1 cup sugar
1½ teaspoons soda
1 cup mayonnaise

1¼ teaspoons baking
    powder
4 tablespoons cocoa
1 cup cold water

Blend all dry ingredients well. Then add mayonnaise well mixed with 1 cup cold water. Bake at 350° for 30 minutes in two 9" layer pans.

Ice with rich chocolate icing.

MRS. KIRK LYNCH (Juanita Kirk)

Sugarless Yellow Cake

3 cups flour
½ teaspoon salt
4 teaspoons baking powder
½ cup butter
1½ cups white corn syrup

2 teaspoons grated orange
   rind
½ teaspoon almond extract
   or 2 teaspoons vanilla
3 eggs
1 cup milk

Orange marmalade or other preserves

Sift flour once before measuring; resift twice with salt and baking powder. Beat butter until creamy; beat 1 cup corn syrup, orange rind and flavoring into butter gradually. Beat egg yolks until light, then add to batter. Beat for one minute. Add sifted ingredients in three parts, alternately with the milk. Beat batter after each addition until well blended. Beat egg whites until stiff but not dry and add ½ cup corn syrup. Fold into batter. Bake in two 9-inch greased pans about 25 minutes in 375° oven. Place marmalade or preserves between layers.

MRS. R. M. ANDERSON (Dorothy Middleton)

Eggless, Milkless, Butterless Cake

2 cups brown sugar
2 cups hot water
2 tablespoons shortening
1 teaspoon salt
1 teaspoon soda

1 package seedless raisins
1 teaspoon cinnamon
1 teaspoon cloves
3 cups sifted flour
1 teaspoon hot water

Boil together sugar, water, lard, salt, raisins and spices for five minutes. When cold add the flour and the soda dissolved in a teaspoon of hot water. This makes two loaves, bread pan size. Bake in 325° oven about 45 minutes. This cake is good texture and keeps moist for some time.

MRS. JOHN LAURENS (May Rose)

Almond Paste for Fruit Cake

1 pound blanched almonds,
   ground fine
1 pound confectioners sugar

2 egg whites, unbeaten
1 teaspoon rose water
2 teaspoons almond extract

Combine egg whites with the sugar; add flavoring and cream well; add almonds. This covers top of a 6-pound fruit cake generously.

MRS. JOHN LAURENS (May Rose)

Uncooked Fruit Cake Icing

2 pounds xxxx sugar
3 small or 2 large egg
   whites

Orange or almond extract
   or rose water may
   be added

Juice of 1 or 2 lemons

Combine ingredients. Beat and continue beating until consistency to use for spreading and decorating. Flavor to taste. Should cover 10-pound cake.

MISS VALERIA CHISOLM

White Icing for Fruit Cake

2 cups granulated sugar
1 cup water

2 egg whites
8 marshmallows

3 tablespoons lemon juice

Beat egg whites stiff. Boil sugar and water until it will spin a thread. Add half of this to egg whites. Leave other half to simmer slowly. Beat syrup and eggs, add flavoring and marshmallows, one at a time. Add remaining syrup and continue to beat until creamy, then spread over cake. Will cover top and sides of 10-pound cake.

MRS. WILLIAM MARTIN (Bettina Parker)

Never-Fail Icing (Seven Minute)

1 cup granulated sugar   3 tablespoons water
½ teaspoon cream of tartar   2 unbeaten egg whites
1 teaspoon vanilla

Put all ingredients but vanilla in top of double boiler under which water is already boiling. Beat until it stands in peaks.

For fruit icings (such as orange, pineapple, etc.), use 3 tablespoons of the juice in place of water and 3 tablespoons grated or chopped fruit in place of vanilla.

MRS. JACK T. WALKER (Margaret Ficken)

Orange Icing

1¾ cups granulated sugar   Zest (rind) of ½ orange
⅓ cup cold water   Zest (rind) of ½ lemon
Yolks of 3 eggs   1 teaspoon orange juice
1 teaspoon lemon juice

Dissolve granulated sugar in cold water. Stir until partly dissolved, then boil without stirring until it spins long hairs when a fork is dipped into it. Into the thoroughly beaten yolks, vigorously stir the zest of orange and the zest of lemon. Pour syrup very slowly over the eggs and when it begins to thicken, add orange and lemon juices.

MRS. T. LADSON WEBB, JR. (Anne Moore)

Easy Caramel Frosting

¾ cup firmly packed   ¼ cup granulated sugar
    brown sugar   ½ cup milk
1 tablespoon butter or oleo

Boil first 3 ingredients until syrup forms a soft ball in cold water (232°). Add butter. Cool to lukewarm (110°). Beat until thick and creamy. If icing has been cooked too long add a few drops of heavy cream. If using this receipt for a large layer cake, double the ingredients.

MRS. HAROLD PETTIT (Corinne Neely)

Chocolate Icing (For Cakes or Layer-Cake)

"This is a receipt from the famous Theus family of bakers. The Theus trio came to Charleston from New Orleans. They sold cookies and cakes, pies and pastries here in the eighteen seventies and eighties. Even in those days their special cake, which had to be ordered days in advance, cost three dollars!—and you furnished your own quart of cream! This chocolate icing was for a lesser cake, but, as far as my knowledge goes, this is the only receipt of theirs which has survived."

1 cup granulated sugar	1 tablespoon vanilla essence
¼ pound bitter	Pinch salt
cake-chocolate	4 tablespoons (approx.)
⅛ pound butter	cream

2 egg yolks

Dissolve sugar in cream. Add chocolate, butter and salt. Cook very slowly until all ingredients are dissolved. (Beginners may prefer to use a double-boiler). Add beaten egg yolks by first pouring hot mixture over them and then returning to saucepan. Continue to cook very slowly—do not boil—until mixture is thick. This will be about five minutes. Remove from stove . Add vanilla essence and beat until cool enough to spread on cake. This will ice, thickly, a two layer cake.

MRS. CLEMENTS RIPLEY (Katherine Ball)

Smooth Fudge Frosting

3 tablespoons shortening	10 tablespoons milk
3 tablespoons margarine	2¼ cups sugar
1½ tablespoons corn syrup	¼ teaspoon salt
3 squares chocolate	1½ teaspoons vanilla

Combine all ingredients except vanilla. Cook in heavy saucepan until it boils rapidly (low heat) and boil 1 minute only. Cool before adding vanilla, then beat till smooth. Will frost a 9″ cake.

MRS. A. FRANZ WITTE, JR. (Lula Thomas Jenkins)

COOKIES

Do, Chile! I ain' got time fuh mek fancy cooky. Teck dis penny en' go git uh horse-gunjuh.

> I do respect that iron man
> Who, when he's faced with cookies, can
> Confine himself to one or two
> And leave the rest for me and you!

Rolled Sweet Wafers

Cream ½ cup of butter and ½ cup (little over) of sugar then add:

One egg

½ cup milk (or enough to make it like cake batter)

One teaspoon vanilla

One cup plain flour, by degrees

Put batter in hot wafer iron (greased on both sides) with teaspoon. Turn to cook on each side. Take out with knife and *roll at once.* Keep in tin can, or will get soft immediately. Yield: 1½ doz.

MISS THEODORA GREGORIE

Scones

"Among the rich and crumbly delights to serve with jams and marmalade, are Scones, those our Grandmothers loved to make; not too sweet, not too hearty, but just right as a morsel of goodness to go with the hospitable gesture of a cup of tea and a good gossip."

2 cups flour

2 eggs

½ cup cream

4 tablespoons butter

1 teaspoon salt

5 teaspoons sugar

3 teaspoons baking powder

Sift dry ingredients, rub in the butter with fingertips. Beat eggs, add cream and mix gently with flour mixture. Roll out to one half inch in thickness; cut in shapes. Brush with white of egg. Bake about 15 minutes in a moderate oven 375°. Yield: 2 dozen.

MRS. LOUIS Y. DAWSON, JR. (Virginia Walker)

Benne (Sesame)

"According to legend among descendants of negro slaves along the coast of Charleston, benne is a good luck plant for those who eat thereof or plant in their gardens. It was originally brought in by the slaves from West Africa to this Coastal region."

Benne Seed Wafers

2 cups brown sugar
1 cup plain flour
½ teaspoon baking powder
¼ teaspoon salt
¾ cup toasted benne seed

1 egg, beaten
1 block butter, or ¾ cup
    cooking oil or oleo
1 teaspoon vanilla
(see p. 356, No. 51 for toasting)

Cream the butter and sugar, add beaten egg, then flour sifted with salt and baking powder Add vanilla and benne seed. Drop by teaspoon or less on greased cookie sheet. Bake in moderate oven 325°. Cook quickly. Allow to cool one minute before removing from pan. This makes a transparent wafer. Yield: about 100.

MRS. GUSTAVE P. RICHARDS (Lizetta Wagener)

Benne Cookies

¾ cup butter
1½ cups of brown sugar
2 eggs
¼ teaspoon baking powder
1¼ cups flour

½ cup toasted benne seeds
    (see p. 356, No. 51 for
    toasting)
1 teaspoon vanilla

Cream butter and sugar together and mix with other ingredients, in the order given. Drop with a teaspoon on waxed paper in pan far enough apart to allow spreading. Bake in moderate oven 325° for 30 minutes. Yield: 7 dozen.

MRS. MAYNARD MARSHALL (Harriott Simons)

Very Thin Benne Cookies

1½ cups dark brown sugar
1 egg
¾ cup flour
¼ teaspoon baking powder

¼ teaspoon salt
1 cup benne seed
¾ cup melted butter
   (1½ sticks)
1 teaspoon vanilla

Cream butter and sugar. Add egg slightly beaten; add flour with baking powder, salt, add benne seed. Add vanilla. Drop with a coffee spoon in pan lined with aluminum foil. Bake in 300° oven till brown. Let cool before removing from pan.

MRS. L. L. OLIVEROS (Evelyn Kenan)

Cookies

1 cup butter
½ cup brown sugar
½ cup white sugar
1 egg beaten
2 cups of flour

¼ teaspoon of salt
½ teaspoon soda
½ teaspoon of vanilla
1 cup finely cut pecan nut
   meats

Cream butter; add sugar and egg. Sift in flour which has been sifted with soda and salt, then add nuts and vanilla. Form in rolls, wrap in waxed paper and allow to stand in refrigerator over night. Slice and bake in hot oven. (400°F.). Yield: 90 cookies.

Coconut can be used instead of nuts. A teaspoon of cinnamon can be added when nuts are used for variety. Or sprinkle sugar, cinnamon and nutmeg on cookies before baking.

MRS. WALTER A. DAVIS (Genevieve Lockwood)

Nut Cookies

¼ pound butter
½ cup brown sugar
½ cup white sugar

½ cup flour
1 egg
¼ pound pecans, cut fine

Cream butter and sugar. Add egg, then flour sifted, then the nut meats cut fine. Drop on greased cookie sheet with teaspoon. Bake in moderate oven (350°); cook quickly. Yield: 50 cookies.

MRS. J. WALKER COLEMAN (Felicia Chisolm)

Brownies

1½ sticks butter	1 cup nut meats
2 cups sugar	1 heaping cup flour
4 squares chocolate	½ teaspoon salt
4 eggs (beaten together)	1 teaspoon vanilla

Cream butter, add melted chocolate and all other ingredients. Spread on greased cookie pan and bake 20 to 25 minutes in 350° oven. Cut in squares while hot. Yield: about 20.

Mrs. W. Lucas Venning (Ruth Gibson)

Brownies

¼ pound butter	2 cups sugar
2 or 3 squares unsweetened chocolate	1 cup flour
	1 cup nuts chopped
2 eggs	1 teaspoon vanilla

Melt butter and chocolate over low flame. Pour over sugar and mix. Add eggs, and flour which has been sifted, vanilla and chopped nuts. Put in greased pan (about 7x10) and bake very slowly for about 30 minutes in oven at 350°. Cut into squares when taken from oven. Let cool before removing from pan. Yield: about 30.

Mrs. Gustave P. Richards (Lizetta Wagener)

Brown Sugar Brownies

1 cup dark brown sugar	1 teaspoon baking powder
¼ cup melted butter	⅓ teaspoon salt
1 egg, well beaten	1 teaspoon vanilla
1 scant cup flour	¾ cup nut meats

Cream together brown sugar and butter. Add the egg. Sift together the flour, baking powder and salt. Add and mix with sugar and butter. Add vanilla and nuts. Pour into greased 8-inch square tin. Bake 20 to 25 minutes in 350° oven. Cut in squares. Yield: 16.

Mrs. Thomas P. Stoney (Beverly DuBose)

Coconut Brownies

½ cup soft butter or oleo	2 eggs, beaten
1 cup sifted flour	½ teaspoon vanilla
4 tablespoons brown sugar	1 cup coconut
1½ cups brown sugar	1 cup pecans
½ teaspoon baking powder	

Mix first three ingredients (butter, flour, 4 tablespoons brown sugar.) Bake in 9″ square pan in 350° oven for 15 to 20 minutes. Then mix other ingredients, adding each in the order listed. Spread this on top of first mixture and bake again for 25 or 30 minutes. Makes 2 doz.

Mrs. A. Franz Witte, Jr. (Lula Thomas Jenkins)

"Lady Baltimore" Cookies

1 cup shortening	1½ teaspoons salt
1½ cups sugar	1 teaspoon cinnamon
3 eggs	1 teaspoon allspice
½ teaspoon soda	1 teaspoon cloves
2 teaspoons water	1 teaspoon nutmeg
3 cups flour	1½ cups raisins
½ cup broken nut meats	

Cream shortening, sugar and eggs together. Dissolve soda in water and add. Mix and sift flour, salt and spices and add to the first mixture. Add raisins and nuts and mix thoroughly. Drop by teaspoons on greased pans. Bake in 350° oven 15 or 20 minutes. This receipt makes about 70 cookies.

Mrs. Wilson Walker (Gladys Hay)

Kiss Cakes

2 light cups of sugar
4 egg whites
1 level tablespoon cornstarch

1 teaspoon vanilla
Dash of almond extract
1 cup broken pecans

Beat egg whites very stiff. Add sugar a little at a time and beat well after each adding. Very important to add only small amount of sugar at a time! Sprinkle in cornstarch. Flavor with vanilla and a dash of almond extract. Then add the pecans. Drop on waxed paper by the tablespoon and bake in a very slow oven 250° about 45 minutes. (The longer they cook, the better.) They are done when you can lift them off paper without breaking. Yield: 2½ dozen.

MRS. J. WALKER COLEMAN (Felicia Chisolm)

Brown Sugar Nut Kiss Cakes

1 egg white
1 cup light brown sugar, well packed

1 cup pecans, chopped fine

Beat egg white stiff but not dry. Mash out sugar smooth, add to egg white slowly, beating all the while with egg beater. Add the nuts and stir in well. Drop on well-buttered cookie sheet small teaspoonfuls about two inches apart. Bake 15 minutes in oven 350°. Makes 24-28 cookies.

MRS. JOHN LAURENS (May Rose)

Date Kisses

1 cup white sugar
3 egg whites

½ pound of pecans
1 package dates

1 teaspoon vanilla

Beat eggs until stiff; add sugar. Cook in double boiler until it will stand in points when dropped from spoon. Then remove from fire, add nuts, dates, and vanilla. Drop on well-greased cookie sheet about 2 inches apart. Bake 45 minutes in a slow oven (300°F.). Yield: 36.

MRS. WALTER A. DAVIS (Genevieve Lockwood)

Groundnut (Peanut) Cakes

From "The Carolina Housewife," a very early and rare cook book published in Charleston between 1850-1860.

Blanch 1 pound of groundnuts; beat them very fine in a marble mortar, adding a little brandy while pounding to prevent oiling. Then add ten eggs, one pound of sugar, and one pound of butter. Beat the whole well together; make a puff paste, lay it on your tins, and fill them with the mixture; grate lump sugar over them, and bake in a slow oven.

Mrs. H. P. Staats (Juliette Wiles)

Ginger Bread Man or Ginger Cookies

½ cup shortening
½ cup brown sugar
½ cup molasses
½ cup sour milk
½ teaspoon vinegar

1 teaspoon ginger
2 teaspoons cinnamon
3½ cups flour
½ teaspoon salt
1 teaspoon soda

Cream shortening, add sugar gradually. Stir in molasses, add 1¼ cups flour sifted with soda, salt and spices. Stir thoroughly and add remaining flour alternately with milk and vinegar (mixed). Chill dough; roll about ⅓ inch thick on floured board; use ginger-boy cutter. Place on baking sheet and bake at 375° for 10-15 minutes. Yield: 26 boys.

Mrs. I. Ripon Wilson, Jr. (Marguerite Bennett)

Moldy Mice (Sand Tarts)

1 stick butter
1 cup flour
1½ teaspoons vanilla

1 tablespoon sugar
½ cup chopped pecans
x x x x sugar

Mix butter and sugar. Flour nuts and put together. Roll in small bars about the size of your thumb. Bake 425° about 15 minutes. When done roll in sugar while very hot. Yield: 3 dozen.

Mrs. W. H. Barnwell (Mary Royall)

Praline Cookies

3 tablespoons butter
1 cup medium brown sugar
1 egg, well beaten

1 tablespoon vanilla
1 cup pecan halves
2 tablespoons flour

Melt butter and blend in sugar, add egg, nuts, flour, vanilla and mix well. Prepare a well-greased heavy cookie sheet, drop one half teaspoon of batter for each cookie, placing them five inches apart. Bake about ten minutes in a moderate oven, then loosen edges of each cookie with wide spatula and lift onto wire cake rack to cool and crisp. This delicious receipt, a truly Southern treat, makes 2½ dozen cookies.

MRS. HOWARD READ (Adelaide Higgins)

Walnut Wafers

½ pound brown sugar
½ pound walnuts (broken, not chopped)

5 tablespoons flour
¼ teaspoon baking powder
2 eggs

Pinch of salt

Mix brown sugar and eggs, beat, and add other ingredients. Drop on buttered pan with teaspoon. Bake in moderate oven 350° for 8-12 minutes. Yield: 3-4 dozen.

MRS. HENRY ELLERBE (Margaret Lucas)

Stickies

Make a biscuit dough and roll out thin. Spread with butter or margarine and cover with brown sugar. On top of this sprinkle cinnamon. Start from side and roll (like jelly roll). Cut roll into slices about ¼ inch thick. Place in well-buttered pan and on top of each slice put a little brown sugar and cinnamon. (This is for those who really like Stickies sticky!) Bake in moderate oven 450° until brown; remove from pan while hot. Dough, using 2 cups flour, yields 24.

MRS. I. RIPON WILSON, JR. (Marguerite Bennett)

Rum Cookies

1 pound of brown sugar
¼ pint brown corn syrup
1 coconut (medium),
   grated

2 cups flour
½ teaspoon soda
1 tablespoon good rum

Mix in order listed. Drop on greased tins by teaspoons and bake in a moderate oven 350° to a golden brown. When slightly cooled, loosen from tin. (If allowed to become cold on tin, they become brittle and break.) Yield: 100.

MRS. WALTER B. METTS (Jane Stauffer)

Whiskey Cookies

3 small boxes of vanilla
   wafers
2 tablespoons cocoa
1½ ounces whiskey

1 cup chopped pecans
4 tablespoons dark corn
   syrup
Powdered sugar

Roll wafers on a board with rolling pin until pulverized. Mix other ingredients and blend thoroughly with wafers. Form into small balls and roll in powdered sugar. Yield: 2 dozen.

MRS. MARY H. BAILEY (Mary Huguenin)

Male Cookies

1⅓ sticks butter
2 cups brown sugar
1 cup flour (measure
   before sifting)

1 teaspoon vanilla
Pinch salt
2 eggs, beaten together
1 cup chopped nuts

Cream butter and sugar; add eggs and flour, vanilla and nuts. Cook in biscuit pan in a slow oven (250°) about 40 minutes. When cold cut in small pieces and roll in powdered sugar. Yield: 2½ doz.

MRS. A. L. WARDLAW (Lelia Elliot)

Magnolia Gardens' Pancake Cookies

1 egg, separated
½ cup brown sugar
½ cup white sugar
½ teaspoon vanilla
¼ pound butter

½ cup finely chopped
   pecans
1 cup sifted flour
1 tablespoon flour
Pinch of salt

Cream butter and sugar together. Add yolk of egg. Then add 1 cup flour and a pinch of salt. Mix pecans with a tablespoon of flour and add to above mixture. Beat egg white until stiff. Add that and vanilla last of all. Take a teaspoon of the mixture, dip in ice water, and spread with a spatula on greased cookie pan. Heat oven to 350°. Turn off oven as soon as cookies are put in. Bake until lightly browned. Yield: 21 cookies.

MRS. NORWOOD HASTIE (Sara Simons)

Almond Cookies

½ cup butter
1 cup sugar
1 egg
1¾ cups flour
2 teaspoons baking powder

Frosting
1 egg white
Blanched almonds
1 tablespoon sugar
¼ teaspoon cinnamon

Pinch of Salt

Cream butter, add sugar gradually, and the egg, well beaten; then flour sifted with baking powder and a little salt. Chill, toss one half of mixture on floured board and roll ⅛ inch thickness, and cut with doughnut cutter. Then proceed with other half of mixture in same manner. Brush over with white of egg mixed with sugar and cinnamon. Split almonds and arrange three halves at equal distances on each. Place on cookie sheet and bake in slow oven for 8 minutes. Yield: 2 dozen.

MISS NANNIE P.deSAUSSURE

Queen Anne Cookies

¼ pound butter
¼ pound sugar
¼ pound flour
2 eggs
½ teaspoon baking powder
Chopped nuts

Cream butter and sugar thoroughly. Add eggs one at a time, then flour and baking powder. Have cookie sheets greased and floured lightly. Spread the mixture very thin with spatula. Sprinkle with chopped nuts (pecans, peanuts or almonds) then with sugar, bake in a moderate oven about 400° until a delicate brown. Cut in squares and remove from baking sheet immediately. Makes about 80 two-inch cookies. Store in air-tight tins.

MRS. WALTER B. METTS (Jane Stauffer)

Chocolate Crispies

2 squares of unsweetened
   chocolate
½ cup butter or shortening
½ cup sifted flour
2 eggs, unbeaten
½ teaspoon vanilla
½ cup nut meats,
   finely chopped

1 cup sugar

To melted chocolate, add butter, sugar, eggs, flour and vanilla, beating well. Spread mixture on baking sheet 12x16 inches or in three 8x6 pans. Sprinkle with nuts. Bake in hot oven 15 minutes. While warm, mark into 2-inch squares. Cool, then break into the squares. Makes 9 crispies. (Secret—spread as thin as possible.) These keep well for several days.

MRS. KINLOCH McDOWELL (Annie Bissell)

Butter Cookies

½ cup butter (1 stick)
½ cup sugar
1 cup flour
1 egg yolk
1 teaspoon vanilla
Good pinch salt

Soften butter to room temperature and mix other ingredients thoroughly into butter; use hands if necessary. Pinch off small pieces of mixture and roll into balls the size of large marble. Place on cookie sheet. Make a small depression in each. Fill this with some tart jelly or preserves. Bake in 350° oven. Watch carefully as they burn easily. (Cooking time: 20-30 minutes). Yield: 50.

MRS. WILLIAM HASKELL (Jeannie Heyward)

Ice Box Cookies

1 cup butter or substitute	3½ cups sifted flour
2 cups brown sugar	2 eggs
1 cup chopped pecans	½ teaspoon salt

1 teaspoon soda

Cream butter and sugar, add eggs and mix well. Sift salt and soda into flour. Add nuts, add to first part and mix. Put dough on well-floured board and knead until smooth. Roll into round roll of desired size; roll in wax paper. Place in refrigerator over night. When ready to bake, slice very thin and bake in moderate oven (350°) until crisp. Makes about 5 dozen cookies.

Mrs. E. H. B. Perry (A. Ruth Perry)

Butterscotch Squares

¼ cup butter	¾ cup flour
1 cup brown sugar	1 teaspoon baking powder
1 egg	½ teaspoon vanilla

¼ cup nuts

Cook butter and sugar together until smooth and well blended. Cool until lukewarm. Add egg (unbeaten) and beat well. Add flour sifted with baking powder. Add vanilla and nuts and bake in oven at 350° until done. Cut in squares, cool before removing from pan. Yield: 24.

Mrs. Henry Ellerbe (Margaret Lucas)

Oatmeal Cookies

1 cup sugar	1 teaspoon vanilla
2 eggs	1 tablespoon butter
2 teaspoons baking powder	2½ cups raw oatmeal

Cream butter and sugar; add yolks of eggs, oatmeal, baking powder and vanilla. Beat egg whites stiff and add last. Drop on buttered tin far apart, and bake in 325° oven until golden brown. Yield: 4 dozen.

Mrs. Louis T. Parker (Josephine Walker)

Louise Boller

1 heaping cup sugar
4 cups cake flour (sifted)

2 sticks butter or oleo
1 beaten egg

Sift sugar and flour in large bowl; mix butter in with fingers, then add the egg, and knead well. Roll into little balls press an almond on top and bake on greased cookie sheets at 300° until light brown. Yield: 100.

MRS. ASHMEAD F. PRINGLE, JR. (Helen Johansen)

Lemon Cookies

Juice and gratings of
one lemon
1 cup butter
2 cups sugar
2 eggs

1 quart of flour (4 cups)
¼ teaspoon soda dissolved
in ½ cup milk or water
1 teaspoon lemon extract
2 tablespoons baking powder

Cream butter and sugar; add eggs, soda, milk (or water) baking powder and flour sifted together; also lemon juice, rind and extract. Roll out thin, adding more flour. Cut with cookie cutter. Bake on greased cookie sheet in slow oven for 20 minutes. Yield: about 100.

MRS. HERBERT RAVENEL SASS (Marion Hutson)

Hillsborough Plantation Date Squares

1 cup granulated sugar
½ cup butter
2 eggs, well beaten
¾ cup flour

¼ teaspoon baking powder
1 teaspoon vanilla
1 cup dates, cut up fine
1 cup nuts, chopped fine

Cream butter and sugar, add eggs, then flour and baking powder, which have been sifted together. Add vanilla, then dates and nuts. Put into a well-greased baking pan, spreading thin enough to cover the bottom of the pan. Bake in 325° oven 15 or 20 minutes. Cut in 1½ inch squares while still warm. Yield: 36 squares.

MRS. ERNEST W. KING (Isabel Simmons)

Pfeffernusse

1 pound butter	½ can mixed cake spice
1 pound shortening	Grated rind of two oranges
2 pounds blanched and ground almonds	1½ ounces of potash
	1 ounce cardamon seed
2 pounds light brown sugar	2 lumps of hartshorn
	6 pounds plain flour
2 cans dark corn syrup	3 eggs
3 teaspoons baking soda	Warm water

Warm shortening and butter, add sugar and eggs, then syrup which has been warmed. Then add baking soda mixed with a little warm water, then the ground almonds and orange peel. Add the flour, to which the potash, cardamon seed, spice, and hartshorn have been added. Mix well. This takes strong hands, but can be partly mixed with electric beater. Pack in a large bowl. The whole mixture does not have to be cooked at once. When finished they are delicious. Make a month before Christmas. Roll very thin, cut with small cookie cutters and cook in oven 300° about 15 or 20 minutes, depending upon your oven. Keep in tin cans. This makes a large amount of cookies. For a small family it is advisable to cut the receipt in half. Yield: several hundred.

Mrs. Henry J. Mann (Florence Hossley)

Christmas Cookies with Almonds

¾ pound butter	2 eggs
½ pound sugar	Almonds
¾ pound flour (3 cups sifted)	Cinnamon

Sift together flour and sugar, cut butter in and knead thoroughly. Add one egg and knead again; let stand covered in ice box one hour. Roll out as thin as possible on floured board and cut with round cutter. Put a little beaten egg on middle of each cookie, add a few thin slices of almond and sprinkle with sugar and cinnamon mixed. Bake in medium oven until light brown.

Mrs. Ashmead F. Pringle, Jr. (Helen Johansen)

Anise Christmas Cookies

1 pound butter	2 eggs
1 pound shortening	1 teaspoon soda
1 cup granulated sugar	3 pounds flour or more
½ teaspoon salt	1 lemon rind, grated
1 cup brown sugar	1 nutmeg, grated
2 cups black molasses	2 ounces cardamon

1½ ounces anise

Cream butter, shortening and sugar; add eggs, molasses, then dry ingredients. Allow to stand in refrigerator for two days, to allow spice to go through. Roll out on floured board and cut with fancy Christmas cutters. Bake on cookie sheets in hot oven until golden brown (about 10 minutes.) Place in air-tight cans until ready to serve. Yield: several hundred.

MRS. WILLIAM McG. MORRISON (Caroline Sams)

Butter Fingers (Christmas Cookies)

1½ sticks butter	2 teaspoons cold water
¼ cup white sugar or 9 teaspoons xxxx sugar	2 cups flour (plain) that has been sifted
1 cup black walnuts or blanched almonds	2 teaspoons vanilla
	Dash of salt

Cream sugar and butter well, add vanilla and grind the nuts and add to this. Add the cold water, then the flour and salt and knead thoroughly. Roll small amount at a time by hand in a roll the size of your finger, cut in pieces about an inch long. Cook in preheated oven 300°. Cook until light brown, about half an hour, depending on your oven. When cool, dust cookies with powdered sugar. Make only one batch at a time. When cool store in a tight can lined with wax paper. These keep a long time and the flavor improves with age. Yield: 24.

MRS. HENRY J. MANN (Florence Hossley)

Date Dainties

1 cup sugar	1 teaspoon baking powder
2 eggs	1 cup dates (chopped)
1 cup flour	1 cup nuts (chopped)

Separate eggs, beat yolks and add sugar, then cream together. Add flour, baking powder, nuts and dates. Mix well. Fold into stiffly beaten egg whites and bake in waxed paper lined pan in 350° oven for 35 minutes. Yield: 3 dozen.

MRS. WILSON WALKER (Gladys Hay)

Defense Cookies

½ cup white sugar	1 cup plain flour
¼ cup brown sugar	1 teaspoon vanilla
½ cup shortening	½ teaspoon soda
1 egg	½ teaspoon salt

1 bag chocolate morsels

Blend white and brown sugar. Cut in shortening and mix well. Sift flour, measure, then add soda and salt. Sift again. Stir flour well into shortening and sugar mixture. Beat egg well and add to sugar, shortening, flour mixture. Add vanilla, then morsels. Have cookie pans well greased and floured. Drop from teaspoon about an inch apart. Bake in moderate oven 350° about 12 minutes. Yield: 36.

MRS. ROBERT CATHCART (Katherine Morrow)

Sugarless Drop Cookies

½ cup shortening	2¼ cups flour, sifted
⅞ cup light corn syrup	2½ teaspoons baking
2 tablespoons honey	powder
1 beaten egg	¼ teaspoon salt

1 teaspoon vanilla

Add honey, egg and syrup to creamed shortening. Mix well. Sift dry ingredients and add to creamed mixture (about a third at a time) mixing well after each addition. Add vanilla and drop from a teaspoon onto a greased baking sheet. Bake about 12 minutes, or until brown, at 400°. Makes 5 dozen. (Variations on next page.)

ORANGE OR LEMON COOKIES: Omit vanilla and add grated rind of 1 orange or lemon to creamed shortening. SPICE FRUIT COOKIES: Sift with dry ingredients: 1 teaspoon cinnamon, ½ teaspoon allspice, ¼ teaspoon cloves or nutmeg. Add ¾ cup raisins to finished batter before baking.

MRS. R. M. ANDERSON (Dorothy Middleton)

Harbor View Apiaries' Honey Bars

1 cup honey	1 cup chopped nuts
3 eggs, well beaten	1 pound chopped dates
1 teaspoon baking powder	1 teaspoon vanilla

1⅓ cups flour

Mix honey and well-beaten eggs together. Add baking powder and flour sifted together, then the chopped nuts, dates and flavoring. Bake in a long flat tin. Mixture should be ¼ inch deep. Cut in strips ½ inch wide and 3 inches long. Before serving, roll in powdered sugar. These are fine for the holidays as they can be made ahead of time and will improve in flavor. Bake at 350° for 15-20 minutes. Yield: 72.

MRS. WILMER THOMPSON (Mary B. McIver)

Sugarless Chocolate Chip Cookies

½ cup butter	1 teaspoon baking powder
½ cup honey	¼ teaspoon salt
1 small egg	½ teaspoon vanilla
1 cup sifted flour	½ cup semi-sweet
¼ cup nut meats, chopped	chocolate chips

Cream butter and honey until light and fluffy. Add egg and beat well. Sift flour, baking powder and salt twice. Add flour mixture to butter mixture; then add vanilla and blend all well. Fold in chocolate chips and nuts. Chill and drop by teaspoonfuls on greased cooky sheet. Bake at 375° for 12 minutes. Yield: 3 dozen.

MRS. WILMER THOMPSON (Mary B. McIver)

ST. MICHAEL'S CHURCH 1752

CANDIES

Unnuh got de sweet toof, enty?
Now there is grape-fruit, crystallized,
And candied orange-peel,
And sugared lemon-rind is found
'Most anywhere you deal.
But you need dry and sunny weather
To manufacture good peach leather.
Also, I've heard, (without negation),
You have to use an incantation!

Benne (Sesame) Brittle

2 cups granulated sugar
1 teaspoon vanilla extract

2 cups parched benne seed
(see p. 356, No. 51 for toasting)

Melt the sugar in a heavy frying pan or saucepan over a low heat, stirring constantly. When sugar is melted, remove from stove and add benne seed and vanilla *quickly*. Pour into a well-buttered pan to about ¼ inch depth (a medium size biscuit pan is right.) Mark into squares while warm and break along lines when cold.

MRS. R. W. ACHURCH (Sue R. Thomas)

Soft Benne (Sesame) Candy

Good now and during "The Running Thread" era.

1 pound light brown sugar
  or ½ pound dark
  brown and ½ pound
  granulated
Pinch of salt

1 cup water
⅓ cup freshly toasted
  benne seed (See p. 356
  No. 51 for toasting)
1 teaspoon butter

Boil sugar and water as if for fudge, testing by beating a little in a saucer. When it is the right consistency, add the butter and a pinch of salt. Beat until it is thick enough to mix in benne seed, and pour on waxed paper. Cut into large squares, as it breaks easily.

MISS KATHERINE DRAYTON MAYRANT SIMONS

Peach or Apricot Leather

"This conserve is a favorite in Charleston. It is usually made with dried peaches, but I prefer apricots."

1 pound dried peaches or   1 cup sugar
    apricots

Wash the peaches or apricots and soak in water overnight. Cover with water (allow room, for they will swell) and boil as they are, until tender. Drain. Then run them through meat chopper, add the sugar, mix well and return to the stove to melt the sugar. Spread the mixture fairly thin on tin cookie sheets. Next you will substitute, as best you can, the conveniences—I have a table with a galvanized iron top and screen frame to cover it. Place sheets on table in hot sunshine and move with the sun. Tin attracts it. When not too dry, sprinkle with graunlated sugar. Cut in strips, roll into little rolls. Then roll in sugar and enjoy.

MISS ELLEN PARKER

Groundnut Cakes

(from Carolina Housewife)
"This is really a candy"

"Formerly these groundnut cakes were sold by our Maumas on street corners or on the Battery on July 4th and other special occasions. The Maumas were picturesque, with their turbaned heads, waving a short fly brush made of dried grasses."

1 quart molasses   1 cup brown sugar
4 cups shelled peanuts   ½ cup butter
    (roasted)

Combine all ingredients, except nuts, and boil for one half hour over a slow fire. Then add the roasted and shelled peanuts and continue cooking for fifteen minutes. Drop on lightly greased cookie sheets, or on a piece of marble. Make little cakes of the candy and let harden. For peanuts you may substitute benne seed.

MISS ELLEN PARKER

Peanut Brittle

From "De Bonnes Choses à Manger"

3 cups sugar	Small piece paraffin
3 teaspoons soda	1 cup corn syrup (light)
⅔ cup vinegar	⅔ cup water

1 quart raw peanuts

Mix sugar, water, syrup and vinegar. Add raw peanuts and paraffin. Boil until brown and peanuts pop or until it is very brittle in water. Take from fire, add soda. Stir well and pour on buttered slab. When cold, break into pieces.

MRS. DANIEL RAVENEL (Ruth Howe)

Khandova

2 cups granulated sugar	1 heaping tablespoon
2 tablespoons cornstarch	butter
½ cup milk	12 English walnuts
1 heaping tablespoon	(chopped)
coconut	18 large chopped raisins

Mix sugar and cornstarch and moisten with milk. Cook to soft ball stage. Add other ingredients and cook a minute. Take from fire and beat until cool, then knead smooth and form into balls. Roll in granulated sugar.

MRS. JOHN M. MITCHELL (St. Clair Thomlinson)

To Crystallize Grapefruit

Clean grapefruit skins and cut in strips. Cover with salted water (1 pint of water to each tablespoon of salt). Let boil 20 minutes. Drain off this water and cover with fresh water (do not measure) and boil 20 minutes. Do this again with fresh water. Drain off the third water and for every whole grapefruit use 1 cup granulated sugar. Let simmer until all the sugar is taken up and skins are clear. Roll in dry sugar and put in sun or heated oven (which has been turned out) to dry.

MRS. HENRY ELLERBE (Margaret Lucas)

Scotch Toffee

2 cups sugar
2 cups nuts
2 large cakes bitter
chocolate
¾ pound *creamery* butter

Put sugar and butter in heavy saucepan over fire; when butter has melted, add 1 cup chopped nuts, folding mixture constantly with wooden spoon, on low heat for 20 to 25 minutes; this should become very thick. Pour on cookie tin that has been placed on top of four wide magazines. Use spatula to spread as thin as possible. When cool it should be brittle. Turn candy completely over with spatula. Spread half of melted chocolate over this and cover with ½ cup finely chopped nuts and press in. Turn this again and spread remaining chocolate and cover with nuts.

MRS. M. BISHOP ALEXANDER (Ferdinand Williams)

To Glaze Nuts

1 cup sugar
½ cup of water
⅓ cup light corn syrup

If almonds or pistachio nuts are to be used, they should be blanched and the almonds should be delicately browned in the oven. Freshen other nuts in the same way if necessary.

Cook the sugar, corn syrup and water, stirring until the sugar is dissolved. Continue cooking without stirring until 300°F. temperature is reached. As sugar crystals form on the sides of the pan, they must be wiped away with a wet cloth. The cooking should be done in a small saucepan, and the latter part of the cooking done over a low flame, so that the syrup will not discolor. The proper shade is a delicate straw color. When the syrup is done, remove from the flame and set into boiling water to prevent hardening. Stir the syrup as little as possible when dipping nuts to prevent crystallization. When the syrup becomes too thick for dipping, it can be reheated but care must be taken that it does not brown.

MISS JULIA M. REES

Homemade Fruit Candy

"One Christmas of my childhood in Summerville we were unable to get Ladevese's Fruit Bars. My Mother did not like chocolate, which was all the Christmas candy we had, and I made this in a hurry and by ear for her. I like it better than the bought bars because the sugar foundation is soft and not of the groundnut-cake hardness of the bars sold in shops."

1 pound dark brown sugar	1 cup granulated sugar
2 cups of chopped and mixed	Water
nuts, raisins, citron,	
dried figs (and cherries,	
if you like)	

Cut fruit and nuts very small, as if for black fruit cake. Almonds, pecans, walnuts may be used (not peanuts). Mix them well with the different kinds of fruit. Cover sugar with water and boil until ready to be beaten to fudge-like consistency. Do not beat too long, as this quantity of nuts and fruit will cool and harden quickly. Add nuts and fruit and pour on waxed paper, making it as thick as mixture allows. Cut into bars of what ever size desired and wrap in waxed paper as soon as cool.

MISS KATHERINE DRAYTON MAYRANT SIMONS

The Piper of Hamlin blew tunes that were dandy
And lured all the children as slick as you please,—
But he was a piker compared to the candy-
Confectioner, Charleston's beloved Ladeveze!
Three generations, with jump, skip and hop,
Sped, clutching their pennies, to Ladeveze' shop!

Mrs. Pierre Stoney's Mint Drops

"These mints are similar to those which were made and sold by Ladeveze. They are delicate enough for very small children."

1 pound fine granulated sugar	6 drops oil of peppermint
6 tablespoons cold water	Little over ½ teaspoon cream of tartar

Put sugar in a porcelain saucepan with the cold water—first laying aside 3 spoonfuls of the sugar in a bowl to which add enough water to moisten (2 - 3 teaspoonsfuls—this is not part of the water measure above) also the cream of tartar and the mint. Mix sugar and water in saucepan and set to boil. Let it boil 3 minutes, then stir in the mixture from the bowl and stir until it gets thick and white, like icing. Drop quickly by teaspoon on marble slab and leave until pretty hard. You can then easily slip them off with your fingers.

MRS. ARTHUR J. STONEY (Anne Montague)

Good Mint Drops

2¼ cups sugar	2 egg whites
½ cup water	10 drops mint extract
¼ teaspoon cream of tartar	

Boil sugar and water until it threads. Pour onto stiffly beaten egg whites and beat with cream of tartar until stiff enough to drop from a spoon. Add mint. Use two teaspoons together and drop onto buttered marble slab or dish.

MRS. LIONEL K. LEGGE (Dorothy Porcher)

Cream Candy

1 quart of sugar	½ teaspoon of vanilla or
1 teaspoon butter (level)	few drops mint extract
½ pint of milk	

Cook all ingredients together until syrup will form a soft ball when dropped in cold water. Pour on buttered plates and pull with floured fingers. When the mixture begins to harden, pull in strips the size of little finger and cut with scissors into inch lengths.

MISS JULIA M. REES

Super Fudge

1 cup creamy milk	2½ cups sugar
4 squares bitter chocolate	1 teaspoon vanilla
Dash salt	1 cup pecans

Small lump of butter

Blend chocolate and milk together over low heat. When melted, beat with egg beater. Add sugar and salt and beat with egg beater over a low heat until mixture starts to boil. Remove beater and *do not touch* after the boiling begins. Cook until mixture is thick and makes a very firm ball when dropped in cold water. Remove from heat and place pan in cold water and allow to cool. Add butter. When candy is cool add vanilla and beat with a wooden spoon until it is creamy. Add nuts and pour into a slightly greased pan. (This fudge takes more time and care but the extra beating adds to its velvety smoothness.)

MRS. W. T. HARTMAN (Betty Blaydes)

Vanilla Fudge

A boon to those allergic to chocolate.

2 cups granulated sugar	¼ teaspoon salt
4 tablespoons light corn syrup	1 cup milk
	⅔ cup cream

1 teaspoon vanilla

Place sugar, cream, milk, syrup and salt in saucepan. Cook slowly, stirring constantly until mixture boils. Continue cooking, stirring occasionally, until soft-ball stage is reached. Cool and add vanilla. Beat until mixture thickens and loses its gloss. Pour into greased pan and when cool cut in squares.

MRS. JOHN M. MITCHELL (St. Clair Thomlinson)

Divinity Fudge

3 cups brown sugar   ¾ cup corn syrup (white)
  (dissolved in one cup   2 stiffly beaten egg whites
  of boiling water)   1 teaspoon vinegar
1 cup chopped walnuts

Let sugar, water and syrup cook slowly until it strings. Pour on egg whites, to which the vinegar has been added. Beat until it is stiff enough to stand when dropped on a dish, add nuts and pour out.

MRS. JOHN C. SIMONDS (Frances Rees)

Walnut Fudge

3 cups granulated sugar   1 cup of walnuts
1 cup sweet milk   (chopped)
Butter the size of an egg

Put 2 cups of sugar, milk and butter over the fire and let this mixture come to a boil. Put the other cup of sugar into a saucepan and set over the fire and stir constantly. When melted and a rich brown color, slowly pour the first mixture, while boiling, into it, beating all the time. Cook to the soft-ball stage. Remove from fire and beat, then add nuts. Pour out and mark into squares.

MISS VIRGINIA MITCHELL

Peanut Butter Fudge Dreams

1 cup white sugar   1 cup brown sugar
2 tablespoons butter   1 cup marshmallows
¼ pound peanut butter   1 cup milk
1 teaspoon vanilla   Few grains salt

Cook sugar, milk and salt to the soft-ball stage. Add marshmallows, peanut butter and butter, just before removing from the stove. Cool, add vanilla and beat, then pour into a buttered pan.

MRS. JOHN M. MITCHELL (St. Clair Thomlinson)

Chocolate Roll

1 cup nuts   1 cup seedless raisins

¼ pound dipping chocolate   2 tablespoons milk

16 marshmallows   Few drops peppermint

Melt marshmallows in milk over hot water. Stir until creamy, then stir in the melted chocolate, seedless raisins, nuts, and peppermint. Form into roll, cool and slice.

Mrs. M. L. McCrae (Ena Mae Black)

Sticky Chocolate Caramels

½ pound bitter chocolate   ½ pound of butter

2 pounds brown sugar   2 teaspoons vanilla

Enough milk or water to moisten

Put all ingredients, except vanilla, in pot. Boil, stirring constantly. Test by dropping a little from spoon on marble slab. When it is chewy, remove from fire; add vanilla and pour on well buttered marble slab. Cut in squares.

Mrs. E. K. Pritchard (Julia Myers)

Martha Washington Candy

½ pound confectioners sugar   ½ teaspoon hot water

⅛ pound butter   ½ teaspoon vanilla

3-4 squares bitter chocolate

Combine ingredients and knead until mixture can be rolled out. Form into balls and dip in melted bitter chocolate.

Miss Virginia Mitchell

319

Nut Patties

1 cup sugar	⅛ teaspoon of salt
¼ cup light corn syrup	½ cup brown sugar
2 tablespoons of butter	⅓ cup of water

1½ cups of nut meats

Cook sugar, corn syrup, and water together, stirring until sugar is dissolved. Continue cooking, stirring enough to prevent scorching, until the temperature of 300°F. is reached. Remove from fire, add salt, butter, and nut meats, stir only enough to mix well. (If much stirring is done it will sugar the brittle). It is desirable to have the nut meats warm before adding so that the candy will not harden before it can be put in the pans. Set in a pan of hot water and, with a large spoon dip out the candy and drop into lightly buttered patty tins, making the candy about one-fourth inch thick. When thoroughly cold, invert the tins, and tap with knife handle to loosen the patties. It is customary to use unbroken nuts, A mixture of different nuts is good.

MRS. JOHN C. SIMONDS (Frances Rees)

Soft Pop-Corn Balls

½ cup sugar	1½ quarts of popped corn
2 tablespoons light corn syrup	½ cup brown sugar
	⅓ cup of water
½ tablespoon butter	½ teaspoon salt

Cook the sugars, syrup, and water, stirring until the sugar is dissolved. Continue cooking, without stirring, until a temperature of 240°F. is reached. Add the butter and stir only enough to mix it through the candy. Have the pop-corn in a large bowl so that when the syrup is added, there will be enough room for thorough mixing. Pour the cooked syrup slowly on the salted pop-corn. Mix well and form into balls with the hands, using as little pressure as possible. These balls are rather soft; if firmer balls are desired, cook syrup to 242°F.

MRS. JOHN C. SIMONDS (Frances Rees)

Pecan Pralines

4 cups granulated sugar   5 cups chopped pecans
1 cup light cream   1 teaspoon salt

Boil 3 cups of sugar with cream until it forms a soft ball. Meanwhile, caramelize the remaining cup of sugar in an iron skillet. Combine boiled sugar and cream with the caramelized sugar, being sure the pot is very large as the caramelized sugar foams a great deal when added to the cream and sugar. Add salt and nuts and beat vigorously until creamy. Drop by spoonfuls on buttered paper.

MRS. CARLTON G. DAVIES (Harriet Goodacre)

Fondant

1 egg white   2 squares unsweetened
2 tablespoons cold water   chocolate (melted)
3½ cups sifted confectioners   1 teaspoon vanilla
    sugar (about)   Walnut meats

Beat egg white slightly and add water, chocolate, vanilla and enough sugar to make fondant shape. Roll into small balls, flatten and put half of a walnut on each.

MRS. JOHN M. MITCHELL (St. Clair Thomlinson)

Coconut Bars

2 cups granulated sugar   ¼ pound shredded
½ teaspoon cream of tartar   coconut
                ½ cup water

Mix sugar, cream of tartar and water; put this mixture over the fire and stir until it comes to a boil, then stop stirring and cook until it forms a ball when dropped into water. Take from the fire and beat until it whitens, then add the shredded coconut and continue beating until it becomes thick. Pour into buttered pan and when cool cut into bars.

MRS. HAROLD G. DOTTERER (Harriet Lipscomb)

Mrs. Rees' Nougat

1 cup sugar	½ cup water
½ cup strained honey	3 tablespoons light corn
2 egg whites	syrup
½ cup pistachio nuts	2½ cups almonds

1 teaspoon vanilla

Blanch the almonds and pistachio nuts and shred coarsely. Brown almonds in a slow oven. Cook the sugar, water and ½ of the corn syrup together, stirring until the sugar is dissolved. Continue cooking to the temperature 290°F. Remove from the fire. During the last few minutes of cooking the syrup, beat the egg whites until stiff. Add the hot syrup gradually to the egg whites, beating all the while. While adding the first syrup to the egg whites, begin cooking the honey and remainder of the corn syrup together. Continue cooking until 290°F. is reached. Remove from the fire and add at once to the egg white mixture, pouring it in gradually and beating continuously. Add nuts and cook over hot water until the mixture dries, stirring while cooking. Test the candy by taking a small amount out in a spoon. When it holds its shape when cold, and is not sticky to the touch, it is done. Add vanilla, pour into pans which have been lined with nougat wafers (gold-fish food), cover with wafers. Place a smooth pan or board on this, with a heavy weight upon it. Let stand for twelve hours or longer. Cut in pieces and wrap in waxed paper.

Mrs. John C. Simonds (Frances Rees)

Coconut Drops

1¾ pounds sugar	1 grated coconut
1½ gills water (¾ cup)	Few drops rose water

Put the sugar and water on the fire to boil and when the syrup becomes sugary, add the coconut and cook until it bubbles and the grease boils out. Take off fire and flavor with the rose water and drop on greased pan.

Mrs. Harold G. Dotterer (Harriet Lipscomb)

JULY IN CHARLESTON

PICKLES & RELISHES

People ain' fuh know groun' artichoke good fuh mek pickle; 'stead dey gib um tuh de pig!

Almost too numerous to choose
Are condiments that people use
To titillate or prickle;
But Charleston views the rest with calm
And firmly sticks to heart-of-palm
The tart palmetto pickle.

(Agate or enameled ware should be used in making pickles.)

(Monosodium glutamate added to any food, except sweets and egg dishes, improves the flavor.)

Pickle making is the time for experimenting. You may use any vegetable you like and add to any sauce you like. Vary the seasonings to your taste—i.e. more mustard, hot peppers, etc. Be sure not to overcook—five to ten minutes is enough for most vegetables.

Palmetto (Heart of Palm) Pickle

4 quarts heart of palm
½ gallon vinegar
1 ounce celery seed
1 ounce mustard seed
1¼ ounces powdered
    mustard

1½ pounds sugar
1 lemon (juice)
2 tablespoons turmeric
1½ cups flour
Red pepper (to taste)

Trim the heart of the palmetto palm until you reach the tender white part. (The upper portion is white and tender and usually used for pickle; however the lower portion, though bitter to taste, may be used also.) Cut the tender white portion into small pieces. Soak in salted water (two tablespoons salt to one quart of water) for two days. Drain. Wash well. Drain again. Mix all other ingredients and boil slowly for ten minutes. Add heart of palm and heat through. Put in sterilized jars and seal while hot. Yield: 8 pints. (Jerusalem artichokes could be subsituted.)

Mrs. E. M. Seabrook (Fannie Lee Anderson)

Plain Whole Artichoke Pickles

1 peck Jerusalem artichokes	1 cup salt
1 gallon vinegar	String of hot peppers or
1 pound white sugar	bell peppers

1 ounce whole black peppers

Wash and clean artichokes. Soak overnight in salt water. Dry with a cloth. Fill jars, adding a hot pepper or a ring of bell pepper. Boil other ingredients for 5 minutes, then cover the artichokes with this mixture and seal while hot. Yield: 8 quarts.

MRS. MARY H. BAILEY (Mary Huguenin)

Chopped Artichoke Pickle

3 quarts Jerusalem artichokes	*For sauce:*
1 quart onions	1 cup flour
1 large cauliflower	6 tablespoons dry mustard
6 green peppers	1 tablespoon turmeric
1 gallon water	2 quarts vinegar
1 pint salt	4 cups sugar

Slice or chop artichokes and onions. Cut peppers fine and break cauliflower into flowerets. Mix all together and cover with salt and water. Let stand twenty-four hours. Pour into colander and drain well. Mix all dry ingredients for sauce and add enough vinegar to make a paste. Heat rest of vinegar and pour over mustard mixture. Return to stove and boil until it thickens, stirring constantly. Add vegetables, bring to boil and seal in jars while hot. Yield: 8-10 pints.

MRS. EDWARD M. ROYALL (Harriet Maybank)

Whole Artichoke Pickles

1 peck Jerusalem (root) artichokes	2 teaspoons turmeric
1 cup olive or cooking oil	3 pounds sugar
1 package mustard seed	1 gallon cider vinegar
1 package celery seed	1 or 2 red pepper pods
	½ pound powdered mustard
2 tablespoons whole black peppercorns	

Scrub artichokes with a wire brush, cutting off any soft spots. Soak in strong brine for three days. Rub dry with a rough cloth. Pack in sterile jars. Sauce: Mix oil and mustard thoroughly. Add vinegar by degrees until half is used. Mix in sugar and when dissolved add rest of ingredients. Bring to a boil, and pour immediately on artichokes and seal. Let stand 6 weeks before using.

Mrs. McIver Wilbur (Susan Prioleau Wilbur)

Great Grandmother's Whole Artichoke Pickle

"This receipt has long been a family favorite."

1 peck Jerusalem artichokes	1 small lump alum
1 gallon vinegar	2 tablespoons celery seed
1 cup brown sugar	2 tablespoons allspice
1 cup powdered mustard	2 tablespoons cloves
	4 tablespoons mustard seed

Wash and scrape artichokes and let them stand over night in water to which salt has been added (1 tablespoon to each quart). Drain. Soak for a day in water to which the alum has been added. Rinse well. Soak mustard seed in small amount of vinegar. Boil rest of vinegar and spices a few minutes. Let cool; add mustard and mustard seed. Put artichokes in a crock and add liquid mixture. Let stand at least a week before using. Dip artichokes out as desired. When supply is exhausted, more artichokes may be added to same liquid.

Mrs. Louis T. Parker (Josephine Walker)

Pickled Okra

2 pounds okra (approx.)
2 cups white vinegar
1 cup water
1 tablespoon sugar
2 tablespoons salt
Green food coloring (if
    desired)

Dill weed
Hot peppers
Garlic buds
Onion slices
Powdered mustard
Tumeric

Use small fresh okra. Wash, drain, and pack tightly in jars, stem end down for 1 row and stem end up for another. To each jar add seasonings to your taste such as ½ teaspoon dill weed, 2 slices hot pepper, garlic bud, onion slice, powdered mustard, and/or tumeric. Boil for 3 minutes vinegar, water, salt, and sugar. Food coloring may be added. Fill jars and seal while hot.

MRS. JAMES M. HAGOOD (Louisa Taber)

Cabbage Pickle

6 pounds hard cabbage
4 quarts green peppers
    (about 1 dozen)
3 quarts white onions
1 cup salt
1½ quarts cider vinegar

1 cup water
5 cups sugar
2 ounces pickling spice
    (put in cloth bag)
1½ tablespoons celery seed
1 teaspoon turmeric

Cut vegetables fine, sprinkle with the salt and let stand over night. In the morning, drain off all water. Add 1 cup water to vinegar. Let all ingredients come to a boil, pour over vegetables and cook for 25 minutes (about) after it starts boiling. Pour into sterilized jars and seal. Yield: 8-10 pints.

MRS. THOMAS P. STONEY (Beverly DuBose)

Mrs. Robinson's Bread and Butter Pickles

1 gallon cucumbers (small)
2 green peppers
8 small white onions
½ cup salt

Pickling syrup:
5 cups sugar
1½ teaspoons turmeric
½ teaspoon ground cloves
1 teaspoon celery seed
2 tablespoons mustard seed
5 cups vinegar

Select crisp, fresh cucumbers. Wash, but do not pare. Slice cucumbers and onions paper thin and cut peppers into fine shreds. Mix salt with the vegetables and bury pieces of cracked ice in the mixture. Cover with weighted lid and let stand for three hours. Drain thoroughly. Mix dry ingredients with vinegar and pour over vegetables. Place over low heat and paddle occasionally, using a wooden spoon. Heat the mixture to scalding, but do not boil. Pour into hot jars and seal. Yield: 7 pints.

Mrs. J. M. Rivers (Martha Robinson)

Pickled Onions

5 medium onions
1 cup salt
2 quarts water

12 whole black peppers
1 small clove garlic
(optional)

White vinegar (about 1 cup)

Peel and slice onions paper thin. Dissolve salt in water and soak onions one hour. Remove to colander and wash well. Add black peppers. Put in quart jar and cover with vinegar. Add garlic, if desired. Excellent for green salads and easy on the digestion.

Mrs. James M. Hagood (Louise Taber)

Cranberry Sauce

1 pound cranberries   2 cups sugar

Wash and remove over-ripe berries. Drain thoroughly, and put in saucepan. Water adhering to berries is all that is needed. Add sugar and cook over low flame. Cook 8 minutes after boiling begins. Cover and remove from fire. Do not remove cover for at least 20 minutes. Yield: 2 pints.

MRS. DAVID MAYBANK (Marion Taber)

Cranberry Sauce

UNCOOKED

2 cups cranberries   1 large orange

1 cup sugar

Quarter orange; remove seed and core. Put all fruit through meat grinder. Add sugar. Let stand in refrigerator for a day or two.

MRS. J. WALKER COLEMAN (Felicia Chisolm)

Spiced Grapes

8 pounds grapes   4 sticks cinnamon
4 pounds sugar   1 ounce whole cloves
3 cups vinegar   2 blades mace

Remove and set aside skins of grapes. Cook pulp in vinegar with spices tied in cheese cloth until grapes are soft. Mash through fine sieve, keeping out seeds. Add skins. Bring to a boil and add sugar, bag of spices. Cook until thick. Put into glasses and seal. Delicious with venison.

MRS. LAWRENCE LUCAS (Nell Hall)

Spiced Red Tomatoes

8 pounds ripe tomatoes 4 pounds sugar
1 pint vinegar   2 tablespoons powdered
            allspice
1 tablespoon powdered cloves

Weigh tomatoes after peeling and then crush. Boil all ingredients until thick—not watery. (Thickens more when cold.) Seal in jars while hot.

Mrs. Henry Clay Robertson, Jr. (Elizabeth Lebby)

Red Pepper Jam

1 dozen red peppers   1½ pounds sugar
1 pint vinegar   1 tablespoon salt

Chop peppers fine, and sprinkle with salt. Let stand three or four hours. Rinse well, then cover with sugar and vinegar. Boil slowly until thick, stirring often to prevent sticking. Makes four or five glasses. Delicious served with cream cheese and crackers.

Mrs. Johnson Hagood (Jean Small)

Pepper Relish

12 red peppers   1 pint vinegar
12 green peppers   2 cups sugar
12 medium size onions 3 tablespoons salt

Run peppers and onions through meat chopper. Cover with boiling water and let stand for five minutes. Drain and add vinegar, sugar, and salt. Boil for five minutes. Put in jars and seal.

Mrs. W. T. Hartman (Betty Blaydes)

Pepper Jelly

1 quart bell peppers 14 cups sugar
 (Seeded)   Red, green or yellow food
1 cup hot peppers   coloring
1½ quarts vinegar   2½ cups certo

Grind peppers in blender with small amount of vinegar. Add vinegar, sugar, and food coloring. Boil 5-10 minutes. Add 2½ cups certo. Boil 1 minute. Seal in jelly jars with parafin. Serve with crackers and cream cheese.

Mrs. James M. Hagood (Louisa Taber)

Slann's Island "Legaré Sauce"

1 (No. 2½) can tomatoes
1 quart onions, cut fine
1 clove garlic, cut fine
1 nutmeg, grated
8 tablespoons salt
1 ounce celery seed

1 ounce white mustard seed
1 ounce cloves
1 ounce allspice
2 pounds light brown sugar
2 tablespoons curry powder
2 quarts vinegar

Put all ingredients into an agate vessel and boil on a slow fire until tomatoes are pulp. Pour through a strainer and bottle. Delicious with meat or fish.

MRS. ERNEST W. KING (Isabel Simmons)

Chili Sauce

2 pecks tomatoes
18 green peppers
3 pints vinegar
8 tablespoons salt
9 tablespoons sugar

2 teaspoons mustard
2 teaspoons celery seed
1 teaspoon allspice
18 cloves
1 tablespoon mace

Pinch of cayenne pepper

Scald tomatoes and add all other ingredients. Boil steadily for 2 hours. Put into clean hot jars and seal at once.

MISS MARGARET WALKER

Mustard

2 ounces powdered
mustard
1 tablespoon sugar
2 tablespoons vinegar

½ teaspoon Worcestershire
1 teaspoon salt
1 tablespoon olive oil
Few drops hot sauce

Blend mustard, sugar and salt. Add vinegar and remaining ingredients. Mix well, making a smooth paste.

MRS. MARY H. BAILEY (Mary Huguenin)

Green Tomato Pickle

1 peck green tomatoes
2 quarts onions
2 quarts vinegar
½ tablespoon cayenne
   pepper
1 tablespoon dry mustard
1 teaspoon turmeric

2 pounds brown sugar
½ pound white mustard
   seed
½ ounce ground mace
1 tablespoon celery seed
1 tablespoon ground cloves
½ cup olive oil

Slice tomatoes and onions very thin. Place on large platters and sprinkle with salt. Let stand overnight. Drain through collander. Add one quart vinegar to vegetables and boil slowly until tender and clear. Drain. Mix sugar, mustard seed, celery seed and cloves with vinegar and boil five minutes. Mix drained vegetables with cayenne pepper, mustard and turmeric and add to vinegar mixture. Mix well, add olive oil, and seal in jars. Yield: 8 quarts.

MRS. EDMUND RHETT HEYWARD (Sarah Boykin)

Sweet Green Tomato Pickle

½ peck green tomatoes
   (20)
2 stalks celery
10 green peppers
24 large white onions
2 large cabbages
1 cup salt

3½ quarts white vinegar
8 pounds brown sugar
3 tablespoons whole cloves
16 tablespoons mustard
2 teaspoons cinnamon
½ teaspoon red pepper
8 tablespoons ginger

Pare tomatoes and chop fine; cut stem from green peppers, remove seeds and chop fine, shred the cabbage, chop onions and celery fine.

Mix ingredients. Add salt and let stand overnight. Drain. Make a syrup of vinegar, brown sugar and spices. Scald the syrup, add the chopped mixture and simmer, after it has been brought to boiling, for forty minutes. Yield: 8 pints.

MRS. LOUIS Y. DAWSON, JR. (Virginia Walker)

Chow-Chow

"Long have gourmets desired this receipt and now we think it's 'High Time to Tell It' ".

4 quarts green tomatoes	*For dressing:*
2 quarts small white onions	2 quarts vinegar
12 green peppers (sweet)	5 tablespoons ground
Several small hot red peppers	mustard
(according to taste)	5 tablespoons turmeric
6 red peppers (sweet)	6 tablespoons flour
1 head cauliflower	5 cups granulated sugar
Water	1 tablespoon celery seed
2 cups salt	1 tablespoon mustard seed
1 bottle of little sour gherkins	1 pint water

Cut up vegetables; cover with water and salt and let stand over night. Next morning boil three minutes and drain for quite a while. Combine all ingredients for dressing. Boil until creamy, pour over pickles and add gherkins. Yield: 8 quarts.

MISS ALVES LONG

Green Tomato Chow-Chow

1 head hard cabbage	4 tablespoons flour
1 quart onions	3 tablespoons ground
1 quart bell peppers	mustard
1 gallon green tomatoes	2 tablespoons white mustard
2 quarts vinegar	seed
¾ cup salt	1 tablespoon celery seed
2 tablespoons turmeric	3 cups sugar

Chop vegetables fine. Sprinkle with salt and let stand over night. Drain. Mix turmeric, flour and mustard with enough water to make smooth paste. Let vinegar come to boil and add mixture. Add all other ingredients including vegetables. Boil 10 minutes. Seal in jars while hot. Yield: 12 pints.

MRS. WILLIAM BARNWELL (Mary Royall)

Iced Green Tomato Pickles

(From Mt. Pleasant's Famous Recipes)

7 pounds green tomatoes	1 teaspoon ground cloves
2 gallons water	1 teaspoon ginger
3 cups powdered lime	1 teaspoon allspice
5 pounds sugar	1 teaspoon celery seed
3 pints vinegar	1 teaspoon mace
1 teaspoon cinnamon	

Soak sliced tomatoes in lime water 24 hours. Drain. Soak in fresh water for 4 hours, changing water every half hour. Drain well. Make a syrup of sugar and vinegar and add spices. Bring syrup to a boil and pour over tomatoes. Let stand overnight. Next morning boil for an hour or until tomatoes are clear. Add several drops of green vegetable coloring to the liquid. Seal in jars while hot. Yield: 8 pints. (Use plain yard lime.)

MRS. JOHN GRAY (Esther Gregorie)

Crisp Watermelon Rind Pickle

1 watermelon rind	1 ounce stick cinnamon
1 quart vinegar	1 ounce whole cloves
5 pounds sugar	1 vial lime

Prepare rind by removing all red and green. Cut in squares. Soak over night in water to which lime has been added. Drain, but do not wash. Cover with water and cook two hours. Drain again and cook slowly for 1 hour in syrup made of remaining ingredients. Syrup should cover rind. Seal in jars while hot. (Lime available at drug stores).

MRS. FRANCIS C. FORD, JR. (Elizabeth Coker)

Sweet Pickled Watermelon

1 watermelon rind
4 cups vinegar
8 pounds sugar

4 tablespoons whole cloves
4 tablespoons cinnamon
   sticks

Cut skin from watermelon; cut rind into small pieces about 2 inches square. After cutting melon, soak in 1 cup salt and enough water to cover for 12 to 15 hours, then pour off and boil in fresh water. Boil sugar and vinegar 10 minutes. Add spices tied in bag. Simmer until syrupy, about two hours. Add melon and simmer 1 hour. Fill jars and seal. Yield: 12 pints.

Mrs. A. Kinloch McDowell (Annie Bissell)

Pickled Peaches

2 pounds sugar
2 cups vinegar

2 sticks cinnamon
2 tablespoons whole cloves

4 quarts peaches

Boil sugar, vinegar, and spices for 20 minutes. Drop peeled fruit in a few at a time, and cook until tender. Pack in hot sterilized jars, adding syrup to ½ inch of the top; seal. Yield: 4 quarts.

Mrs. R. C. Stoney (Adela Holmes)

Sweet Pickled Figs

5 quarts ripe figs
Alum (size of pigeon egg)
Water (to cover)

1 pint apple vinegar
1 pound sugar
1 tablespoon cloves

Leave stems on figs. Let stand overnight in 2 quarts water and 2 tablespoons salt. Dry carefully, bring to boil in alum water. Wash thoroughly in several waters. Lift out and dry on towel. Add spices and sugar to vingear and bring to a good boil. After five minutes add figs and boil three minutes. Remove from fire and pack in jars.

Mrs. Thomas B. Bennett (Margaret R. Fraser)

Mrs. Mayberry's Chutney

12 green tart apples	1 pound brown sugar
12 large green tomatoes, or	2 tablespoons salt
24 small green tomatoes	½ teaspoon red pepper
4 onions (sliced thin)	1½ tablespoons curry
1 pound seeded raisins	powder
1 quart vinegar	2 tablespoons pickling spice

Core and chop apples and tomatoes. Tie pickling spice in bag. Add other ingredients. Boil about twenty minutes, or until apples look transparent. Take out fruit and let syrup boil until it thickens. Pack in jars and seal while hot. Yield: approximately 12 pints.

MRS. FRANCIS McINTIRE (Emmie Mayberry)

Chutney

4 pounds mangoes or hard green peaches (pears could be used)	1 pound preserved ginger, in syrup
2 tablespoons white mustard seed	2 pounds sugar
	2 quarts vinegar
1 tablespoon ground dried chile pepper	1½ cups raisins
	1 clove garlic

Peel and cut fruit, and add one quart vinegar. Boil for 20 minutes. Combine sugar and second quart of vinegar and boil until it is a thick syrup. Pour off most of the liquid from the fruit and add to this syrup. Boil this combination until it is thick. Combine this thick syrup with the rest of the ingredients and fruit except the ginger, and cook thirty minutes. Add chopped ginger and its syrup and cook ten minutes longer. Bottle. The flavor is improved if it is placed in the sun for several days. This India Chutney is almost identical with a very famous brand of chutney. Yield: 5-6 pints.

MRS. ADRIAN R. MARRON (Polly Ficken)

Pompion (Pumpkin) Chips

1 firm, medium-size,   1 dozen lemons
    dry pumpkin   1 cup sugar to each
                            2 cups chips

Peel pumpkin and cut into thin pieces, one-half inch square. Add sugar and the lemon juice (save the skins). Let stand overnight. Boil until the chips look clear and transparent. Take chips out and boil syrup until it thickens a little. Cut up lemon skins and boil separately until soft. Add the chips and lemon skins to the thickened syrup and bring to a boil. Place in jars and seal. Yield: 6-8 pints.

Mrs. Philip G. Porcher, Sr. (Mary Cordes)

Three Fruit Marmalade

1 grapefruit   1 lemon
1 orange   Sugar

Cold water

Grate lightly the rind of each whole fruit. Cut rind in very thin narrow pieces and chop pulp, except center. Keep this center and the seeds of all fruit separate and tie in a cloth bag. Measure the mixture of pulp and rind and add three times the amount of cold water. Let stand overnight and next day boil rapidly for thirty minutes. Boil with bag of seed, remove seed after boiling, weigh and add its equal weight of granulated sugar. Let stand several hours, then boil rapidly, stirring constantly. Test frequently until it jells. Put in glasses or jars and seal while hot.

Miss Louisa B. Poppenheim

Fig Preserves

2 quarts firm figs
4 pounds sugar
1½ cups water

2 lemons, sliced
1 ounce stick cinnamon
24 cloves

Wash fruit carefully in colander. Let sugar and water come to a boil. Add lemons and figs, and spices tied in a bag. Boil slowly until figs are tender and clear, about one hour. Lift fruit carefully into sterilized jars and cover with juice. Seal while hot. Yield: 3 pints.

MRS. JOHN WELCH (Julie Pringle)

Pear Chips

8 pounds pears, after peeling
   and slicing
7 pounds sugar

1¼ ounces root ginger
   (whole)
2 lemons
3 oranges

1 pint water

Grind oranges and lemons, using all except seeds. Dissolve sugar in water; add all ingredients and cook until pears are clear and syrup thickens. Seal in jars while hot. Delicious on ice cream. Yield: 10 pints.

MRS. LAWRENCE STONEY (Jane Saunders)

Ginger Pears

9 pounds pears
6 pounds sugar

3 ounces crystallized
   ginger

4 lemons

Pare fruit; cut in thin slices after removing core. Mix pears and sugar. Place over low heat in large kettle. Stir until sugar is melted and syrup formed. Simmer until fruit is clear, stirring occasionally. Add grated rind of two lemons and juice of all four. Add ginger cut in small pieces and simmer until thick. Put in sterilized jelly glasses and cover with paraffin, or seal in sterilized pint jars, while hot. Approximate yield: 18 jelly glasses.

MRS. JOHN LAURENS (May Rose)

PHOEBE PASSES MY GATE

SHORT CUTS

W'en you ain' got time fuh tarry, bus' open a can!
The soup is served, the candles lit,
The family prepares to sit,
When suddenly three guests arrive;
(Which makes you eight. You've chops for five!)
Don't blench with fear or flush with rage;
Turn swiftly to the proper page;
Select a quick receipt to serve
And dish it up with joy and verve!

SHORT CUT RECEIPTS

c = cup   T = tablespoon   t = teaspoon   lb. = pound

CLARET PUNCH—Combine equal amounts of domestic claret and dry ginger ale. Serve very cold.

> Mrs. John Bennett (Susan Smythe)

TEEN AGE PUNCH—Combine equal amounts of grape juice and ginger ale. Pour over a large lump of ice in punch bowl and serve.

> Mrs. David Maybank (Marion Taber)

CHEESE STRAWS—To a package of pie crust mix add 1 c. grated cheese, ½ to 1 t. red pepper, blend thoroughly and add amount of water called for on pie crust package. Roll dough thin and cut in strips. Bake for eight minutes in a hot oven (450°).

> Mrs. Frank B. Gilbreth, Jr. (Elizabeth Cauthen)

CINNAMON WHEELS—Make pastry from pie crust mix. Roll dough thin, sprinkle with two T. cinnamon and spread generously with soft butter and 1½ T. of sugar. Roll up and cut in 1″ sections. Dot top of each with butter. Bake 8-10 min. in a hot oven (450°).

> Mrs. Frank B. Gilbreth, Jr. (Elizabeth Cauthen)

HORS-D'OEUVRE BISCUIT—Mix pastry from one package of pie crust mix. Roll in small balls and press each with bottom of a jigger glass to make a depression. Bake in hot oven. Fill with caviar, anchovy paste or if a sweet is desired, marmalade or jelly.

> Mrs. Arthur J. Stoney (Anne Montague)

CHEESE BISCUIT—Blend one package of pie crust mix (dry) with one jar of sharp cocktail cheese and ½ t. of red pepper. Roll thin and cut with small biscuit cutter. Press ½ nut on each. Bake in hot oven until golden brown. Yield: 36.

Mrs. Robert W. Achurch (Sue Thomas)

BENNE WAFERS—Prepare pie crust mix as directed on package, add 1 c. parched benne seed. Roll thin and cut in rounds. Bake in hot oven and salt while hot. Yield: several dozen.

Mrs. Bohun B. Kinloch (Betty Austin)

CRAB SOUP—Combine 2 cans of cream of celery soup, equal amount of milk, 1 lb. of crab meat, salt, pepper and a pinch of mace. Heat and add sherry to taste. Serves 6-8.

Mrs. J. Walker Coleman (Felicia Chisolm)

BORSCH—Save all juice from 2 bunches boiled beets; add an equal amount of canned consommé. Simmer for half hour; add 1 t. vinegar and a few pieces of beets cut small. Add sherry to taste and serve topped with a daub of sour cream. Serves 4.

Mrs. Charles W. Waring (Margaret Simonds)

ONION SOUP—Sauté 6 large onions, sliced, in butter; cover with water and simmer gently for about ½ hour. Add 2 cans of bouillon or consomme and serve with a piece of toast in each bowl well sprinkled with Parmesan cheese. Serves 4.

Mrs. Charles W. Waring (Margaret Simonds)

CRAB SOUP—Combine 1 lb. crab meat, 1 can tomato soup, 1 can green pea soup, 1 can bouillon. Let come to a boil and add ½ c. sherry wine. Serves 6-8.

deSaussure Dehon

OYSTER STEW—Heat 1 can of ready-to-serve celery soup to boiling point . Add ½ pint small oysters. Bring to boiling point again, add sherry to taste and serve. Serves 2.

Mrs. Robert W. Achurch (Sue Thomas)

TUNA SURPRISE—Combine 2 cans of condensed mushroom soup, 1 can tuna fish and ½ cup sherry wine. Place in casserole and cover top with potato chips. Bake in moderate oven. Serves 4-6.　　　　　Mrs. Frank B. Birthright (Lila Rhett)

CRAB OR SHRIMP CROQUETTES—Mix 2 cups of crab meat or ground shrimp, or 1 of each, with 1 can of condensed cream of mushroom soup. Season with ½ t. mace, 1 T. Worcestershire and sherry to taste. Add cracker meal to stiffen enough to form flat cakes. Coat cakes with more cracker meal and brown in butter. Serves 4.　　　　　Mrs. Robert W. Achurch (Sue Thomas)

DEVILED CRABS—Combine 1 lb. crab meat, 2 T. melted butter and 1 c. mayonnaise dressing. Add 2 eggs, well beaten, salt, pepper and Worcestershire to taste. Fill crab shells, sprinkle with bread crumbs and bake 5 minutes in a hot oven. Yields: 8-10.
　　　　　Mrs. William A. Hutchinson (Eva Austin)

EASY LOBSTER NEWBURG—Melt 1 T. butter, add 1 T. flour and cook a few minutes. Mix 1 egg yolk and 1 c. light cream and add to butter and flour, stirring constantly. Add salt, pepper, mace, nutmeg, Worcestershire to taste, 1 large can lobster and lastly 1 wine-glass of sherry. Serve on toast. Serves 4.
　　　　　Mrs. Lionel Legge (Dorothy Porcher)

SHRIMP AND CRAB MEAT CREOLE—Alternate in glass baking dish, 1 pound cooked shrimp, 2 T. butter, buttered and toasted bread crumbs and 1 pound crab meat. To one can condensed mushroom soup add 2 t. catsup, 1 T. Worcestershire, 1 pinch cayenne pepper, ½ t. salt and pour over all. Top with more crumbs and bake in oven for 20 to 30 minutes. Serves 10.
　　　　　Miss Caroline L. Porcher

BROILED OYSTERS—Toast 1 or 2 pieces of bread for each serving. Butter toast, cover each piece with as many raw oysters as it will hold. Salt and pepper lightly. Cut bacon strips in half and cover oysters. Put under flame to broil bacon. Garnish with lemon slices and serve with dressing made by blending 2 T. each of tarragon vinegar, chile sauce, tomato catsup, 1 T. of Worcestershire sauce and a little hot sauce, and heating thoroughly.
　　　　　Mrs. Arthur J. Stoney (Anne Montague)

FISH CASSEROLE—Into a casserole, put in layers, 1 can flaked fish, 1 can condensed mushroom soup, 1 small package potato chips crumbled. Bake covered in moderate oven until thoroughly heated. Do not overcook. Serves 4-6.

Mrs. Arthur J. Stoney (Anne Montague)

FRIED OKRA—Chop fresh okra fine and fry in bacon grease until brown, stirring constantly. Salt to taste.

Mrs. Ernest King, Jr. (Mary Elizabeth Johnson)

FRENCH-FRIED ONIONS—Make a thick batter of prepared pancake flour and evaporated milk. Soak Bermuda onions, thinly sliced, in ice water until crisp. Dip rings in batter and fry in deep hot fat.

Mrs. Wilmer L. Thompson (Mary Bissell McIver)

QUICK HOPPING JOHN—Fry 2 slices of bacon and 1 slice of onion; add to 1 can field peas. Wash 1 c. rice, add to other ingredients with salt and pepper to taste. Steam 2 hours. Serves 6.

Mrs. Gerald Thomas (Lottie Johnson)

RICE AND CHICKEN CASSEROLE—Combine 2 c. cold chicken, 2 c. cooked rice, 1 green pepper, cut in strips and put in greased casserole. Mix 1 can condensed mushroom soup with 1 c. chicken gravy and 1½ c. water. Pour over mixture in casserole. Bake in moderate oven 30 min. Serves 6.

Mrs. Gerald Thomas (Lottie Johnson)

LUNCHEON DISH—Add 1 c. cream sauce or 1 can condensed cream of chicken soup to any left over vegetables. Put in buttered ramekins. Place a poached egg on top and sprinkle with grated cheese. Place under broiler until cheese has melted.

Mrs. Ralph Mills (Elizabeth Stevens)

SPOON BREAD—Mix 1½ c. corn meal, ¾ t. salt, 2 level t. baking powder, 1 level t. sugar, 3 c. milk, 1 egg. Have heating in a 500° oven, 2 heaping T. butter in a casserole. Add this melted butter to mixture and cook in same casserole 15 min. at 450°. Heat 1 c. milk while this bakes, and pour over mixture just as cooking is finished. Serves 6.

Mrs. James Hagood (Antoinette Camp)

SPANISH RICE—Fry 4 strips of bacon, remove from pan and brown 1 large, or 2 or 3 small onions and 2 chopped green peppers in drippings. Add drained tomatoes from No. 2 can (2½ c). Salt and pepper to taste and simmer until blended. Alternate cooked rice (left over or minute) and left over meat or chicken, cut in small pieces, in greased casserole. Pour tomato, onion and pepper mixture, to which has been added bacon broken in pieces, over rice and meat. Bake in moderate oven about 30 min.

MRS. WILLIAM L. MENGEBIER (Clelia Matthew)

QUICK CHICKEN à la KING—Heat 1 can of condensed mushroom soup. Add 2 cans chicken and 2 drained pimientos cut fine. Season to taste. Serve in patty shells or on toast. Serves 4.

MISS NANCY McIVER

BLUSHING BUNNY—Put 1 can condensed tomato soup and 1 c. grated cheese in double boiler and cook until smooth. Add 1 beaten egg, Worcestershire, salt and pepper to taste . Pour hot over toast. Serves 4.

MRS. FRANK B. BIRTHRIGHT (Lila Rhett)

A QUICKIE—Heat together 1 can condensed cream of chicken soup, 4 hard cooked eggs, chopped, and 2 to 4 slices of bacon fried crisp. Serve hot on toast. Serves 4.

MRS. FRANK B. BIRTHRIGHT (Lila Rhett)

CRANBERRY AND APPLE TARTS—Grind 1 lb. raw cranberries, picked over and washed ,and 4 crisp apples. Combine and add sugar to taste. Use in patty shells made of prepared piecrust-mix. Top with whipped cream. The apple and cranberry mixture makes a wonderful molded salad, using orange juice for liquid and adding chopped nuts.

MRS. ROBERT W. ACHURCH (Sue Thomas)

MINCEMEAT OR MARMALADE TURNOVERS—Mix 1 package of prepared pastry; roll thin and cut in rounds. Place 1 t. of prepared mincemeat or marmalade on each round, fold into semicircles and crimp edges with fork. Bake in hot oven until brown.

MRS. JOSEPH YOUNG (Elizabeth Jenkins)

TIPSY PARSON—Soak squares of sponge cake with rum. Cover with sherry flavored, sweetened whipped cream. Top with a cherry.

Mrs. Daniel Ravenel (Ruth Howe)

CHOCOLATE ICE CREAM—Mix 1 pt. of cream, whipped, and ½ pt. prepared chocolate sauce. Freeze in refrigerator.

Mrs. John Bennett (Susan Smythe)

SYLLABUB—Whisk together 1 qt. heavy cream, ½ pt. sweet milk, ½ pt. sherry wine and sugar to taste.

From "Over the Teacups"

ORANGE SPONGE—Saturate a sponge cake layer with orange juice, cover with sweetened whipped cream. Decorate with grated nuts or orange rind.

Mrs. Arthur J. Stoney (Anne Montague)

KITTY'S COFFEE DESSERT—Melt 40 marshmallows in ½ pt. black coffee over hot water. Cool. Then stir in ½ pt. cream whipped. Set to jell for three hours and serve topped with whipped cream. Serves 6.

Mrs. William Popham (Louisa Stoney)

PINEAPPLE ICE CREAM—Whip 1 pint of heavy cream lightly, add 1 pint coffee cream and 1 can crushed pineapple. Sweeten to taste. Freeze in refrigerator, stirring once during freezing. Serves 6-8.

Mrs. John Frost (Laura Green)

LEMON SHERBET—To 1 quart of milk add slowly, stirring constantly, ½ c. lemon juice with sugar to taste. When partially frozen, beat well and return to refrigerator. Cut down on sugar if less sweet sherbet is desired. Serves 6.

Miss Sallie Carrington

ORANGE MOUSSE—To 1 pint of heavy cream whipped, add 1 6-oz. can of frozen orange juice concentrate and 1 pint coffee cream. Sweeten to taste and freeze. Serves 6.

Mrs. Wm. H. Barnwell (Suzanne Pringle)

UPSIDE UP CAKE—Preheat oven to 450°. Mix 2 c. prepared biscuit mix with ¾ c. cream and 2 T. sugar. Drop lightly into buttered square or oblong baking dish. Cover dough with fruit or berries which have been sprinkled with sugar. Dot top of fruit with sugar and butter creamed together. Bake 15 or 20 min. or until dough appears done. Serve with slightly sweetened whipped cream, or two t. of sugar to a cup of cream warmed, makes a nice sauce; season with almonds, nutmeg or vanilla, depending on fruit. Serves 6-8.

MRS. ARTHUR J. STONEY (Anne Montague)

STRAWBERRY ANGEL—Split a bought angel food cake in half crosswise. Spread top of one section with sliced strawberries (frozen or fresh); cover with sweetened whipped cream. Place second section on top, covering all with whipped cream and filling center with strawberries. Serves 8.

MRS. JOHN WELCH (Julie Pringle)

QUICKIE BROWNIES—Melt 3 squares of unsweetened chocolate and add 1 can condensed milk, 2 c. of vanilla wafer crumbs and 1 c. chopped nuts. Spread ¾ in. thick in buttered pan and bake in oven at 300° about 30 min.

MRS. T. PRIOLEAU BALL (Teresa Daniel)

STICKIES—Mix prepared pastry and roll out to about ¼ inch. Spread with brown sugar and chopped nuts and dot liberally with butter. Roll up and cut in ½ in. slices. Bake in medium hot oven until brown. These must be removed from pan while hot to keep from breaking.

MISS FRANCES JENKINS

BENNE COOKIES—Beat an egg; add ½ c. sugar, 2 T. flour, 2 T. melted butter, 1 t. vanilla and enough parched benne seed to make a stiff mixture. Drop on a pan that has been greased and dredged with flour. Bake in moderate oven. Remove from pan after slightly cooled, but not cold. They become brittle very quickly. Chopped nuts or rice flakes may be substituted for benne seed. Yield: 3 dozen.

MRS. ROBERT W. ACHURCH (Sue Thomas)

APPENDIX

Do, gracious! Dese bin all de ting wuh I done fergit!
Appendices are postscripts with added information,
  Yet modern books possessing them create a mild sensation.
Still, Charleston hostesses have found these items applicable
And so we have included them in hopes they're serviceable.
We trust you'll read and will approve
The appendix we did not remove.

TABLES OF MEASURE

Dry Measure	Liquid Measure
8 ounces — 1 cup	3 teaspoons — 1 tablespoon
3 teaspoons — 1 tablespoon	½ fl. ounce — 1 tablespoon
16 tablespoons — 1 cup	16 tablespoons — 1 cup
2 cups — 1 pint	½ cup — 1 gill
2 pints — 1 quart	4 fl. ounces — 1 gill
8 quarts — 1 peck	4 gills — 1 pint
4 pecks — 1 bushel	2 pints — 1 quart
1 barspoon — ¾ teaspoon	4 quarts — 1 gallon
	1 jigger — 1½ ounces
	1 pony — 1 ounce

Average Can Size

No. 1 — 1¹/³ cups	No. 3 — 4 cups
No. 2 — 2½ cups	No. 10 — 13 cups
No. 2½ — 3½ cups	No. 303 — 2 cups

OVEN HEATS

250° — Very slow	350° — Moderate
300° — Slow	375° — Moderately hot
325 ° — Moderately slow	450° to 500° — Very hot

TEMPERATURE DEFINITIONS

180°	— Simmering point of water
212°	— Boiling point of water
234° to	
240°	— Soft ball stage for syrups
255°	— Hard crack stage for syrups
320°	— Caramel stage for syrups
220°	— Jellying point for jams and jellies

At altitudes above 3000 feet, lower air pressure causes differences in the boiling point of water and syrups. Consult government bulletins for details.

Gracious! Ef e ain' be sumpin new ta learn ebery day!

The following conversion factors (equivalents) are presented as a convenience for those persons who would like to convert their favorite receipts to metric units.

CONVERSION FACTORS — U.S. CUSTOMARY TO METRIC

VOLUME		MASS (WEIGHT)
1 teaspoon	= 5 ml	1 ounce (av.) 28.4 g
1 tablespoon	= 15 ml	1 pound (av.) 454 g
1 cup	= 240 ml	
1 ounce	= 30 ml	
1 pint (fluid)	= 473 ml	
1 quart (fluid)	= 946 ml	
1 pint (dry)	= 551 ml	
1 quart (dry)	= 1.1 litres	

To convert customary units to metric units, multiply by the conversion factor. Round the results.

The only units needed for expressing volume and mass in receipts when using the metric system are:

VOLUME	MASS (WEIGHT)
millilitre (ml)	gram (g)
litre (l or *l*)	kilogram (kg)

The above units will be used for the sale of all packaged and bulk food items in stores.

Metric receipts should not be converted back to the customary system. It is better to obtain a few metric volume measures for use with metric receipts.

This page contributed by the U.S. METRIC ASSOCIATION, Inc.

TABLE OF EQUIVALENTS

Almonds, chopped	4½ cups	3½ lbs. unshelled
Asparagus	20 stalks	1 lb.
Bananas, skins on	3 large	1 lb.
Beans, fresh green	1 qt.	3¼ lbs.
Beans, dried	1 cup	½ lb.
Bread crumbs	1 cup	2¾ oz.
Butter	2 cups	1 lb.
Butter	1 stick	½ cup
Butter	size of egg	about ¼ cup
Chocolate, bitter	1 square	1 oz.
Cheese	¼ lb., grated	1 cup
Cheese	4½ cups	1 lb.
Coffee	1 lb.	40-50 cups
Corn meal	3 cups	1 lb.
Crab meat	2 cups	1 lb.
Currants, dried	2¾ cups	1 lb.
Dates, pitted	2 cups	1 lb.
Eggs, whole	5	1 cup
Egg whites	8	about 1 cup
Egg yolks	16	about 1 cup
Figs, chopped	3 cups	1 lb.
Flour, bread	3½ cups	1 lb.
Flour, whole wheat	4 cups	1 lb.
Flour, cake, sifted	4½ cups	1 lb.
Lard	1 cup	½ lb.
Lemon, juiced	1	2 to 3 tbs.
Milk, skim	1 cup scant	½ lb.
Nut meats, chopped	4 cups	1 lb.
Okra, chopped	4 cups	1 lb.
Okra, whole	1 qt.	1 lb.
Orange, juiced	1	6 to 8 tbs.
Peanuts, chopped	3 cups	1½ lbs.
Pecans, chopped	3 cups	2¼ lbs. unshelled
Prunes, dried	2½ cups	1 lb.
Raisins, seeded	2½ cups	1 lb.
Raisins, seedless	3 cups	1 lb.
Rice, uncooked	1 cup	3 cups cooked
Rice, uncooked	1 cup	½ lb.
Shrimp, raw	1 plate	about 1 lb.
Shrimp, cooked	2 cups	1 lb.
Sugar, granulated	1 cup	½ lb.
Sugar, confectioners	3½ cups sifted	1 lb.
Sugar, brown	2½ cups packed firmly	1 lb.
Sugar, loaf	55 to 70 lumps	1 lb.
Tomatoes, average	4	1 lb.
Walnuts, black	3 cups chopped	5½ lbs. unshelled
Walnuts, English	4 cups chopped	2½ lbs. unshelled
Water	1 cup	½ lb.

HELPFUL COOKING HINTS

1. To whip ½ pt. coffee cream: soak 1 t. gelatin in 1 T. cold water. Heat 3 T. coffee cream and pour over gelatin stirring until dissolved; cool and add remaining ½ pt coffee cream. Whip when very cold. Use same proportions for larger amonuts of cream.

2. Corn syrup or honey may be substituted for ½ amount of sugar called for, if ¼ less liquid is used.

3. To bring out flavor of fowl and make it tender: rub fowl inside and out with 1 t. each of salt, pepper and soda. Keep in refrigerator overnight.

4. To keep cakes fresh put an apple cut in half in container.

5. To bake ham: put ham in paper bag, twisting ends of bag and place in biscuit pan. Remove bag ½ hour before ham is done, skin and decorate ham as desired.

6. To clear bacon grease for subsequent use: pour while liquid, but not hot, into a can containing cold water. Burnt portion will drop to bottom of can.

7. To flour chicken for frying: shake in paper bag with flour. Cookies may be covered with confectioner's sugar in the same way.

8. Put a clove of garlic in a bottle of bought French dressing to improve flavor.

9. Left over cheeses of all kinds may be put from time to time into a jar containing a little wine. When enough to be used has accumulated it will have a very intriguing flavor.

10. Season sea food, especially crab and shrimp dishes, with a little mace.

11. Cut down odor of cabbage, cauliflower, etc. when cooking by adding a little vinegar to cooking water. Vinegar also prevents white of poached eggs from spreading.

12. Add 1 t. of salt water to keep egg white from escaping a cracked shell when being boiled.

13. Roll pastry between two sheets of wax paper. When the top paper is peeled off, the pastry may be easily turned into a pie pan and other paper removed.

14. To make fresh bread slice easily: place loaf in ice box and chill thoroughly.

15. To melt chocolate: grease pot in which it is to be melted and place over boiling water.

16. To make croquettes light and creamy inside: use cream sauce instead of eggs.

17. To peel a coconut: drain milk, place nut in oven until hot to touch, remove and tap all over with a hammer, particularly at ends, give one hard knock and shell will crack open. Lift shell off, peel brown skin and cool before grating or grinding.

18. To measure molasses: grease cup in which it is to be measured.

19. To measure shortening: subtract amount of shortening required from 1 cup; fill cup with water to amount of difference and add shortening until water level measures 1 cup. Lift shortening from water and you will not have wasted any on sides of cup.

20. To vary taste of vegetables: add a pinch of dried thyme to fresh carrots; cook a sprig of fresh mint with green peas; add ¼ t. minced fresh marjoram to butter when melting and pour over cooked spinach.

21. To remove excessive taste of salt from food: while cooking add 1 t. each of vinegar and sugar, or in soup, add a few slices of raw potato.

22. A bit of sugar in batter of pancakes or waffles will make them brown more quickly.

23. Sugar may be softened by placing in warm oven for 10 or 15 minutes.

24. To make nut meats come out whole: soak nuts in salt water overnight before cracking.

25. Sprinkle salt in frying pan before frying meat to prevent fat from splashing.

26. To sour sweet milk: add 1 T. vinegar or lemon juice to each cup and let stand for a few minutes.

27. To freshen sour milk: add ½ t. baking soda and use 2 t. less of baking powder than receipt calls for.

28. Peel an onion under running water to keep back the tears.

29. To rid vegetables of insects: add a pinch of borax and a little vinegar to the water in which they are washed.

30. To peel dried fruits: wash in warm water, drain, then cover with boiling water and let stand until cool.

31. To freshen wilted greens: douse quickly in hot and then ice water, with a little vinegar added.

32. To keep parsley fresh for a long time: wash and store in tightly covered jar in refrigerator.

33. To blanch almonds: cover shelled almonds with boiling water, allow to cool, slip off skins.

34. Wrap a cloth moistened with vinegar around cheese to keep it fresh.

35. To keep macaroni from boiling over: put a T. of butter in water.

36. To make potatoes light and fluffy: add a pinch of baking soda as well as hot milk and butter.

37. Add a little salt to flour before mixing to prevent lumping.

38. Use a nutmeg grater to remove burnt edges from cake.

39. Heat molasses and butter together—1 T. butter to each cup of molasses—for use on waffles or pancakes. Tastes good and saves butter.

40. Adding sugar to water in which some vegetables are cooked improves flavor: for sweet potatoes add 1 heaping t.; for peas, cabbage, turnips, beets and corn add 1 level t.

41. To preserve yolks of eggs in refrigerator: slide into a bowl and cover with cold water.

42. Dry celery in warm oven and store in tightly covered jar for use as seasoning.

43. To keep layer cake from crumbling when being sliced: cut square in center of cake before slicing from outside edge.

44. Dipping citrus fruit in hot water before squeezing will increase amount of juice that can be obtained.

45. A pinch of salt added to the sugar in making icings will prevent graining.

46. 12 qts. punch makes 96 cups.
One gal. of punch, 32 servings.
A 12 lb. ham serves 20.
To serve cold sliced turkey or chicken to 25 people, allow 20 lbs. of poultry, drawn weight.
A 4 lb. chicken—drawn weight—makes 4 cups of diced chicken. One gal. of ice cream will serve 30 people if served with scoop. An 11 in. casserole of scalloped potatoes serves 8 generously.

47 Fruit cake almond paste may be quickly made by buying the almond paste from a pastry shop; adding an equal amount of granulated sugar and diluting to proper consistency with rose water.

48. French fry carrots like potatoes for a change.

49. Wild ducks are easier to pick if dipped in, or painted with, melted paraffin. When it is cool pull the paraffin off; the feathers come too. Allow 1 cake of paraffin for each duck.

50. If water called for in package pie-crust mix is reduced, a much tenderer pastry will result. In a damp climate the liquid may be reduced as much as one half.

51. To roast or parch benne seeds, put in heavy pan on top of stove or in oven until dark brown.

MENUS

Dis-yah de way de buckra like he bittle su'b-tuh-um.

Charlestonians dine at two o'clock,
An early English custom.
(Suggestions that they dine at eight
Apparently disgust 'em!)
But call it dinner, supper, lunch,—
The hour does not matter,—
Sometimes the strain of planning meals
Can cause the nerves to shatter!
These menus, planned for eating, drinking,
Will spare you hours of painful thinking!

"TWO O'CLOCK" DINNER

She-Crab Soup (p. 46) or Carolina Crab Soup (p. 46)
Chicken with Brandy (p. 108)   Rice (p. 157)
Spinach Soufflé (p. 183)   Best Beets (p. 173)
Muffins (p. 199)
Plain Whole Artichoke Pickle (p. 326)
Wine Jelly (p. 243)   Benne Wafers (p. 292)

Shrimp Cocktail with Sauce (p. 98)
Lavington Plantation Wild Duck (p. 139)   Wild Rice Casserole (p. 163)
Spiced Grapes (p. 330)
Boiled Red Cabbage (p. 176)   Beets with Orange Sauce (p. 174)
Celery and Green Olives   Rum Bumble (p. 239)

Brown Soup (p. 53)   Shrimp Supreme (p. 79)
Rice Ring (p. 162   Green Peas (p. 187)
Biscuits (small) (p. 191)   Syllabub (p. 229)

Okra Soup (p. 56 or p. 57)
Ida's Broiled Chicken (p. 118)   Chicken Hemingway (p. 118)
Rice (p. 157) and Gravy (p. 129)   Candied Sweet Potatoes (p. 181)
Spinach in Cream (p. 185)
Fig Ice Cream (p. 251)   Lemon Cookies (p. 303)

Shrimp Soup (p. 47)
Fillet of Veal (p. 112)   Rice (p. 157) and Gravy (p. 129)
String Beans with Almonds (p. 173)
Fresh Corn (cut off cob, with diced green pepper)
Magic Butter Rolls (p. 206)   Chow-Chow Pickle (p. 334)
Lemon Ice Cream (p. 253)   Rum Cookies (p. 299)

Crab Cocktail with Sauce (p. 98)
Baked Lamb Steaks (p. 115)   Rice Croquettes (p. 161)
Succotash (p. 176)
Rolls (p. 206)   Apple Meringue (p. 236)

Mrs. Alston Pringle's Mock Terrapin Soup (p. 54)
Channel Bass (p. 94)
Scalloped Irish Potatoes and Onions (p. 181)
New Cut Plantation String Beans (p. 173)
Cole Slaw with Cream Dressing (p. 219)
Pineapple Fritters with Sauce (p. 246)

Créme Vichyssoise (p. 61)   Shrimp Croquettes (p. 75)
Ring of Red Rice (p. 158 and 162) with Green Peas in center
Middleburg Plantation Corn Pudding (p. 174)
Chopped Artichoke Pickle (p. 326)
Grandma's French Biscuits (small) (p. 192)
Pineapple Sherbert (p. 258) (double receipt) in melon mold, surrounded by pitted black
cherries, with fresh seedless grapes at each end of platter.

LUNCHEON OR SUPPER

Mrs. C. C. Calhoun's Chafing Dish Oysters (p. 88)
Green Salad with Minute Egg Dressing (p. 217)
Waffles (p. 207)   Rum Pie (p. 270)

Cream of Spinach Soup (p. 59)
Hunter's Chicken (p. 121) and Rice (p. 157)
Mixed Green Salad with French Dressing (p. 218)
Rolls (p. 193)   Lemon Pudding (p. 229)

Creamy Fish Chowder (p. 51) (served from tureen)
Grapefruit and Avocado Salad with Grapefruit Dressing (p. 217)
Cheese Daisies (p. 192)   Pecan Pie (p. 267)

Oysters and Sweetbreads in Patty Shells (p. 90)   Spoon Bread (p. 197)
Asparagus Mousseline (p. 214)
Southern Spicy Gingerbread with Lemon Sauce (p. 244)

Cypress Gardens' Egg Plant and Cauliflower (p. 176) (first course)
Veal Paté (p. 128)   "Crowded House" Cucumber Salad (p. 209)
Biscuits (p. 191)   Chocolate Soufflé (p. 242)

Chicken Croquettes (p. 122)   Hominy Surprise (p. 156)
Mixed Green Salad with Anchovy Dressing (p. 219)
Chopped Artichoke Pickle (p. 326)
Orange Ice and Vanilla Mousse (p. 257)   Mocha Cakes (p. 279)

Chicken Tetrazzini (p. 120)
Ring of Cucumber Jelly (p. 212); center filled with Purple Cabbage Slaw
and Cream Salad Dressing (p. 219)
Biscuits (p. 191)   Mrs. Dill's Bucket Dumpling (p. 245)

Créme Vichyssoise with Curry (p. 61)
Fiddler's Green Stuffed Avocados (p. 209)   Hot Rolls (p. 205)
Peppermint-Stick Ice Cream (p. 253)   Chocolate Sauce (p. 260)

Iced Spinach Soup (p. 60)
Meeting Street Crab Meat (p. 84) in individual baking dishes
Hearts of Artichoke Salad with Bahamian Salad Dressing (p. 216)
Sherry Tarts (p. 271)

BUFFET SUPPER OR LUNCHEON

Low-Country Oysters with Mushrooms (p. 90) and/or
Baked Ham with Ham Paste (p. 136)
Red Rice (p. 158)   Green Tomato Chow-Chow (p. 334)
Mixed Green Salad with Roquefort Dressing (p. 218)
Hot Rolls (p. 193)   Angel Food Charlotte Russe Cake (p. 231)

Buffet Supper Shrimp (p. 77) and/or Chicken Mousse (p. 125)
Asparagus Casserole (p. 171)
Tossed Green Salad (p. 210) with Aunt Em's Salad Dressing (p. 219)
Hot Rolls (p. 205)   Hampton Polonaise (p. 227)

Jellied Chicken Loaf (p. 126) and
Deviled Crabs (p. 81) or Shrimp Salad (p. 210)
Picnic Pride Rice (p. 162)
Whole Tomatoes filled with Chopped Celery, Green Pepper, Mayonnaise (p. 216)
Cold Asparagus on Lettuce, French Dressing (p. 218)
Cheese Biscuits (p. 192)   Lady Baltimore Cake (p. 277 or p. 278)

Jellied Daube Glacé (p. 127)
Carolina Deviled Sea Food (p. 80)
Tomato Aspic Ring (p. 213) (double receipt) with Mayonnaise (p. 216)
Curried Rice (p. 160)
Grandma's French Biscuits (p. 192)   Huguenot Torte (p. 235)

Popham Shrimp Pie (p. 71)   Baked Ham (p. 111)
Tossed Green Salad (p. 210) with French Dressing (p. 218)
Garlic French Bread (p. 198)   Coffee Mousse (p. 257)

Chicken Country Captain (p. 123) and/or Ham Mousse (p. 126)
Asparagus and Egg Casserole (p. 172) Fruit Salad (p. 215) Rolls (p. 209)
Angel Ice Box Cake (p. 302) or Baba au Rhum (p. 238)

Sullivan's Island Shrimp with Rice (p. 70)
Beef á la Mode (sliced and cold) (p. 103)
Mixed Green Salad with French Dressing (p. 218)
Rolls (p. 210)   Watermelon Balls with Raspberry Ice (p. 260)

Shrimp Curry (p. 77)   Rice (p. 157)
Green Tomato Pickle (p. 333)   Corned Tongue (p. 107)
Tossed Green Salad (p. 210)   with French Dressing (p. 218)
Magic Butter Rolls (p. 206)   Charlotte Russe (p. 232)

359

RECIPE INDEX

363

369

370

373

Standard English translations for the Gullah lines used in the *Charleston Receipts*

Pg. 13

"If you take a heap of hard liquor, you are going to think deep and talk strong."
(If you drink too much liquor, you will voice strong opinions.) English idiom.

Pg. 29

"Young married women in this day are never satisfied with old-fashioned dishes, they always want to make some new kind of mixture."

Pg. 45

"Crabs have to walk into the pot by themselves, or they are no good."
(Live crabs must be cooked in boiling water. If the crabs are already dead, they are not good to eat.) English idiom.

Pg. 67

"She has a heavy pan full of mullet and she has both shrimp and crabs, and she has hominy and other things."
(Cry of the Seafood Hucksters)
"Lady get your dishpan, here comes the shrimp-man!
Shrimp, Shrimp! Raw, raw, shrimp.

Fish! fresh fish! I have porgy!
Oh the porgy walk, and the porgy talks,
the porgy eats with knife and fork!
Porgy! Porgy! fresh fish!"

Pg. 103

"If there is no meat on the table, the dinner is worthless."

Pg. 153

"When a man is hungry, he takes some eggs or cheese and things and eats until he is full, but a woman is bound to make work and trouble. She cooks!"

Page 171

(Cry of Vegetable Hucksters)

"I've got okra, tomatoes and sweet potatoes.
Soup! Carrot! Carrot!
Fresh cabbage! Vegetables!
Vegetable man!"

Pg. 191

"The girl brought him a big plate piled up with butter cakes. He put two or three on his plate and covered them with molasses and started to eat."

Pg 209

"Salad? That's when they take grass and things and arrange them to look fancy, like a girl dressed to go to church."

Pg. 223

"When the preacher eats at a woman's house, he eats the best, nothing else will suit."
(When a woman invites a preacher to eat at her house, she will serve him only her best food. She isn't satisfied to serve him anything less.) English idiom.

Pg. 251

"Miss Sally, if I churn it for you, can I lick the dasher?"

Pg. 263

"When you are making a pie crust, you take flour and put in enough to take up the slack."
(Add enough flour to the shortening so that you can handle it.) English idiom.

Pg. 275

"No, Mam, I don't measure. I just judge by my own experience. I take my flour and my brown sugar and two or three 'glub' of molasses. What do I mean by 'glub'? The sound molasses makes when it is poured from a jug."

Pg. 291

"Do, chile! I don't have time to make fancy cookies. Take this penny and go get a horse ginger cake."
(A ginger cake shaped like a horse by the baker.) English Idiom.

Pg. 311

"You have a sweet tooth, do you not?"
(You want some candy, don't you?") English Idiom.

Pg. 325

"People don't know that ground artichokes make good pickles, instead they give them to the pigs."
(People don't know that artichoke tubers make good pickles, instead they give them to the pigs.) English Idiom.

Pg. 343

"When you don't have time to wait or waste, open a can!"

FAMILY FAVORITES

Recipe   Page No.

_____

_____

_____

_____

_____

_____

_____

_____

_____

_____

_____

_____

_____

_____

_____

_____

_____

_____

FAMILY FAVORITES

Recipe   Page No.

_____

_____

_____

_____

_____

_____

_____

_____

_____

_____

_____

_____

_____

_____

_____

_____

_____

_____

FAMILY FAVORITES

Recipe   Page No.

_____

_____

_____

_____

_____

_____

_____

_____

_____

_____

_____

_____

_____

_____

_____

_____

_____

_____

Also by the Junior League of Charleston, Inc.

Charleston Receipts Repeats
Party Receipts
Charleston Receipts Album

To learn more about The Junior League of Charleston,
visit their Web site at www.jlcharleston.org.

FRP.INC

FRP creates successful connections between organizations and individuals through custom books.

 Favorite Recipes® Press

Favorite Recipes Press, an imprint of FRP, Inc., located in Nashville, Tennessee, is one of the nation's best-known and most-respected cookbook companies. Favorite Recipes Press began by publishing cookbooks for its parent company, Southwestern/Great American, in 1961. FRP, Inc., is now a wholly owned subsidiary of the Southwestern/ Great American family of companies, and under the Favorite Recipes Press imprint has produced hundreds of custom cookbook titles for nonprofit organizations, companies, and individuals.

Other FRP, Inc., imprints include

 BECKON BOOKS   The Booksmith Group   CommunityClassics®
A DIVISION OF FRP

Additional titles published by FRP, Inc., are

Favorite Recipes of Home Economics Teachers

| Cooking Up a Classic Christmas | Recipes Worth Sharing | More Recipes Worth Sharing | The Hunter's Table | The Vintner's Table |

Junior Leagues In the Kitchen with Kids: Everyday Recipes & Activities for Healthy Living

Almost Homemade

The Illustrated Encyclopedia of American Cooking

To learn more about custom books, visit our Web site, www.frpbooks.com.

Classic JUNIOR LEAGUE® COOKBOOK COLLECTION

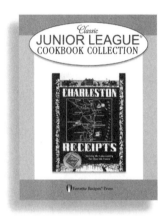

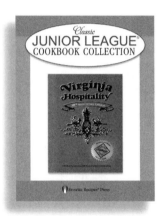

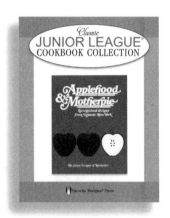

This collection includes six of the most well known and respected Junior League cookbooks of all time; combined there are more than 2,000 pages with 4,000 regionally inspired, tried-and-true recipes. Collectively, over 2,000,000 copies of these cookbooks have sold over a span of 60 years.

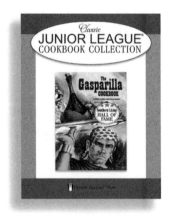